This book is an excellent tool for anyone in business without a business degree and who needs to understand the bigger picture of their entire enterprise.

Guy W. Wallace, CPT, Vice President, Performance Improvement
Wachovia – A Wells Fargo Company

If you want to understand your organization in a hurry, I've never seen a book on the subject that is both this serious and easy to understand. It was a one-book review of my whole MBA degree. Anyone with a job (or looking for one) ought to read this one. It helps you understand what managers and executives are worried about. It will help you make a bigger contribution to your organization's success, and promote your own career. This is so important it ought to be passed out to all knowledge workers as part of their initial orientation. It is an essential tool for self-management.

Bill Daniels, CEO, American consulting & Training, Inc.
co-author of The Change-ABLE Organization
ISPI Gilbert Distinguished Professional Achievement Award.

This book is the Rosetta Stone for organizational anthropologists or for anyone with a desire to connect the dots. The "Seven Logics" have the capacity to reveal the innermost workings of any organizations. Putting them into use is like seeing the morning fog lift from the organization. Silber and Kearney individually are unique contributors within the Performance Improvement field. Together they create a formidable brain trust with tremendous insight.

Jim Schultz, CPT, President, Pretty Good Consulting, and
Div. V.P. Performance Development Walgreen Co. (Retired)

Having Organizational Intelligence is a crucial first step in meeting the Certified Performance Technologist Standard # 4 "Utilize partnerships or collaborate with clients and other experts as required." The Business Glasses Model provides a clear, concise, comprehensive and do-able way of seeing the organization the way the client does. This provides a basis for collaborating with clients on projects that meet their needs, and working with them in their language.

Judith Hale, PhD, CPT, ISPI Director of Certification
author of Performance Consultants Fieldbook, 2nd Edition
ISPI Gilbert Distinguished Professional Achievement Award..

The Organizational Intelligence framework is complete and easy to reference, a great enhancement to the rules of thumb I've used to research my clients in the past."

Timm J. Esque, CPT, Partner, Ensemble Management Consulting

The authors have done a remarkable job in synthesizing and clearly explaining the evidence-based practices from fields we typically ignore (e.g., finance, marketing, management, human resources, organization design). The Business Glasses model allows practitioners in our field to apply these practices to gathering baseline data about their own organizations. They can use these data as a basis for deciding on needed interventions and evaluating organizational performance improvements after those interventions.

Dr. Richard E. Clark, professor of educational psychology and technology in the Rossier School of Education at the University of Southern California, co-director of the Center for Cognitive Technology; co-author of Turning Research in Results; *ISPI Gilbert Distinguished Professional Achievement Award.*

About This Book

Why is this topic important?

Experts in the Human Resources and HPT fields have been saying for 30 years that a key to consulting well with any client is to understand their business and speak their language. But the fact is that most practitioners of Training, Human Performance Technology, Instructional Design, Organization Development, and Human Resources, though they are experts in their field, *do not* understand the logic and language of business and of the organization in which they work. Clients expect us to understand business in general, their business in particular, and the issues they face, and to propose solutions (or initiatives) that are practical and aligned with their business needs. Yet we still typically do not meet these expectations. We do not have **Organizational Intelligence**—the ability to think effectively about an organization, from a business point of view.

What can you achieve with this book?

By the end of this book you will have Organizational Intelligence. You will be able to understand, and talk about your work in terms of: the language of business, how the organization works, what issues your clients (internal or external) are really concerned about, gather information about your organization, identify the key issues facing your organization, identify what key measures your organization is concerned about, determine what the current and desired states of those measures are, and determine what the gaps in organization performance are.

This book is unique in helping you meet these objectives because it is easy to read and understand, right and left brained (we use pictures), theory and research based but practical, immediately applicable to your job, and full of tools you can use to apply the information in each chapter.

This book is aimed directly at your needs if you are an employee or consultant or student in the fields of Training, Human Performance Technology, Instructional Design, Organizational Development or Human Resources. The content in this book is also aimed at you if you are in other "staff" positions in the organization (Information Technology, Facilities, Public Relations, etc.)—experts in your technical area, but lacking an understanding of how you fit into the business. And finally, this book is for every line manager/supervisor who has been promoted and is as confused as you are.

How is this book organized?

Chapter 1 explains the purpose of this book, introduces the business logic model, and shows how to use it to get better results as a consultant, whether you are internal or external. Chapter 2 proposes how to gather credible data in a practical and useful way. Chapter 3 introduces you to external logic, so you can understand the business environment your client is operating in. Chapters 4 through 9 address the organization's six internal logics: the economic, strategic, customer, product, process and structural logics that drive goals, measures and decision-making in each part of the organization. Chapter 10 presents a case study showing how the business logic model was applied to a real organization to create context and a baseline before doing performance improvement work. Each of these business logic chapters ends with a summarizing job aid, a couple of worksheets, sample completed worksheets based on a real client engagement, and an assignment for applying what you have learned to a client organization of your own.

About Pfeiffer

Pfeiffer serves the professional development and hands-on resource needs of training and human resource practitioners and gives them products to do their jobs better. We deliver proven ideas and solutions from experts in HR development and HR management, and we offer effective and customizable tools to improve workplace performance. From novice to seasoned professional, Pfeiffer is the source you can trust to make yourself and your organization more successful.

Essential Knowledge Pfeiffer produces insightful, practical, and comprehensive materials on topics that matter the most to training and HR professionals. Our Essential Knowledge resources translate the expertise of seasoned professionals into practical, how-to guidance on critical workplace issues and problems. These resources are supported by case studies, worksheets, and job aids and are frequently supplemented with CD-ROMs, websites, and other means of making the content easier to read, understand, and use.

Essential Tools Pfeiffer's Essential Tools resources save time and expense by offering proven, ready-to-use materials—including exercises, activities, games, instruments, and assessments—for use during a training or team-learning event. These resources are frequently offered in looseleaf or CD-ROM format to facilitate copying and customization of the material.

Pfeiffer also recognizes the remarkable power of new technologies in expanding the reach and effectiveness of training. While e-hype has often created whizbang solutions in search of a problem, we are dedicated to bringing convenience and enhancements to proven training solutions. All our e-tools comply with rigorous functionality standards. The most appropriate technology wrapped around essential content yields the perfect solution for today's on-the-go trainers and human resource professionals.

Pfeiffer
www.pfeiffer.com
Essential resources for training and HR professionals

ORGANIZATIONAL INTELLIGENCE

ORGANIZATIONAL INTELLIGENCE

A Guide to Understanding the
Business of Your Organization
for HR, Training, and
Performance Consulting

Kenneth H. Silber, PhD, CPT
Lynn Kearny, CPT

Pfeiffer

A Wiley Imprint
www.pfeiffer.com

Published by Pfeiffer
An Imprint of Wiley
989 Market Street, San Francisco, CA 94103–1741—www.pfeiffer.com

For additional copies/bulk purchases of this book in the U.S. please contact 800–274–4434.

Pfeiffer books and products are available through most bookstores. To contact Pfeiffer directly call our Customer Care Department within the U.S. at 800–274–4434, outside the U.S. at 317–572–3985, fax 317–572–4002, or visit www.pfeiffer.com.

Pfeiffer also publishes its books in a variety of electronic formats. Some content that appears in print may not be available in electronic books.

Library of Congress Cataloging-in-Publication Data

Silber, Kenneth H.
    Organizational intelligence : a guide to understanding the business of your organization for HR, training, and performance consulting / Kenneth H. Silber, Lynn Kearny.
        p.   cm.
    Includes bibliographical references and index.
    ISBN 978-0-470-47231-6 (cloth)
        1. Organizational learning. 2. Personnel management.   3. Employees—Training of.
    4. Business logistics. I. Kearny, Lynn. II. Title.
    HD58.82.S56 2009
    658.3124—dc22

                                                                                        2009034415

Printed in the United States of America

Printing   10 9 8 7 6 5 4 3 2 1

CONTENTS

LIST OF TABLES

Tables

To the late Dr. James D. Finn, my mentor and a forgotten HPT
pioneer, who taught me to see systemically with the left side of
my brain and always ask the hard questions

To Judy Hale who taught me that you can see however you choose
to and has been a friend and colleague for more than 20 years

To Lynn Kearny who taught me to see with the right side of my brain
and helped me write in understandable English

To my wife Belinda Silber, who taught me to see with my heart
and whose love, acceptance, patience, and support helped me
write from that special place

KHS

To my husband, best friend, and lifelong companion,
Cress Kearny, who has seen me through the late nights and
early mornings without giving
up on me

To my friend and mentor, Roger Addison, who has
staunchly supported my use of drawings to crystallize HPT concepts

To my friends and colleagues, Walter Ratcliff and Carol Haig,
for their unswerving support

To Ken Silber who talked me down out of the trees when
I was sure I could never understand a balance sheet or any
of that financial stuff

LBK

PREFACE

This book fills a need that has existed for 30 years; it has been 10 years in the writing.

A Little History

We have to say a word or two about each of those numbers.

How could a need exist for as long as 30 years? Since the mid-1970s, many experts in the human resources (HR) and human performance technology (HPT) fields have been pointing out that:

- A key to success in HR or HPT practice is to consult well with clients.
- A key to consulting well with all clients is to understand their business and speak their language.

When one of the authors decided to start a consulting practice, experienced advisors said, "Be sure to go to your local business library and do your homework on a potential client before your first visit." We all hear the same advice today, only the place to do our homework is the Internet. Unfortunately nobody provides very clear direction about what that homework is, other than to "learn about the business." Professional societies, like the International

Society for Performance Improvement (ISPI), American Society for Training & Development (ASTD), the Organization Development Network (ODN), and Society for Human Resource Management (SHRM), have been exhorting members for years to become business partners to line managers and really understand the business. Successful practitioners of training, human performance technology, instructional design (ID), organization development (OD), and human resources (HR) must understand the logic and language of business and of the organization in which they work.

Yet most do not. In workshops and courses the authors have conducted between 2002 and 2008 involving approximately 2,000 training/HPT/ID/OD/HR practitioners—people like you—the authors have found that fewer than 20 percent can answer very basic business questions about the organizations they work in or work with as consultants, about the strategic issues facing the organization, and about how they, as HR/training practitioners, contribute to the organization's bottom line (or even what the bottom line is or how it is calculated). Few know where to find documentation about what the business is doing, what its plans and challenges are, and how it is measuring up (including documentation that is public and required by the government).

If the training/HPT/ID/OD/HR practitioners do not understand key business concepts or the business language their clients use, they can't understand their client's most urgent concerns, and their clients are likely to dismiss their recommendations as naive. Clients expect training/HPT/ID/OD/HR practitioners to educate themselves about the business issues and to propose solutions (or initiatives) that are practical, that are aligned with the client's goals, that take current business constraints into consideration, and that are not likely to interfere with other, non-HR initiatives.

Yet training/HPT/ID/OD/HR practitioners still typically do not meet these expectations. Their training programs at universities and professional association meetings continue to focus on teaching the technical parts of their discipline, not on how to become a business partner. Though Stack (1994) and Charan (2001) have written books on understanding the financial aspects of business and calculating return on investment (ROI), there are **no books** to help training/HPT/ID/OD/HR practitioners understand all the elements of a business (not even in the *Dummies* series).

As already stated, the authors have been told this by over 2,000 practitioners to whom they have offered sessions and workshops on this topic since the late 1990s. Any time exhortations to make improvements continue for a decade or more without changing performance, we look for a cause. Why aren't there remedies? One reason is that it's hard to grasp a complex subject without a map. People in HR, OD, training, and HPT are model users, and models are maps. So perhaps what is needed is a Business Logics Model. Practitioners all recognize the need and have been anxiously awaiting this book.

We will have more to say about the importance of understanding how a business works in Chapter 1.

Which brings us to the second number: 10 years to write this book. The delay is not because the authors write slowly. It is partly because of the way the model this book is based on developed and partly because of the way the model was tested and revised before we published it.

About 10 years ago, Ken was developing a model of organizational metrics based on the Kaplan and Norton's *The Balanced Scorecard* (1996). It was extremely linear, verbal, and matrix driven (not surprisingly, given Ken's left-brained orientation). Around the same time, 2,000 miles away, Lynn was further developing a model (started in 1994) of how to understand organizations based on Albrecht's *The Northbound Train* (1994) business logics. It was beautifully presented (not surprisingly, given Lynn's right-brained orientation) but missing numbers.

Aha, we said to one another at a conference of the International Society of Performance Improvement. We are working on the same idea from two different perspectives that should be merged to provide a whole picture. We commenced to merge our work, and two years later we had developed such a model and workshop (Silber and Kearny, 2001). We received feedback from the workshop audience, revised the model and presentation, and presented it again every year at ISPI, revising it each year. We finally were comfortable enough to publish it as a chapter in the *Handbook of Human Performance Technology*, 3rd ed. (2006).

This book is both an expansion of that *Handbook* chapter and yet another revision of the model.

This Book Is for You If . . .

This book is aimed directly at your needs if you are what we call a training/ HPT/ID/OD/HR practitioner. This phrase sounds a little weird and takes up a lot of space on the page (as evidenced on the previous page), so our publishers have suggested we use only one of these terms at a time throughout the book, and we have agreed.

This broad group includes anyone who works in any of the following fields:

- *Training*: These practitioners engage in a wide spectrum of formal training in adult learning theory and techniques; they design and deliver training in large and small organizations. Most have learned on the job and are often very good at what they do. This group includes many members of *ASTD*.

- *Human performance technologists*: These practitioners do systematic analyses of organizational problems, and they select, design, and evaluate interventions that go beyond training. Some have formal training, and some have acquired their skills in the trenches: HPT is a new field and is still being defined. This group includes the members of ISPI.
- *Instructional designers*: These practitioners have formal training (usually MA degrees) and systematically design and evaluate training for classroom or e-learning delivery in large organizations; this group includes the members of AECT (Association for Educational Communications and Technology) and other e-learning–focused organizations.
- *Organizational development*: These practitioners focus on the interpersonal and social side of the functioning of an organization; their expertise varies from no formal training through MA and PhD degrees; this group include the members of ODN (Organization Development Network).
- *Human resources*. These practitioners focus on performing all the HR functions within an organization; this group is, in large organizations, the umbrella organization under which training, ID, HPT, and OD fall. Their expertise is reflected in two levels of certification (PHR and SPHR) and varies from no degree to MA and PhD degrees; this group includes the members of SHRM.

However, we do not see the audience as limited to practitioners in these fields.

Another audience consists of *graduate (MA/ PhD) students* in all these fields. Since part of the genesis of the book comes from articles about training students in the ID/HPT fields, it makes sense that it would help students know how to understand organizations *before* they went into them. Thus, this book is an excellent text for either an introductory course in any of these fields or a course in how to consult in business, along with Block's *Flawless Consulting* (2000).

Another audience is all the people in *staff positions* in their organizations (information technology, facilities, public relations, etc.). People in these fields are the same as those in HR-related fields: experts in their technical area but lacking an understanding of how they fit into a business.

Consultants make up another audience for this book: those who do HR-related consulting and who are looking for a quick way to understand a new client organization.

Salespeople can also greatly benefit from this book. Their bread and butter depends on a thorough understanding of their customers and prospects. Whole sales teams have attended past workshops in Business Logic; this book provides both a framework and a logical deepening and broadening of the target organization analysis they need, especially for large-ticket item sales.

And finally—dare we say it?—there is an audience for this book among all those *line managers* or *supervisors* who have been sent to the three-day training course on finance for nonfinancial managers and who have left just as confused as they were when they walked in.

The Tone of This Book

We have written this book in a tone that we hope makes it:

- *Personal*: We use the pronouns *we* and *you* just as if we were sitting around talking about this stuff.
- *Easy to read*: Lynn has worked hard (as has Pfeiffer) to shorten Ken's long sentences.
- *Right and left brained*: We present all the ideas in the book both in running text paragraphs, as well as in tables with icons and bulleted points to highlight the key ideas.
- *Theory and research based*: This is *not* the trend-of-the-day or what-these-two-wacko-authors-think. It's well documented.
- *Practical*: However, the theory is brought down to the what-I-can-do-with-it level, and the book is full of everyday examples of the concepts we are talking about.
- *Simple to understand*: We have boiled everything down to a limited number of key concepts with lots of examples.
- *Reader friendly*: Though we are dealing with complex ideas, even the feared financial numbers, we have tried to empower rather than intimidate you.
- *Applicable to your job*: You'll notice immediately that you can understand concepts that others in the organization are talking about and even use them yourself.
- *Full of tools*: We practice what HPT practices, and we give you job aids to help you implement the model.

How to Use This Book

We believe this book is useful as both a learning and a reference tool. And how you use it depends on what you already know.

Let's assume this is all new to you. Then, not surprisingly, we suggest that you read the book from front to back *but not* that you read it all at once. First, there is too much information to absorb all at once. So take it, as you would any pizza that the model resembles, one slice at a time. And don't just read it. At the end of chapter, there is a section for you to do an activity, applying the content of the chapter to your own organization. We suggest you actually do that activity, not skip over it. And complete it before taking on the next chapter.

Now let's assume you have some knowledge but are missing knowledge about a part of the model. Perhaps something has just come up that requires you to understand some part of the model by tomorrow's meeting. In that case, start with that logic. The model is circular, and it does not really matter where you start or in what order you go. (*Caveat:* The model is also systemic, so it *does* matter that you look at all seven logics to understand an organization, but it does not matter where you start.) Again, however, we suggest you complete each chapter, as you would complete each meal with a dessert, with doing the activity of applying the content to your own organization.

Finally, let's assume that you already know the content or that you have read the book a while ago and forgot the content. Then we have two options for you. First is the chapter route. We suggest you go the chapter that describes the logic you are concerned with, skip the text, go directly to the tables that summarize the major ideas of the chapter, and then go to the end of the chapter for the measures. The second option is the job aid route. Skip the book entirely and go directly to summary job aid online at www.Pfeiffer.com/go/kennethsilber (password: professional).

Happy understandings!

Ken Silber, Chicago, Illinois
Lynn Kearny, Oakland, California
March 31, 2009

ACKNOWLEDGMENTS

Thanks to the entire crew at Wiley: to Matt Davis for seeing the importance of the book and to Lindsay Morton and Liah Rose and her staff for being so willing to work with us in the design of this complicated book and overseeing the transformation of our manuscript to the beautiful and readable book you have in your hands.

Thanks to our friends who understand accounting for helping us out with Economic Logic (though we are responsible for any errors): Daniel Cousineau, MBA; Joe Durzo, Ph.D.; Don Kirkey, MBA; Deb Pavelka, Ph.D.; and Jim Schultz, MBA.

Thanks to the students at Northern Illinois University and Capella University who used prior versions of this book in HPT classes, and to Capella's TPI program, Dr. Jamie Barron chair, for being the first program to incorporate this book into its Introductory HPT class.

Thanks to ISPI, the organization itself, the convention attendees, and especially Roger Addison, for giving us the opportunity to present the ideas contained in this book for eight years at ISPI conferences to bring them up to their present level.

Thanks to our uncited friends and colleagues who provided feedback, ideas, and even hard-to-find books through e-mails, phone calls, and package deliveries: John Lazar, Carol Haig, Miki Lane, Anne Apking, Timm Esque, Clare Carey, Mary Norris Thomas, Walter Ratcliff and John Swinney.

ORGANIZATIONAL INTELLIGENCE

PART ONE

INTRODUCTION TO THE BUSINESS LOGICS MODEL

CHAPTER ONE

WHY AND HOW TO USE THE MODEL

This chapter, which introduces the book and Model, is divided into four sections:

- What organizational intelligence is and the objectives of the book as they relate to it
- Why organizational intelligence is important
- An overview of the Business Logics Model we use to develop organizational intelligence
- Suggestions on how to use the Model

What Organizational Intelligence Is and How This Book Will Present It to You

Organizational intelligence is the ability to think effectively about an organization from a business point of view. This subject is taught in business schools or, in the case of many line managers, learned in the trenches as they work up to higher levels of responsibility for the organization's profit and loss. Line managers who don't acquire this way of thinking don't rise very high.

When we talk about *business* in this book, we certainly include the corporate sector, the usual context in which people use the word *business*. But a business is *any* organization that offers a product or service to customers and receives income. It is any organization that has expenses it must meet in order to create its product or service and that tries to ensure at least enough income to meets its expenses.

Finally, it has a strategy, processes, and people to make all this happen. Therefore, when we speak of a business in this book, we include government, not-for-profits, educational systems, financial organizations, hospitals, and the like.

What we are calling organizational intelligence, the business way of thinking, becomes second nature to the people who use it. When those who engage in the business way of thinking encounter those who do not, line managers and executives tend to disregard those who do not as naive, inconvenient, and sometimes even dangerous to the business. They become a disturbance to be managed.

Staff specialists like you, from human resources (HR) and organization development (OD) to facilities, public relations, and information technology (IT), have deep expertise in their own fields, but they often lack much background or experience in the general business and financial concepts that go into business intelligence. These business and financial concepts drive high-level decision making in most organizations. Thus, while many of you think very intelligently about specific problems in your area of responsibility, you often fail to frame your ideas and recommendations in the context of your organization's business model, its strategies, and its objectives.

Of course, you care about the organization as a whole, and you are certainly smart enough to appreciate organizational intelligence. You just never got the business background that leadership in the line organization takes for granted. This lack handicaps you, making it difficult for you to influence business decisions or to gain the time and attention of the people who make those decisions—that is, "getting a seat at the table."

The purpose of this book is to address this need by providing you with a clear, simple method for understanding the business of the organization in which you work. The book provides you with a set of business ideas and vocabulary so that you can talk with your clients in terms they understand and about the things they care about. It provides you with the tools for understanding the problems your clients are struggling with and for understanding them from their own perspective. It can help you build credibility and at the same time identify the business issues that are driving your client's decisions. It will help you discover what metrics your client is using to measure success so that you can make better decisions about which projects to tackle and know how to ask for the data that you want. It will also alert you to all parts of the business that your clients must take into consideration and give you some idea of how changes you propose in one area might affect initiatives in another area.

To accomplish all this, the book provides a model—a high-level structure—for assembling an overview of the organization. It also provides a menu of measures that organizations use to determine how they are doing in the different areas of the enterprise.

By the end of this book you will be able to understand and converse intelligently about your performance improvement interventions in terms of:

- The language of business.
- How the organization works.
- What issues your clients (internal or external) are really concerned about.
- How to communicate your ideas in terms your clients care about.

In addition, you will be able to:

- Gather information about your organization.
- Identify the key issues facing your organization.
- Identify what key measures your organization is concerned about.
- Determine the current and desired states of those measures.
- Determine the gaps in organization performance.
- Create performance improvement interventions that are aligned with the business and culture of the organization.
- Communicate those gaps and your proposed solutions for closing them to management in language that management understands and accepts.

Why Organizational Intelligence Is Important

As explained in the Preface, since the mid-1970s, many experts in the human resources and human performance technology (HPT) fields have been pointing out that success in HR or HPT practice depends on your ability to act as a business partner with your client (Bratton et al., 1981; Choayun and Schwen, 1997; Deden-Parker, 1981; Deden-Parker, Bratton and Silber, 1980; Hartt and Rossett, 2000; Hedberg, 1980, IBSTPI, 1999; ISPI, 2002; Katz, 1978; Price, 1978; Silber, 1975, 1978a, 1978b, 1980a, 1980b, 1982a, 1982b, 1998; Silber and Bratton, 1984; Silber and Kearny, 2000, 2001, 2003; Summers, Lohr, and O'Neil, 2002). This means understanding the client's business and being able to discuss it in the client's language.

Clearly, this requires understanding the industry the business operates in, the organization's strategic goals, its financial picture, the competitive landscape, and other related factors. Yet people come to workshops asking how to get clients to understand what we do. They are missing a basic point: They do not add value when they require the client to do extra work to understand them.

For example, how would you react if you wanted to buy a car, and the salesperson at the dealership insisted you learn the principles of materials stress testing so that you could really understand the advantages of the car you're considering? Or how would you react to a doctor who required you to learn the basics of anatomy and biochemistry so that she could explain exactly what was wrong with you and help you prevent the illness from happening again? Acquiring such knowledge would no doubt be useful, but few of us have the time (even if we have the interest) to go deeply into the other person's area of expertise. We just have a problem that's bothering us, and we want it remedied so that we can get on with our real work.

The same is true for our clients. We are actually asking them to learn our language and concepts (which took us weeks to years to learn) before we will even talk to them about their problem. And we imply that, unless they understand us, our language, and our processes (for example, the difference between an organization scan, a performance analysis, and a training needs assessment), they are just not all that smart—despite their MBAs and 6-Sigma black belts. We can come across as arrogant, snooty, and uninterested in clients' problems when we demand they understand us on our own terms.

Instead, we can add value by understanding the client's business and language and by framing our recommendations using their concepts and vocabulary. When we propose ideas to clients (internal or external), they must consider our recommendations in the context of many other aspects of the business. Clients must consider how those ideas align with the strategic direction of the organization, what resources their implementation will require, how their management peers will react to the ideas proposed, and what other changes in the organization will have to be made to accommodate the recommended changes. They must think of all the elements of the organization that will be impacted. The conversations that clients have about these issues, both among themselves and with others, are carried out using business concepts and business language.

If we don't understand the business concepts and the business language our clients use, how can we understand their most pressing problems? If we make recommendations that do not take the big business issues that clients face into account, how can they trust our recommendations? It would be like trusting your boat to a person who was technically proficient at managing a sailboat, but who knew nothing about currents, tides, and ship traffic. The risk is simply too great.

Clients expect us to make recommendations that address their key goals and objectives, in language that they understand. They expect us to recommend actions that won't derail other key business initiatives in their areas. They also expect us to find out about these issues as part of our research and to take them into consideration when making recommendations. They expect us to state both the cost and the payoff of any recommendation we make in business terms so they can evaluate it and make an informed decision and so that they can defend their action if challenged by their bosses or peers.

This is the same level of service you would expect from your attorney or financial adviser: You expect them to know their own territory, to understand your situation, and to advise you of both the risks and rewards of any course of action they recommend to you. A competent (and ethical) attorney will not encourage you to file a lawsuit without informing you if she thinks the opposition will make mincemeat of you in court. As HR-related advisors, we owe the same level of professional service to our clients.

This book provides a set of business ideas and vocabulary that will let you talk with your clients in terms they understand and about the issues they care about. It offers tools for understanding the problems most clients are struggling with from their own point of view. Use it to build credibility and to identify the business issues that drive your client's decisions. Use it to make better decisions about what projects to take on and to decide what data you need to ask for. It will make you aware of the other parts of the business that your client must take into consideration before agreeing to act, and it will give you an idea of how changes you propose in your client's area of responsibility might affect initiatives in other parts of the organization.

The Business Logics Model

Being able to do all this does not require an MBA, an education in marketing and accounting, or a one-day "finance for non-financial managers" workshop. With a useful model and your existing analytical abilities, you can get enough of an overview of the organization to ask intelligent questions and determine where to find the answers you need. That's what the Business Logics Model does for you. It is offered in this book at two levels: the one-day, quick overview level, and a more detailed level that you would use to build a much deeper understanding of the business over time.

Overview of the Model

One of this book's authors set out to find a business model that would work at the overview level. The search was initially for a model that business managers commonly used, but it turned out there wasn't any widely used and recognized business model that looked at the whole organization. There were financial models, strategy models, marketing models, HR models, and models for almost every subcomponent of an enterprise, but nothing that pulled it all together. What was needed was a 360-degree model that would give the user a CEO's or a general manager's view of the business as a whole. Clearly, a new model had to be created.

Ultimately, a model was developed based on business logic, as expounded by Karl Albrecht in his 1994 management text, *The Northbound Train*. This information was supplemented by concepts from other respected business writers, like Michael Porter. To make the concepts easier to grasp and remember, the information was chunked into logical elements and provided with icons to aid both understanding and visual memory. The first version of this model was created in 1994.

The other author undertook to find a model that would allow HR practitioners to identify commonly used business measures, so that they could anchor their analytical and evaluative efforts with measures that were important to the business and that were already being collected. The measurement model selected and adapted is the balanced scorecard (Kaplan and Norton, 1996).

Since the late 1990s, we have been field-testing, successfully using, and continually improving the model with input from clients and colleagues. The result is the Business Logics Model, which contributes a new, unique, and easy to understand way to frame and organize information about an organization.

The Model is summarized several ways. First, in the left column of Table 1.1 is a graphic representation of all the Business Logics; the six in the circle are what we call Internal Logic, and the box around the circle is what we call External Logic. In the right column of Table 1.1 are the definitions of the Logics. Second, the measurement aspects of the Model are presented in Table 1.2. It contains the seven logics, the subelements of each logic, and a number of measures an organization can use to determine its performance in each.

External Logic

External Logic looks at both the general business environment and the industry the business belongs to. An external scan has become a basic part of how organizations think about their business, especially when developing, reviewing, and updating their strategic plans. A scan looks first at the Business Environment, considering general trends in five areas: economic, demographic, political/legal, technological, and sociocultural. Then it looks at Industry Structure; for example,

TABLE 1.1. THE BUSINESS LOGICS MODEL

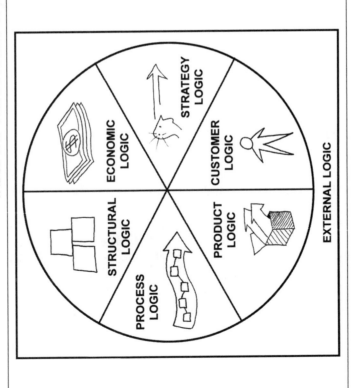

External Logic: Opportunities and threats the organization faces due to forces in its own industry and general trends in the world around it

Economic Logic: How the organization makes a profit and achieves growth

Strategy Logic: The purpose of the organization, the direction it is moving in, and its plans for getting there; includes the organization's culture

Customer Logic: How the organization locates, acquires, and keeps customers

Product Logic: How the organization's products or services appeal to the customer; how they are differentiated; and the company's image with its customers

Process Logic: How the organization creates, produces, and delivers its product/service

Structural Logic: The organization's infrastructure; how it organizes itself to accomplish its work

TABLE 1.2. SAMPLE MEASURES FOR BUSINESS LOGICS

Logic	Subelements	Sample Measures
External	Substitutes; New Entrants; Technological Trends	Number identified by organization; number addressed by plan
Economic	Cost Structure; Financial Focus; Profit Source	Selling, general, and administrative expenses (SG&A); cost of goods sold (COGS); earnings before interest, taxes, depreciation, and amortization (EBITDA); profit per source
Strategy	Mission; Culture; Core Competencies; Growth	Identified? Accuracy and alignment? Measurability?
Customer	Market Strategy; Customer Relations Strategy	Size of market share; new customers; complaints
Product	Niche/Broad; Differentiation; Image	Quality; price; knowledgeability; novelty
Process	R&D; Production; Logistics; Postsale	Cycle time; waste; cost; coordination
Structural	Structure; Information Technology; Learning/Innovation	Alignment; percentage of knowledge captured; rewards

Intel belongs to the semiconductor industry and Genentech is part of the biotech industry. Industry Structure looks at six factors impacting the industry:

1. The threat of new entrants
2. The bargaining power of suppliers
3. The bargaining power of buyers
4. The threat of substitutes
5. The intensity of the rivalry
6. Whether the industry is growing or shrinking

For example, when banks were still regulated, competition among them was restrained and gentlemanly, but the banking industry is now a shark tank. The six Business Environment trends are part of most standard business planning models (ISPI, 2005; Jain, Trehan, and Trehan, 2006; Kotler, 1991; Rummler and Brache, 1990. Industry Structure is based on Michael Porter's *Competitive Strategy* (Porter, 1980).

We will look at these in detail in Chapter 3. Just as you wouldn't analyze an individual job holder in isolation from her environment, you can't understand what's happening in an organization without understanding the business environment it's operating in.

Internal Logic

Internal Logic provides a high-level structure, allowing you to build an overview of how the business works from the inside. It is divided into six business perspectives, which we call logics because they represent a coherent way of thinking about a related set of issues. Each Internal Logic is accompanied by a set of measures commonly used by businesses. The six Internal Logics are as follows:

1. *Economic Logic:* How the organization makes a profit and achieves growth
2. *Strategy Logic:* The organization's purpose, the direction it is moving in, and its plans for getting there, including the organization's culture
3. *Customer Logic:* How the organization acquires and keeps customers
4. *Product Logic:* How the organization's products or services appeal to the customer, how they are differentiated, and the organization's image with its customers or its brand
5. *Process Logic:* How the organization creates, produces, and delivers its products and services
6. *Structural Logic:* The organization's infrastructure and its knowledge management, learning and innovation, and human relations functions.

Each of these logics is further broken down into several elements that are further defined and described in this book. A chapter is devoted to each logic with its elements and its possible measures. You will find a fairly detailed explanation of each, along with examples. At the end of each chapter you will find a quick reference job aid that summarizes the key elements, along with more examples and a menu of measures.

How to Use the Model

This Model is scalable. That means you can use it at different levels in the organization: the whole company, a suborganization within the company, and even your own department.

- First, it can be used to understand the whole organization, whether it is a company in which you work or one for which you might consult.
- Second, it can be used to understand a subunit in the company, such as the client's department.
- Third, it can be used to develop a scorecard for the business: a set of measures that the business uses to assess how well it is doing. These are the uses we will focus on in this book.

- Fourth, it can be used as a framework for both understanding your own department, and doing comprehensive strategic planning for your department.

1. Using the Model to Understand an Organization

The Model will help you get an overview of an organization as a business (as opposed to as a social system, a performance system, a branding exercise, etc.). It provides a framework for organizing relevant information about what the organization is trying to accomplish and for assessing whether the big pieces hang together logically or are at war with each other.

We believe that, even if you work in an organization and think you know it, it is a good idea to have a complete, high-level overview of the entire company using the Business Logics Model. We would be surprised if it turned out that, when you were done with the analysis, you had not learned several important things that you did not know before.

To use the Model this way, collect all the information in each of the external and six Internal Logics. (Don't panic; you can do this in one day even if you start out knowing nothing at all about the company; just do the information collection as we explain in Chapter 2 and as the Case Study in Chapter 10 shows.) Then put it all into the worksheets we provide. Finally, look at the big picture of the organization and see if there any issues of disconnects or misalignments.

2. Using the Model to Build a Scorecard for the Business

Numbers are used to keep score. Organizations use measures to determine how well they are doing: Sales and costs are two of the most obvious measures. Kaplan and Norton (1996) pointed out in *The Balanced Scorecard* that businesses need to track and report more than financial data, which are trailing edge indicators. Organizations need leading edge indicators of health, measures that provide early warning if things are going off track, that give a clearer picture of what is going wrong and where, and that furnish that information in time to adjust, before bad financials start showing up. Since many businesses already had measures to keep track of most of the important parts of the business, the balanced scorecard approach was logical for organizations to adopt. Because its use has become widespread, we adapted the Business Logic Model and the balanced scorecard measures into one integrated model.

At the end of each Business Logic section, you will find a menu of possible measures. You can partner with your client (or other experts in the organization) to identify which of the measures listed are used by the business you are working with. To build a scorecard, find which measures are targeted by this year's goals and which are currently being used to track the organization's performance. For measures that are targeted in the organization's goals, provide both the should-be numbers (the goals) and the current numbers (how the organization is doing today). This information is already being tracked and stored somewhere in the organization.

This scorecard can be used as a gap analysis. Use it to help you find opportunities to do projects that will move the numbers that are important to the organization toward the goal. This is key to the business's survival and should be a priority for us.

3. Choose a Target Suborganization Within the Total Company

If your client comes to you with a problem in specific part of the organization (for example, manufacturing), then you might want to focus your business logics and measures analysis at that suborganization level. As we have explained, we recommend doing the whole company first, but if you are doing most of your work with a single division or even a single department, you may save your really detailed research for analyzing and understanding chiefly that suborganization. However, keep in mind that every subunit of the organization has to serve the purposes and goals of the next level up. The department that is completely divorced from the goals and welfare of the division above it will be substantially interfered with from above, especially in a downturn. Always have at least a broad overview of the layers above the suborganization you are working with and understand how your client group fits in.

4. Use the Model on Your Own Department

We assume that if you are reading this book, you are in some type of HR and/or performance improvement department in your organization. You can use the Model to ensure that your department knows, and is aligned with, the organization as a whole.

To use it this way, first you have to apply the Model to the organization as a whole. Then you apply it again to your department, but you define the department (e.g., all of HR, just Training, and the like). Then compare the two analyses, checking for alignment and disconnects. Check measures: Are you measuring the same things that the organization as a whole cares about? (In our experience, this is a big gap for most departments in our area.)

Finally, the next time your department is putting together the plan for next year, use the organization-level model as your baseline and develop your own department's plan to be in alignment with that.

5. Pick a Level of Detail

You can do a basic overview, aim for a detailed understanding, or shoot for a level somewhere between the two.

- *Basic overview:* Decide whether you are going to build just a high-level overview or a detailed understanding of your target organization. If you are an independent consultant or a job interviewee going to see the client organization for the first time, the high-level overview is a practical choice. You can do an adequate job in a few hours spent over a few days. This high-level overview will help you establish credibility and allow you to discuss the business intelligently with business managers and decision makers in the organization. It will also let you identify some opportunities for improving the organization's performance, and it will suggest ways to approach the topic with your clients.
- *Detailed understanding:* On the other hand, if you want to be a player in the organization, you need to build a detailed understanding of the business and how it works. This will take time, and you will most likely build it over a period of weeks. If you go to this level of detail, you will know more about the organization than most of the people in it. You will be able to identify business issues and risks and discuss them intelligently with senior managers. This understanding puts you in a position to become a trusted advisor, a business partner (although it does not guarantee you will become one). You will have a much broader understanding of the organization's challenges and opportunities, and you will be better positioned to make a difference. *Caveat:* Many internal people, including line managers, know little outside their own areas of responsibility. Be aware of this shortcoming, and don't assume that all senior-level managers have an understanding of the business as a whole or have the larger organization's goals and interests at heart. Many do, but some do not.
- *Something in between:* You may choose a combination of an overview of the entire enterprise and a detailed understanding of a particular segment. Or you may decide on an in-between level, getting more detailed information than the overview but less than all the categories of information addressed in this book. You can customize the worksheets and job aids in this book to suit your own objectives.

6. Using the Book to Get a High-Level Overview

At the end of each chapter are:

- A summary job aid that covers in brief what was discussed in the chapter.
- A worksheet showing an example of notes for a high-level overview.
- A blank worksheet.

You will also find a downloadable worksheet in Microsoft Word format on the Web site. Use the job aid to trigger your investigation and gather information only at the level of topics listed there. The example shows the least detail you should obtain; you will probably get a little more. Do your first pass based on your Web research, any phone networking you can do, and your best guesses. Fill out the worksheet to the best of your ability, then take it to a meeting with your client. Ask for a few minutes to confirm or correct what you learned and to fill in any blanks. Most clients respond very positively to this. Don't be surprised when some ask for a copy of the completed document themselves.

7. Using the Book to Get a Detailed Overview

To get a detailed overview, use the book as your guide. As you look at the chapter for each logic, you will see that it is broken into more detail than the summarizing job aid offers. After providing definitions and examples, the chapter lists common issues for each element within that logic. Next is a section titled What You Should Do, which lists three to seven pieces of information for you to obtain. Use the What You Should Do section as your guide when you are building a detailed overview. We suggest you create your own detailed worksheet using Excel, which will let you expand where you need to and record as much information as you think will be useful in the future. We suggest you create an additional column for each element, where you can list issues discovered in your research.

Set a time frame for completing your initial overview: Try to get high-level information first, then fill in as many details as you can. Ask around about any blanks, and seek out experts who can provide the missing information. Try to finish all or most of your analysis within the timeframe that you set; the sooner you have the big picture, the more effective you can be in your work.

8. Uses for the Information You Have Gathered

Caveat: Let's begin with something you should definitely ***not*** do with your analyses. It is likely, whether you apply the Model to the organization as a whole or to just some part of it, you will find many performance problems. That is not surprising: All organizations have them, and that is what keeps us employed.

Armed with this new, systematically derived, systemic view of the organization, do *not* march into the office of the CEO, your VP, or the VP of your client organization, report what you have found out, and say how messed up things are. This is called a career limiting move.

We are not suggesting that you ignore the information you have gathered, but there are better ways to apply it, ones that help the organization improve without getting you fired.

8a. High-Level Overview

If you are interviewing for a job or you are in a consulting sales situation, use the high-level overview you have created to plan your first visit. Identify questions to ask and strategic issues to inquire about during your first conversation with a decision maker. Use the questions to establish your credibility as someone who has done the homework, who understands the organization and its business environment, and who is ready to add value. Use the opportunity to simply ask some intelligent questions, not to pontificate. This is still more of an opportunity for learning than for action, and questions are always more effective than pronouncements.

You may be analyzing a department or division in detail and are doing just the high-level overview for the business as a whole. Use the high-level overview as a map and compass during your work with the division, to keep you from acquiring an overly division-centric outlook. We have all run into so-called silo organizations, in which each division (or sometimes each department) leads an insular existence, without considering how their actions impact the other parts of the organization. In this situation, the high-level overview can help you help your client keep the big picture in view, and it can focus your talks on contributing to the organization as a whole.

When you are working on a problem (such as resolving interdepartmental conflict or trying to improve a cross-functional process), look at the high-level overview you created for misaligned areas of business logic that may be contributing to the problem. For example, one of the authors worked for a bank whose Customer Logic targeted high-net-worth individuals. Although their advertising and products were directed at that target market, their Structural Logic did not support it. Information systems were fragmented, communication between different product lines and operations were poor, and customer-facing employees were given low wages, no career ladders, and little beyond basic training. As a result, the service expectations of high-net-worth individuals were rarely met.

8b. Detailed Overview

Use a detailed overview as you work with specific clients on performance improvement projects to win respect and influence with decision makers. When clients come to you with a problem that they are sure can be solved by the proverbial three-day training class, begin your preparation by reading the high-level assessment you have done for the whole organization. Then do a detailed analysis using the model of the suborganization in which the problem is occurring (for example, if the problem is the retention of sales personnel, then look at the sales, or sales and marketing, department).

Look at the detailed model, both logics and measures, you have completed. Use this to identify the real gaps or discrepancies between logics that you believe are the real causes of current problems. List the benefits of fixing them, the risks of failing to do so, and list alternative solutions.

Then as you meet with your client, begin to present the ideas about the real problems that you have identified. Use the model to show where the real disconnects and misalignments lie. Use your consulting skills along with the model to help move the client from seeing this as a training problem to seeing the real organizational issues involved.

And if you get any static about your ideas, feel free to both blame us and give them a copy of the book to read.

Summary

In this chapter, we have introduced organizational intelligence and the Business Logic Model. You now have an overview of what the Model is, where it came from, and how you can use it. The next chapter will address how to gather data as you are using the Model to build an overview, whether high level or detailed, of a business you are working with.

CHAPTER TWO

HOW TO GATHER DATA

The first question we are always asked when we talk about the Business Logics Model is where can we get all that information. Related questions are, "How much time does it take to collect all that data? Isn't it confidential? Won't I get fired for asking? How will I understand the data? Isn't that too much information to collect? If I am external, where can I find all this information?"

The purpose of this chapter is to go into detail about the last question (finding the information), but let's begin by dispelling some of the myths and fears about collecting data.

Myths and Fears

How Much Time Does It Take to Collect All That Data?

Yes, collecting information will take time, as does any analysis of a problem that we are all trained to do. The data will not magically appear one morning on your computer screen. So the question is how much time will it take? In Chapter 1 we touched on this question. Depending on your organization, the data can be collected in as little as one (yes, that's one) day (as is the case in the Chapter 10 case study). If you need to do a little more research or legwork, it could take as long as a week, but that's spending about two hours per day, not a full 40-hour week. So it's not an onerous task.

Isn't It Confidential? Won't I Get Fired for Asking?

Forgive us if this answer sounds like a sermon. Remember, you are not asking for the secret ingredients of Coca-Cola, the U.S. nuclear launch codes, or the patented chips and screen for the iPhone. All you are asking for is information about how your company runs, much of which is actually required (for public companies and not-for-profits) to be on file with the Securities Exchange Commission, and it is available on the company Web site (especially the investor section). It should also be available to all employees as a matter of course, like the mission/vision wallet cards that are so popular.

If all this information is being kept a secret within the organization (here comes the sermon), you are working in a corporate culture that is not likely to produce productive and satisfied employees. As we point out in the Chapter 9, people these days are talking about sharing information and knowledge management, rather than knowledge hiding.

If your company is unwilling to share this information with you, then you have already identified a performance problem that will likely cause many others. And if it is just you they will not share it with, because you are "only in human resources or training" and don't need to know it, then you have proof that the organization thinks very little of your department and its contribution to the organization. You will be very vulnerable at downsizing time.

This flip side of this coin is what someone once called the Rodney Dangerfield syndrome in our fields: "We get no respect, no respect at all." (If you are too young to have heard him say it on TV, check YouTube.) The result is that we feel we do not deserve to have anything but the training assignments we are given. We are afraid to ask to do analyses and afraid to ask for information. This is a case of our limiting ourselves, rather than the organization doing it to us. As an employee of a company, you have the right to know any of the information that we are suggesting that you gather. (That's the end of the sermon.)

How Will I Understand the Data?

The information that the Business Logics Model asks you to gather is, for the most part, very straightforward. If you cannot understand, for example, the demographics of your customer base, then it is very likely that your understanding is *not* the problem, but rather the way the information is explained or the lack of clarity of those demographics. And if you cannot understand the mission, vision, products and services, and other aspects of the company, how will the customer be able to?

There is one exception: Economic Logic. In Chapter 3, we discuss a specific strategy (our take-an-accountant-to-lunch program) that you can use to overcome your number-phobia and even understand that information.

Isn't That Too Much Information to Collect?

As we've explained, we are not expecting you to spend a lot of time doing this, so you probably won't collect too much information to begin with. But for you overachievers, we have created a way for you to know when to stop.

All the worksheets are specifically designed to give you very little room to write. The idea is *not* to blow them up in size or to put them on several sheets so that you can write more. The idea is to gather and write just enough information to understand each of the logics of the organization. Too much information will overwhelm rather than help you. There is always time to go back and get more information or to locate supporting documents with all the details, when you need them for a specific purpose. As explained in Chapter 1, sometimes you will decide you really want to have an in-depth understanding of the organization. For example, you might have an HPT job where you have been assigned to act as a business partner to one of the executive team, to shadow her in her decision-making meetings, to consult with her on a regular basis, and to ensure that her HPT/HR/process improvement, and related needs are anticipated and met. For such an assignment, you do need to gather and understand a large amount of information, but if you have been assigned such a role, you are expecting some heavy lifting. That is not a role for the faint of heart. As another example, you may be a salesperson dealing in large-ticket item sales: capital equipment, enterprisewide systems, or outsourcing major functions. In this case also, you need a deep understanding of the business and will do a detailed analysis. In these situations you will customize and expand the data collection forms, and you will spend more than a day. But that isn't where most people need to go. Most will need only the general overview that can be done in a day or less.

If I Am External, Where Can I Find All This Information?

Whether you employed by the organization or a consultant to it, you need to understand the same information about the company in order to help it. The issue, as we pointed out in Chapter 1, is the level of detail you need initially. When we consult with an organization, we do a high-level Business Logics Model of the organization before going in for the first meeting. Do we know as much as someone who has worked there for 10 years? Generally, no, of course not. But in some areas, we actually know more about the whole than do most people who work there because they know a lot about their parts of the organization, but not much about the rest. We certainly know enough to sound intelligent about the company and the business issues it faces.

But, we hear you asking, how do you get all the information if you don't work there? The key is that a great deal of the information for External Logic and for five of the Internal Logics is publicly available and easy to access, or easy to deduce from the kinds of business publications that we assume you read. If you are consultant, we assume you are reading the following periodicals, and that reading gives you a start, in addition to the information in the next section of this chapter:

- *Wall Street Journal*
- *BusinessWeek*
- *Forbes*
- Crains' Business publications for specific cities
- Publications for the industry in which the company is found
- The business section of a good newspaper (if any are left by the time this is published)
- HR, training, HPT, and OD publications, where companies talk about their latest Structural Logic innovations

Where to Find the Information

Now, here are some ways to obtain the information asked for in the Model.

Why It's Easy

Finding the information you need for the Business Logics Model is easy, and for a reason. You are looking for information that is important to the organization and that enables it to run. Despite our sermon, companies cannot function if employees do not know or have access to some information, such as the mission, next year's objectives, financial statements, inventory and sales figures for different products, newly awarded patents, organization charts, customer service call wait times, and the like. This information, unlike the so-called butts-in-seats and course-posttest scores we sometimes focus on, is crucial to an organization running and making a profit. This information exists, is collected daily, and is used by the people who need it.

This data is analogous to the data available on the dashboard of your automobile: speed, amount of gasoline remaining, and oil level/temperature. These are all critical for you to know in order to drive, and they are right there for you to see—no searching, asking permission, running special reports, doing statistical calculations. The data we are talking about is what NASA might call mission-critical data. You must have it at your fingertips, and it must be accurate, or you cannot function. So the information we are gathering is not data that will take a complex statistical analysis to run, or three months to pull together. It is in a report somewhere. All you have to do is retrieve it.

Documents

We can use many published sources to learn about a business before we ever talk to the client. Most organizations large enough to afford our services are required to publish information about themselves every year: to inform investors, governmental agencies who fund or oversee them, and other stakeholders. In the United States, the sources of such documents are as follows:

- *Annual reports:* A high-level report of the organization's financial health, the annual report is increasingly used as a communication tool to many stakeholders. These reports are available on most companies' Web sites, under the section for investors. These sections are usually titled Investor Relations.
- *10-K and Form 990 reports:* More detailed reports (our favorite) are published yearly by all publicly traded companies (10K) and not-for-profit organizations (990). They list all the financials (especially the documents we talk about under Economic Logic, broken down by most of the financial concepts you will learn in that chapter), and details about industry structure, competition, market conditions, internal problems (such as lawsuits, R&D issues), key patents and technologies, mission, vision, objectives for the year, products and services, sales figures, and on and on and on. The reports even contain the names and contact information for officers, products, and services. These documents are also available on most companies' Web sites, under the section for Investors, or on the company intranet. If your company does not have this information, the U.S. government does, and you can get it with four mouse clicks and a little typing:
  —Go to http://www.sec.gov/.
  —Under Filings and Forms on the left, click on Search for Company Filings.
  —Click on Company or Fund Name. . . .
  —Fill in the Company Information and Click Find Companies.
  —When all the reports for your company come up, scroll down the list looking in the left column for the 10-K.
  —Click on it, and there you are.
- *Caveat:* Don't just download a 10-K, hit print, and leave the room. The authors learned this the hard way. Some of them run over 500 pages, many of them not very useful for what we're doing here. First open the document and scan for the information you want. The table of contents will help you narrow your search. Then print select portions, or just read them on screen.

- *Hoovers or Mergent:* Hoovers is a popular by-subscription investor publication that profiles all publicly traded companies. It gives several thumbnail analyses of each company with financials, history, a brief thumbnail critique of management, strategy and operations, and comparisons with the company's three top competitors. It's quick, pithy, and fun to read. Hoovers.com charges a lot for subscriptions, in which case you may either have access to a corporate subscription, or you may use a less lively publication called Mergent Online. Mergent Online used to be an investor publication called Moody's and has never been as gossipy as Hoovers, but it has good information. You can access Mergent through most public libraries' Web portals for free.

- *Libraries:* (For younger readers, these are quaint places where they store actual books printed on paper.) The main library in any city will have at least one business librarian and research librarian. These specialists are extremely knowledgeable and helpful with identifying resources about different companies and in showing how to use them. We learned this the hard way—researching prospective employers while unemployed.

- *The company Web site:* Visiting an organization's Web site reveals what the organization wants investors, customers, and prospective employees to believe about them. It communicates the image the organization is trying to project, and, if the site is well organized, it gives useful information about the company's products and services. It also shows locations. The Web sites of most publicly traded companies have a section called Investor Relations, where you can download the annual report and 10K.

- *Company intranets:* Most organizations have realized that the sharing of information among employees is crucial to their success. So, for example, if you work for an insurance company that was involved in the Hurricane Katrina disaster, the information about the number of customers involved, all the meetings with them, claims, payouts, and denials is on the company intranet. In some organizations you have direct access to it, and in some your boss or your boss's boss will have to get the information. But it's there.

- *The Web:* Our mea culpa. We don't know how to text, tweet, or use the Web to find this information as well as we should. We do know that most of the documents and periodicals are available online.
  - Undoubtedly your company subscribes to some Web sites that provide information about your industry, your customers, your products, and related items.
  - And Google and other (yes, there are others) search engines, when used properly, can turn up any information about any company.
  - You can go online to find friends, colleagues, and even strangers who work for organizations you're trying to learn about or who have worked for them. Social networking sites can be very helpful in locating people with the information

you want. Sites such as LinkedIn, Plaxo, Facebook, and many others have groups you can tap into, and search engines for finding people. Many businesses have set up their own pages on Facebook and whole buildings in Second Life, where you can go to find information and people to network with.

— If you are under 30, you already know how to do this; if you are over 50, ask your kids or grandkids, because they know.

- *Departmental reports:* We've saved our second favorite source for last. Every department in the organization puts together reports on a regular basis: production reports, sales reports, orders reports, customer service call volume, strategic planning documents (missions, visions, objectives), among others. These reports are generated to provide upper management in the organization with the important information about how those key business functions of the organization are doing. They contain most of what you need. So all you need is to get access to them (see our preceding sermon if you can't).

People

We can use external experts and networks, as well as internal networks, to gather data for the Business Logics Model.

- *External networks:* These include professional societies (e.g., SHRM, ASTD, ISPI), business schools, the chamber of commerce, sports clubs, and local service organizations (not to mention Web-based networks like LinkedIn), to make informal contacts for obtaining information about an organization. It is likely that within three contacts, you will find someone who has not only worked for that organization, but who has the information you want.
- *Internal networks:* All employees in an organization have an informal network, a group of colleagues with whom they eat lunch, party outside of work, complain about life and the company, and share gossip and information. We all know that, have been part of one, and have learned all the important things we know about the organization in the network. This is an excellent source of both information (which might be slightly limited or biased within the group) and the names of other people whom people in the group know—people who do have the information you need.
- *Managers*: Managers are a good source of information about the areas they are responsible for. However, unless the manager is highly placed or particularly alert and well tuned into the organization, many of them are narrowly focused on their own specialties.
- *Internal experts*: Specialists in various logics of the Model are invaluable resources. Ask accountants or finance people to interpret the financials for you, instead of

spending hours puzzling over numbers. As we promised, we will explain our famous take-an-accountant-to-lunch program in Chapter 4. And remember, as busy as people are, they love to talk about their work (and how good they are). So just popping your head into the office of the product manager for a new and successful product and saying, "I hear the X's are flying off the shelves. Are we doing really doing that well? What are the numbers?" is less likely to meet with a brush-off than a request for the printout of a 20-page PowerPoint presentation of sales figures.

- *Customers*: External customers are the best source for information about how the organization's Customer and Product Logics are actually playing out. So try the same strategy with the customer service people, and ask to listen to some of those monitored phone calls. The tactic works wonders.
- *Others that you can think of:* You know your own organization better than we do, and you should use those unique resources.
- Some companies still have librarians and knowledge managers, who can give you all this information in about an hour.
- Some companies have the company character who has been there since the company opened and who knows not only all the information for the External and Internal Logics, but all the information we don't want to even think about in this Model.
- Some companies belong to industry benchmarking forums that share data on some of the logics across companies.
- And all the other ways you have developed on your own to find out what is going on in the organization.

Data Collection Worksheets

Tables 2.1, 2.2, and 2.3 show you blank copies of worksheets for collecting and saving the information gathered in a high-level overview. As explained earlier in this chapter under how much data to collect, these worksheets are deliberately designed to give an at-a-glance overview of the business and to be doable in a day or less. We recommend starting out by collecting no more information than you can summarize on these sheets:

- The External Scan Worksheet (Table 2.1) is for recording the information you gather about External Logic.
- The Internal Scan Worksheet (Table 2.2) is for recording what you learn about the six Internal Logics. Answer the questions at the bottom of the worksheet when you have filled out the six columns.

TABLE 2.1. EXTERNAL SCAN WORKSHEET

Do environmental scan for the business you are targeting: ■ Business Environment ■ Industry Structure

BUSINESS ENVIRONMENT	KEY THREATS	INDUSTRY STRUCTURE
Economic?		Competitors: Intensity of rivalry?
Demographic?		Bargaining power of suppliers?
Political/legal?	KEY OPPORTUNITIES	Bargaining power of buyers?
Technological?		Threat of new entrants?
Sociocultural?	Is the industry growing or shrinking? How fast?	Threat of substitutes?

- Considering your answers, what appear to be key threats and opportunities for this business?
- How can you test your assessment of the threats and opportunities?

TABLE 2.2. INTERNAL SCAN WORKSHEET

Assess and fill in the logic the business appears to be using.

ECONOMIC LOGIC	STRATEGY LOGIC	CUSTOMER LOGIC	PRODUCT LOGIC	PROCESS LOGIC	STRUCTURAL LOGIC

- Do the logics in the six columns support each other or are they contradictory?
- If they are contradictory, does this have some bearing on the problem you were asked to solve?
- How can you test your assessment that these are the business logic(s) the company is using?
- Now review the logic in the light of your environmental scan. Do the six logics seem to be consistent with external realities?

TABLE 2.3. MEASURES WORKSHEET

Logic	Measures	Target	Current	Gap	Performance Problems	Interventions	Measured Results
Economic							
Strategy							
Customer							
Product							
Process							
Structural							

- What specific measures does the organization use for each type of logic? Write them in column 2.
- What is the target for each measure? Write it in column 3.
- What is the current number for each measure? Write it in column 4.
- What is the gap between target and current number for each measure? Write it in column 5.
- Those measures with the greatest and most critical gaps are the focus of the performance problem analysis and intervention selection that take place next in the performance improvement process.

- The Measures Worksheet (Table 2.3) is for recording at least one significant measure for each of the six Internal Logics. If you want to identify measures for each of the elements within a logic, you can either add rows (see the client examples at the end of each chapter) or build a spreadsheet.

Each of the worksheets is available in electronic form at www.Pfeiffer.com/go/kennethsilber, where you can download them. Or, you may photocopy the forms in this book at 8 1/2" x 11" and use them to take hand-written notes.

The worksheets in Tables 2.1 and 2.2 match the categories in the Model we described in Chapter 1. We'll now talk about the Measures Worksheet (Table 2.3).

Guidelines for Using the Measures Worksheet

The Measures Worksheet serves two purposes. First it assists in achieving the Business Logics Model's goal of understanding the organization in business terms because businesspeople are results oriented, and these measures are the results they use to judge their success. As you can see in Table 2.3, the Measures column has one row for each of the Internal Logics (because, as explained in Chapter 3, it makes no sense to have measures for the External Logic).

Second, the worksheet provides a new and interesting way to display your organization scan or performance analysis results as you work on a performance improvement project. You can display your analysis data in this worksheet and then include the rest of the project information in it as well. It has eight columns. In this book, we will use the first five. The last three are there for you if you choose to use this format (as one of the authors does, using an Excel spreadsheet version) to track the rest of the performance improvement project through to measured results to see if you closed the gap.

- The Logics column is self-explanatory.
- The Measures column asks, in effect, "What measures does your organization use to determine how it is doing on that logic?"
  - If you know, you write them in (more in a bit about how many and how they fit in the box).
  - If you do not know, look at the Measures Table that appears as the next-to-last section of every chapter after Chapter 2, where we provide a representative (not complete) list of possible measures from which most organizations choose. Choose the ones that fit your organization.
  - If you cannot choose from the list provided because you do not have the information, then you take the list to your information sources (those discussed earlier in this chapter) and ask. It's much easier to get an answer

when you show them the list of possible measures than if you just ask, "How do we measure X?"

- The Target column asks you to fill in the number that the organization hopes to reach if it is successful (e.g., in the Economic row, for the measure Profit, the Target might be $1 million). Again, if you don't know the target, put it on your list of questions to ask.
- The Current column asks you to fill the number that the organization is at today (e.g., this profit may be at $850,000).
- The fifth column you fill in is the Gap. For most measures, it requires simple subtraction. For some of the narrative measures, the gap must be worded.

Issues in Using the Measures Worksheet

Astute workshop participants who have used this worksheet have pointed out an issue to the authors: *The answers don't fit into the little boxes.* Yes, we did tell you that the purpose of the Internal and External Logics Worksheets and the Measures Worksheet is to fit everything on three pages and that you should not blow it up to fit more in. Kaplan and Norton (1996) and Stack (1994) are very clear that an organization cannot really track more than four to six (that's 4–6) measures at a time—meaning focus on and improve only four to six at a time. So why does the worksheet in Table 2.4 (which matches the reality of most of you reading the book), take up enough lines so that they do not fit in the little box we gave you.

There are three reasons for this discrepancy, one having to do with the purpose of the book, the second having to do with reality versus theory, and the third having to do with using this worksheet to identify performance problems.

Book Purpose

The purpose of the book is to show you how to use the Business Logics Model, including the measures. Therefore, we have provided an example that includes measures for each of the major elements of each the six logics, so that you can see what a complete measurement analysis would look like. Given the large number of possible measures we discuss in the book, the table runs to several pages. You can see the example measures we have provided for in the table titled Measures for each chapter (the number differs from one chapter to another) and in the completed worksheet for a client example at the end of each chapter. For the practical reasons of wanting to give a clear example without taking up too much space in the book, these client worksheets show only the measures collected for the type of logic in the chapter.

TABLE 2.4. MEASURES WORKSHEET EXAMPLE

Logic	Sample Measures	Target	Current	Gap	Performance Problems	Interventions	Measured Results
Economic	% Variable;	85%	5%	80%			
	COGS	$5/card	$20/card	$15/card			
	Profit Source	50% from lowest income demographic	95% from lowest income demographic	45%			
	Return on Equity	10%	3%	7%			
	Cash Flow	30 days late	120 days late	90 days			
Strategy	Mission/Vision,	Meet all criteria	Meet all criteria	None			
	Culture	Meet all criteria	Meet all criteria	None			
	Core Compets.	Meet all criteria	Meet all criteria	None			
	Growth Strategy	Meet all criteria	Meet all criteria	None			

TABLE 2.4. MEASURES WORKSHEET EXAMPLE (*Continued*)

Logic	Sample Measures	Target	Current	Gap	Performance Problems	Interventions	Measured Results
Strategy (Cont'd)	Pricing Strategy	Meet all criteria	Meet all criteria	None			
	Alignment	Meet all criteria now, and with addition of new customers & products	Meet all criteria now	Evaluate strategy with addition of new products & customers revise strategy or cust/prod to keep aligned			
	Target market segmentation	Demographic and behavioral	Demographic	Add behavioral			
Customer	Niche focus	3 Niches (add 2 Niches to improve cash flow with new product)	1 Niche	2 new Niches			
	New Customers	100/week in existing niche; 1,000/week in 2 new niches	50/week in existing niche;	50/week in existing niche; 1,000/week in 2 new niches			

TABLE 2.4. MEASURES WORKSHEET EXAMPLE (*Continued*)

Logic	Sample Measures	Target	Current	Gap	Performance Problems	Interventions	Measured Results
Product	Differentiation	Novel (focused on target group needs) 1 familiar for new customer	Novel (focused on target group needs)	Familiar for new customers			
	Price	Appropriate for current & new custs;	Approp. for current custs	Approp. for new custs			
	Innovative	Only product for this market	Only product for this market	None			
	Responsive	97% satisfied	97% satisfied	None			
	After-sale service	Within 6 hours; cheery	Within 6 hours; cheery	None			
Process	R&D Innovation	1 new product not borrowed	0 new products	1 new product			
	Quality	10% error rate in credit granting	65% error rate in credit granting	55%			

TABLE 2.4. MEASURES WORKSHEET EXAMPLE (Continued)

Logic	Sample Measures	Target	Current	Gap	Performance Problems	Interventions	Measured Results
Process (Cont'd)	Cycle Time from loan to collection	Average 30 days	Average 120 days	90 days			
	Dispute handling %	5% disagreements escalate to dispute	95% disagreements escalate to dispute	90% disagreements resolved			
	Structure	Meet all criteria for structure type	Meet only 50% of criteria for structure type	50% of criteria			
	System	Knowledge captured and stored	0% Knowledge captured and stored	100% Knowledge			
Structural	HR Mgmt functions aligned	100% functions aligned	50% functions aligned (hiring, promotion not)	50% functions			
	Performance Improvement	HPT/OD solve 90% of problems	Training alone solves 30% of problems (only regulatory)	60% problems			
	Organizational Learning	Meets 90% of criteria; all Type II learning	Meets 0% of criteria; all Type I learning	90% of criteria; 100% change in learning type			

Reprinted with permission of Lynn Kearny, 2009

Theory Versus Reality

In reality, you may choose the same approach, that is, try to find all the possible measures for each logic. We still believe, given how important each of the listed measures is, that you can collect all that information in the day to a week we suggested earlier in the chapter. And if you can, we recommend that approach because, as shocking as it may seem to some of you, sometimes your client is actually focused on the wrong measure. (Dare we also point out trainers who are still counting butts-in-seats and smile sheet scores instead of focusing on measures about how they contribute to the organization's key measures as identified in the *first* five of the six logics?)

On the other hand, we recognize that your knowledge of the organization, your client's sophistication, and your available time may make the selection of one or two key measures in each logic sufficient. If, for example, in Process Logic, your measure is defect rate and your current measure is 50 percent, you may conclude that you need go no further in gathering other measures. You have found the so-called low hanging fruit and are going to work to improve that measure before you even look at other measures.

That is a sage approach as long as you understand the risk that some other measure you did not check, like on-time delivery of inputs, may be impacting or interacting with the measure you have focused on. Like a physician, you want to stop the hemorrhaging before beginning to look inside the wound.

Using the Measures Worksheet for Performance Analysis

As mentioned, you can combine your Business Logics Model analysis with your performance analysis or organization scan to identify the nature and causes of performance problems in the organization, If you do, then your logic would be as follows:

- Get all the key measures the organization uses and then see how the organization prioritizes them.
- Get the target, current, and gap for each measure.
- Look for interactions among the measures and gaps to see if they are independent or related to one another.
- Group and prioritize the gaps along some criterion that will make sense to the client.
- Put all this into a comprehensive, systemic, systematic performance improvement plan for addressing the most important gaps (largest, most interrelated, etc.).
- Because this table does not include all the columns needed for tracking and evaluating an intervention, like Problem Causes and Implementation strategy, recreate the table (perhaps in Excel), with more columns and space to include all the needed information.

- Present this data and my proposed solution to the client as a package rather than as set of piecemeal, isolated recommendations.

To do this, collect the measures, gather all the data, and do not worry at all about the length of the table or the software used to represent it.

Summary

In this chapter, we have tried to do several things.

- First, we've tried to combat the arguments about why you cannot get the information the Business Logics Model calls for. We have, and you can too. You won't get all of it every time, but you'll acquire enough to be very useful.
- Second, we described why getting the information is so easy (it is key business data without which your organization cannot run).
- Third, we have listed the documents and people that can provide you with the information called for in the Business Logics Model (remember our favorites: 10-Ks, department reports, internal networks).

With the overview provided in this section of the book, you are now ready to move into Part II, and learn about each logic in detail.

PART TWO

THE BUSINESS LOGICS MODEL IN DETAIL

CHAPTER THREE

EXTERNAL LOGIC

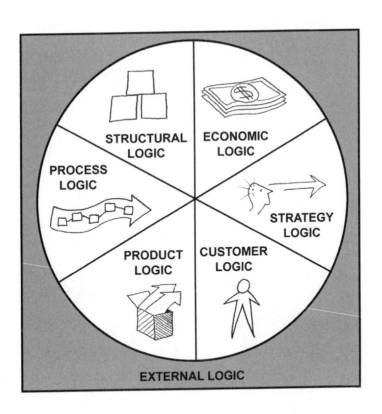

TABLE 3.1. ELEMENTS OF EXTERNAL LOGIC

Business Environment	Industry Structure
Economic	Industry competitors:Intensity of rivalry
Demographic	Bargaining power of suppliers
Political/legal	Bargaining power of buyers
Technological	Threat of new entrants
Sociocultural	Threat of substitutes

External Logic is based on both the common sense and the theoretical notions that organizations do not exist in a vacuum. They exist in an environment that occurs outside the organization, and that environment impacts the organization. Everyone reading this, based on the recent economic crisis, understands, intuitively at least, that what happens either in the outside world or in an industry different from our own has impact on our organizations and on us. From systems theory to marketing theory to management theory to human performance technology, there is a clear recognition that before one can even attempt to understand the insides of an organization, one must first understand the external environment and industry in which that organization functions.

This chapter will give you a detailed look at two sides of External Logic: Business Environment and Industry Structure.

Why External Logic Is Important to You and the Organization

You may be asking yourself, "Why should I spend time worrying about this? It's the job of the executives to understand this stuff. Economics, legal matters, technological advances, demographics, bargaining powers, substitutes—those are all subjects that are way beyond me. I barely understand them when they talk about them on the news." It is probably true that you will never be an expert in these fields. But here's why you need to understand the external environment in which your organization (and you) function.

Let's take the two most obvious aspects of the Business Environment: economic and demographic. As of March 2009, the United States and most of the world were in a major recession. Would your organization just go on doing what it has been doing, making the same products, offering the same services, having the same market strategy? If so, would that be likely to work if, for example, you are in the financial, automobile, food service, entertainment, clothing, or newspaper industry? Clearly the answer is no. The economic crisis is affecting your industry and your organization. And if you and your organization do not understand how, then your resume better be up-to-date. Actually, the only industry that was doing quite well in that economic environment, whether we like it or not, was the alcoholic beverage industry, where year-to-date sales in 2009 were almost double those of the previous year! Chronic, but true. And being aware of how the economic state affects the alcoholic beverage industry, production is up (not down like everyone else's), and the shelves are full. This is *not* a recommendation that you drink, just an example of an industry that understands clearly that economy affects it differently from the way it affects most others.

The second example is demographic. The wave of baby boomers who, assuming their 401K plans are not wiped out, were going to start retiring in 2010, when this book was published. That's millions and millions of 60-something-year-olds, in pretty good health and with a very diverse set of interests, looking for things to do with their active lives for the next 20 or so years. Does your organization know what products and services it can provide to those boomers by creating new services, by assisting in building new types of retirement communities, by inventing new products to help them stay healthy and overcome illness, or by creating new industries and learning communities in which they can spend their free time, so that they can enjoy the next 20 plus years? If not, your resume should be up-to-date.

Companies that understand the external business environment and the structure of their industries can be agile in responding to changing customer demands, and they can be proactive in creating completely new demands as the world shifts. As a sociocultural example, Toyota was able to see the potential of the green movement early on, and its offering of the Prius hybrid car was a major economic and company image coup for them, even while some companies were still denying there was such a movement.

Companies that do not understand the changes in the external environment and how to respond to them are perishing. In only three weeks in February–March 2009, two newspapers folded, and one moved to publishing only online, as the United States moved from getting its news from papers and TV to the Web. Just like buggy whip manufacturers, who at the turn of the twentieth century refused to believe the automobile was going to replace horse-drawn carriages, companies and whole industries are disappearing every year in the twenty-first century.

Based on changes like these, your job is going to change. Who in the HR or ID fields, for example, would have said 15 years ago that many of the employees whom you hire and are responsible for in your own company would not live and work in the United States, but rather in India. Who would have predicted that not only customer service centers and manufacturing would be done overseas, but instructional design and development as well? That impacts you personally and directly. You do your work differently, face different challenges, and have to adapt to different requirements. Succeeding in this global work world requires you to understand the Business Environment and how industries are now structured.

The Elements of External Logic

Each of External Logic's two major elements, Business Environment and Industry Structure, has a number of sub-elements, as shown in Table 3.1 at the beginning of this chapter.

The distinction between the Internal Logics, on the one hand, and the two types of External Logics on the other, is best articulated by Elearn Limited (2005). First they describe the Internal Logics as those element that include:

> the system (inputs, transformation processes, outputs) and all the resources, knowledge and the actions of the decision-makers and employees that make up the organisation. (p. 2)

One of the key points they make is that internal factors may be controlled and deployed to enable the system to operate effectively and efficiently. (p 2).

Next they describe what we call the "closest in" External Logic, the industry, as:

> the organisation's marketplace, where it buys its materials, resources and other inputs and provides good and services to customers. It also include competitors, . . . (pp. 2–3)

They point out that these are factors outside the organization that affect it, but the organization can take some limited action to affect them (less than for internal, more than for what they call Macro Business factors).

Finally, they describe the Macro Business Environment, which they call

> the "playing field" for all businesses in the global and national economy. It is the external environment that provides a general background in which all organisations operate. It is made up of political, economic, social, technological, legal and eco-environmental forces. (p. 3)

This Macro Business Environment has two characteristics. First, it influences both the internal and industry levels. Second, these are forces that the organization certainly cannot control and may not even be able to influence them, as in industry.

Interestingly, for many years, the Industry Structure and Business Environment were referred to as global structures. To use the popular phrase from columnist Thomas Friedman, "the world is flat." There is no more division between "United States and international" at these levels. All the Business Environment and Industry Structure elements refer to their global state, not just to the U.S. state.

This chapter will first discuss the element of Business Environment, explaining the general category, describing and giving examples of each of the five sub-elements in it, discussing issues related to Business Environment, and ending with what you should do about all we have said. Then the chapter will do the same for the second element, Industry Structure.

The Business Environment

Why Business Environment Is Important to You and to the Organization

Though we have discussed the importance of External Logic in general and were clear that Business Environment is a component of External Logic, there is still something to say about the importance of understanding it.

The point is quite simple and clear, according to Palmer and Hartley (2008):

> History is full of examples of organizations that have failed to understand their operating environment, or simply failed to adapt to change in their environment. The result has been a gradual decline in their profitability. . . . On the other hand there have been many spectacular successes where organizations have spotted trends in their operating environment and capitalized on these. . . . (p. 5)

The importance of the Business Environment, the elements of Business Environment, and the issues with the Business Environment, as we present them here, are our own amalgam of the ideas from Palmer and Hartley (2008), Kotler (1991), Jain, Trehan, and Trehan (2006), Rummler and Brache (1995), ISPI (2005), Cummings and Worley (2009), and Elearn Limited (2005), since all present the same concepts using slightly different wording and diagrams. The five factors we have identified that make up Business Environment are summarized Table 3.2.

Economic Environment

The *economic environment* includes all the financial factors that affect the organization as a whole and the spending power of its customers:
Global economic models (capitalism, etc.)

- Global and national economic conditions (inflation, recession, etc.)
- Economic and trade policies (General Agreement on Tariffs and Trade, World Trade Organization, Big 8 Summit, etc.)
- Interest rates
- Unemployment rates
- Levels and distribution of wealth globally and nationally
- Rates of savings and debt among consumers
- Consumer spending patterns (individual, corporate, national, and global)

Taken together, these factors determine how much the organization's customers have to spend on its products and how much therefore the organization (and its competitors) can reasonably expend in doing business.

TABLE 3.2. BUSINESS ENVIRONMENT

Factor		Explanation	Examples
Economic		What changes in the economy are affecting the business?	Inflation/recession (globally, not just United States) Tax rates Interest rates Gross domestic product
Demographic		What are changes in the population makeup?	Increased percentage of older people Migration of people from one country/region to another
Political/legal		What legislation, regulation, legal = precedents, and political = changes have occurred?	Admission of Eastern European counties to European Union Laws related to pollution
Technological		What developments have occurred = in science and technology?	Genetics Biotech Chemistry Physics New materials (microfiber)
Socio/cultural		What changes have occurred in people's cultures, beliefs, desires, actions?	Terrorism Increased global opportunities for women AIDS/HIV

© 2009. Reprinted with permission of Lynn Kearny.

For example, in early 2009, capitalism in the United States, the mixed economic models of some European countries, and the noncapitalist models of the largest nations in Asia were in recession. The world may be flat, but there are many trade barriers and copyright infringement issues. Interest rates are low for those who have money, but many fewer people have money because unemployment rates are high. Wealth is low (most U.S. investors having lost 50 percent of their worth in the last five years), but China's wealth is comparatively high—as long as the United States can repay the $1 trillion debt. And many Arab and Asian countries are buying U.S. property and companies. Most consumers have low savings and high debt, and they spend only on essentials, if they can afford them.

Now before you think the authors spend every day reading *The Wall Street Journal* and watching CNBC, please note that all the preceding information was gleaned from common, everyday sources: the daily newspaper, the daily TV news broadcasts, even *Tonight Show* jokes about how bad things are even for Hollywood plastic surgeons. These sources are hardly esoteric or beyond any reader of this book.

Demographic Factors

Demographic factors consist of information about the population. We will discuss these factors from an internal marketing perspective under Customer Logic, but here we are concerned with population factors worldwide:

- Population growth, now and projected, worldwide (e.g., increasing in India, decreasing in Germany)
- Age distribution (huge baby boomer retirement wave starting in 2010; patterns of growth in birth rates, by country over the last 30 years, during some periods, decline in others)
- Family structure (two-person/two-parent plus children, one-parent plus children, parent(s) plus children plus grandparents, etc.)
- Gender distribution (ratio of males to females)
- Geographic distribution of population (reurbanization of United States; moves in United States from cold northern states to Florida and the Southwest)
- Education levels, in the United States and globally (United States not the highest, especially in science and math)
- Ethnic and racial makeup (the United States now changed so that former "minority" groups, taken together, equal a majority)

All this information is available online with a quick search engine query on the term *demographics*. Although we avoided Web sites like Wikipedia in doing research for this book, the Web does have its place in providing access to masses of demographic data. Some sites our search turned up that look useful in providing companies with present and projected demographic data include that provided by the U.S. government at www.census.gov/ipc/www/idb/ and sponsored sites, some with free as well pay-for data, including www.esri.com/bao and http://www.geolytics.com/.

Political/Legal Factors

Political/legal factors are the elements of international governments and related laws that govern how business functions: the organization, the industry, and the customer. These rules of the game include the following:

- Government policies in the organization's home country (in the United States, changes in policy from the George W. Bush to Barack Obama administrations)
- Intergovernmental relations and alliances (relations between India and Pakistan or between the United States and Russia)
- Intracountry relations among different ethnic and religious and tribal groups (on a scale from friendly to genocidal)
- Stability of governments and geographic regions (how long the current government is likely to be in power, how a change of power might occur, and what changes a change of power woud bring about)
- Legislation that governs business and trade:
  — Within the states and countries of origin (e.g., which Texas state laws govern what can be used as collateral for a loan, and what U.S. federal laws govern which products can be said to be "made in the United States," or what food is "organic"?)
  — Within the region (e.g., North American Free Trade Agreement)
  — Globally (e.g., trade treaties, copyright laws in China impacting U.S. software and CD/DVD companies)
- How the government enforces existing laws
- What nongovernmental groups lobby for laws that impact business
- The attitude of the government toward consumer lawsuits
- Labor-management relations (including unions)

This element of Business Environment is probably the most complex for an organization to keep track of because of its global complexity. Given the number of countries involved in most manufacturing and service supply chains, keeping track requires not only understanding the political situation in almost every region in the world and in most of the countries, but also knowing the laws that govern your industry in every country in which you buy, make, or sell products. Clearly, you will not go to this level of detail every time; you will focus on the legislation that most impacts the organization you are with. Often this takes the form of regulation. What regulations must your target organization comply with, in order to keep its doors open?

Technological Factors

To say we live in a highly technological era, with rapidly changing and improving technologies, is a cliché, as science fiction and fact merge daily. *Technological factors* have a direct impact on both organizations and customers. Here are some considerations:

- The value of science in a culture
- Fields of science in which the "hot breakthroughs" are being made (e.g., biotech)
- The percentage of government and private money available for research and development
- Changes in products and services that incorporate technology (e.g., Blackberry and iPhone versus mobile phone)
- Changes in lifestyles as a result of products and services (e.g., working anywhere, anytime instead of at the office)
- The life span of any technology:
  — The product or service itself
  — The equipment used to create the product or service
- The regulation of technology (who can manufacture, use it; how is its safety ascertained?)
- The protection of technological innovation (e.g., legal, political, force)
- Paradigm shift technologies (e.g., decoding and use of DNA) versus improvement technologies (faster computer chips)

Being familiar with advances in all fields of science and technology is one of the most difficult Business Environment tasks. In some ways, it requires more specialized knowledge than most of us have even to understand the implications of some technological developments. And some technologies we think of using in one way can provide unanticipated insights in other fields. For example, CAT scans of the brain, initially developed to diagnose brain injuries, have now developed an important function for trainers. As neuroscientists use CAT scans to watch the brain as people learn, they are coming to understand a great deal about what learning really is, how it occurs, and what changes it creates in the brain.

It does not take a science fiction writer to see that this has implications for changes in how instruction is designed or even the possibility, as imagined in the film *The Matrix*, of chemically or electronically induced learning. You can learn a lot by paying attention to news and the general buzz about new technologies. You can also learn much from talking with interested people in your organization, asking what technical developments they see coming that will impact (or that are already impacting) the business.

Sociocultural Factors

Sociocultural factors are the basic worldview—the values and beliefs—of people that determine how they see things and act every day. In the United States, for example, one frequently hears about living in a Post–9/11 world. However, for sociocultural factors to act as a useful concept for organizations and customers, we have to recognize that they are more complicated than that example and that many sociocultural factors are at play:

- What are the core values of the predominate culture of a country (each country, not just the United States)?
- What are the core values of subcultures in a country? How do they clash, and where is there common ground?
- What are people's views of the following, and how do these differ by subculture, educational level, religious affiliation, etc. (Kotler, 1991, pp. 150–151; Jain, Trehan, and Trehan, 2006, p. 10)?
    —Themselves
    —Family and marriage
    —Others
    —Organizations
    —Society
    —Language
    —Food
    —Religion
    —Nature
    —The universe
    —Birth and death

Issues Related to the Business Environment

Several issues are related to the Business Environment.

- The missing component
- The inactive factors

- The ever changing factors
- The differential factors

The Missing Component

Only Jain, Trehan, and Trehan (2006) include the natural environment as part of the Business Environment in a separate category (others include elements, like "being green" under sociocultural factors). The argument for its being a separate category is that it is a large category of factors that impact organizations (in all parts of the supply chain) and consumers (what products they will need or buy and which they will not), over which they have little or no control. It includes all the geological, ecological, and meteorological factors of a given country or region, including:

- Climate and weather patterns
- Natural calamities
- Natural resources
- Pollution
  —Natural
  —Human-made
- Topography

The Interactive Factors

The Business Environment factors are not a set of discrete factors, as some of the Internal Logics are. And they interact with each other in both predictable ways (for example, sociocultural and economic factors drive political/legal ones) and in unpredictable ways. The interactions are both complex and uncontrollable; you cannot simply align these factors in a rational way, as you can in an organization's Strategy Logic). Things just happen. The goal, a difficult one for action-oriented CEOs, is to try to understand them and then to use them in the organization's favor, without trying to change the complex interactions.

The Ever Changing Factors

The set of Business Environment factors an organization thinks it understood yesterday is not the same set it faces today. One United States administration has a certain view of bioscience, and fewer than 60 days later a new administration changes it completely. One hurricane misses the United States, and another destroys a city. One day we do not believe in global warming, and the next the man who has spent most of his recent life pushing for ecological change has not only a Nobel Prize but an Oscar and an Emmy.

The Differential Effects

The Business Environment factors and the interactions among them affect different organizations differently. In what the authors consider a perverse example, in March of 2009, amidst a recession, industry layouts, company bankruptcies, global warming, political instability in three regions of the globe, and a host of other serious problems, two industries are making more money that ever before: alcohol sales and movies. Some industries will do very well with the demographic of baby boomer retirements, whereas others may wither and die.

What You Should Do

You should take two actions for this element of External Logic:

1. Find out what the Business Environment looks like for the geographical regions in which your organization creates, produces, or sells products or services. What are each of the five (or six, if you include nature) elements of the Business Environment in which your organization operates?
2. Based on this Business Environment, what are the:
   a. Strengths/opportunities for your organization?
   b. Weaknesses/threats for your organizations?

Industry Structure

An *industry* is "a group of firms that offer a product or class of products that are close substitutes for one another" (Kotler, 1991, p. 222). The structure of the industry involves five competitive forces, consisting of one central force and two pairs of opposing forces (Porter, 1980, p. 4). The central force is that of industry competitors. One pair of opposing forces is the buying powers of suppliers versus those of sellers; the other pair is the threat of new entrants into the industry and the threat of substitute products or services. Kotler (1991) separates the issues of new entrants from the problems of barriers to exiting an industry, and he expands on competitors to differentiate "good" and "bad" ones, and ones to "attack vs. avoid."

Why Industry Structure Is Important to You and to the Organization

Though we discussed the importance of External Logic in general and were clear that Industry Structure is a component of External Logic, there is still something to say about the importance of understanding it. According to Porter (1980, 1985),

TABLE 3.3. INDUSTRY STRUCTURE

Force		Explanation	Examples
Industry competitors: Intensity of rivalry?		How fiercely do firms in this industry compete?	Compare computer software companies' competition with that among oil companies.
Supplier bargaining power		Are key suppliers few (and therefore have high bargaining power over supply and price) or many?	Oil suppliers have high bargaining power; pharmaceutical companies have high power until the patents run out, then it becomes low.
Buyer bargaining power		Are there many equal buyers, each with equal or low power, or few major powers with high power?	Wal-Mart and McDonald's have high bargaining power as buyers.
Threat of new entrants		How easy is it for new competitors to enter the industry (or to change the industry to enter it)?	Gasoline industry has a low threat; computer industry high. Telephone industry had low threat (landlines), but cell phones made the threat high.
Threat of substitutes		How likely is it the industry will be completely obsolete due to a new product that does the same thing and more?	Telephone and computer industries have high threat. For now, auto and oil industries have low threat.

© Lynn Kearny 2009. Reprinted with permission of Lynn Kearny.

Industry Structure is an aspect of External Logic that changes over time, is one of the key components in determining the organization's competitive strategy, and is an aspect of External Logic that can be influenced through that strategy. The interplay of the five elements that make up the industry also determines the attractiveness of an industry; that is, it influences whether a company should enter, stay in, stay in and change, or leave the industry. Therefore, only by understanding the Industry Structure can an organization respond intelligently with an Internal Logic (especially Strategy, Customer, and Product Logics) to existing competition and forces (through cost or differentiation, to be discussed later in the chapter) and to change the industry to better position itself.

For you, understanding the Industry Structure is important because it relates to part of your job. The ways of changing an organization's position in an industry, as well as cost and differentiation, can rest on the number and quality of people in the organization. If more or different types of people need to be added, if people need to learn new job skills, if processes need to be more efficient, if people need to fired, it is more than likely that you will be involved somehow in making that happen. Understanding the business reasons that drive the work you do will make you far more effective at designing solutions that meet the business needs. The five factors we have identified that make up Industry Structure are summarized Table 3.3.

Industry Competitors: The Intensity of Rivalry

Intensity of rivalry refers to the number and type of competitors in the industry, how they compete, and possible strategies for differentiating oneself from competitors.

The first concerns are what dimensions determine the level of rivalry in any industry and how intense the level is. Porter is not suggesting that some industries have no level of rivalry, but in some industries it is far more intense than others. Porter says rivalry is more than just normal competition. It occurs when "one or more competitors either feels the pressure or sees the opportunity to improve position" (1980, p. 17). Competitive moves by one company have effects on the others in the industry, leading to retaliation or countermoves.

Some of the many variables that impact how rivalries in an industry behave, according to Porter (1980, pp. 17–23) and Kotler (1991, pp. 231–233), include:

- *Number of competitors*: In an industry with many equally balanced competitors, it is possible for an upstart to start a rivalry relatively unnoticed, whereas in an industry with few competitors, rivalries are quickly noticed.
- *Growth rate of industry*: The more an industry is growing, the more customers there are, and the greater the opportunity is for all companies to gain additional customers (e.g., initially, the PC market had high growth; now it has slowed).

- *Diverse nature of competitors themselves*: The more similar the competitors (in terms of strategy, personality, etc.), the harder it is to differentiate the companies in the customer's mind (e.g., U.S. auto manufacturers competed at one end of the spectrum, Apple and Google competed with Microsoft at the other end).
- *Differentiation of products*: Are the products offered by different competitors very similar, or is there great diversity? (Although this is a relative notion, there is a greater differentiation in, say, home furniture styles than there is in carpet floor coverings.)
- *Strategic stakes*: How important is it to the strategy of a new company to enter the industry (e.g., Japanese car companies entering the U.S. auto industry's market, India entering the call center industry)?
- *High exit barriers*: If it costs a lot of money to leave the industry, the companies wanting to leave will stay around anyway, increasing the rivalry. (For example, there are huge expenses involved in closing down a nuclear power plant. It may cost less for a utility to keep them going at a loss than to close several plants.)
- *Innovation in the industry*: Is the innovation small and incremental or paradigm changing (e.g., the move from all gasoline-powered autos to hybrids compared to the move from photography on film to digital photography)?
- *Focus of the competition*: On what variable do competitors compete (e.g., price, quality, sales process, postsale service, novelty and innovation, etc.)?

Industry Competitors and Differentiation

The second question is, given an analysis of the industry using those and other factors, what can a company do to differentiate itself from its competitors? Since this question takes Porter (1985) a whole book to answer, the authors will leave the complexities and nuances to those interested in more reading. The basic answer boils down to (pp. 12–14):

- Price
- Differentiation

Kotler (1991, pp. 234–235) and Porter (1985, pp. 221–237) also address which competitors to compete with and which to avoid. They discuss the differences, within an industry, between:

- Strong and weak competitors
- Close and distant competitors

"Good" competitors (who play by the rules, set reasonable prices) and "bad" competitors (who buy market share, upset the industry's equilibrium).

Supplier Bargaining Power

Suppliers are companies that provide component parts, raw materials, labor, or information to the industry or to the companies in it. The Industry Structure issue is how much control does the supplier have over the price of materials that a company (or an industry) buys, compared to the amount of control the purchasing company has? Intuitively, you understand this question because you have experienced it. When your furnace goes out in February in Chicago, or your water pipes burst at 2 a.m., you know that the supplier, not you, has almost complete control over what you will pay because you will freeze or drown if you refuse to pay the price or if you spend a few days shopping around.

What factors impact the prices that a supplier charges? According to Porter (1980, pp. 27–29; 1985, p. 6), some of factors include the following:

- *Uniqueness of what is supplied*: The goods are different from those of other suppliers, and there are no substitutes (e.g., it would be difficult for NASA to change suppliers for the heat-resistant tiles it uses on the space shuttle).
- *Cost of changing suppliers*: Compared with the cost of paying more to the same supplier (e.g., computer manufacturers can change chip suppliers easily because the cost of the change is low, whereas a hospital would have a high cost associated with changing suppliers of CT scan and MRI equipment).
- *Number of suppliers available*: The fewer the number of suppliers that an industry can go to for some component or information, the more the suppliers can charge (e.g., if you have bought or refinanced a house, you know there are only three firms that supply your credit rating data to the mortgage company, giving them high bargaining power on price).
- *Possibility of collapsing the supply chain*: The industry or company has enough money to buy the major supplier if the prices it is forced to pay become too onerous.

Buyer Bargaining Power

The second of the pair of supplier–buyer bargaining powers that squeezes the industry or company is that of buyers. *Buyer bargaining power* can refer either to the end customer or to the industries that use the outputs of your industry. It refers to factors that allow or do not allow the customer to put the industry under price pressure and to the buyer's sensitivity to price. As a consumer of automobiles, for example, you know that you can bargain for the price of your car based on information (dealer costs, end-of-month quotas), the general economy, and how hot the car is that you want.

There are two sets of factors according to Porter (1980, pp. 24–27; 1985, p. 6). The first set consists of those that determine bargaining leverage, and they are very similar to those we just looked at for the supplier, with some additions:

- Uniqueness of the product or service
- Cost (to the customer) of changing suppliers of the product service from the current one
- Number of suppliers available to the customer
- Amount of information the customer has about costs
- Volume of purchases the customer makes
- Possibility of collapsing the supply chain, but in the other direction (the customer starts to produce it rather than buying it)

Other factors can make the customer price sensitive:

- *The ratio of the price for this product compared to the amount paid for all purchases*: If it is large part of the total budget, the customer is more price sensitive than if it is a small part.)
- *Profitability*: The lower the customer's profit level, the more price sensitive the customer is; for example, grocery stores have a very low profit margin.
- *The impact of the product or service on the customer's end product quality*: For example, an auto manufacturer must have high quality—precisely machined engine parts—or the end product, the car, will not be a quality machine.
- *The importance of the brand identity to the customer*: For example, does the customer need to be seen wearing Versace?

Threats of New Competition

The second pair of opposing forces deals with new competition: the threat of new entrants to the industry and the threat of substitute products and services.

Threat of New Entrants

New entrants are new companies entering the industry. As explained, having more suppliers in an industry drives price and profits down. Therefore, it is important for an industry to know if it has appropriate barriers to entry, which include (Porter, pp. 7–17; 1985, p. 6):

- *Government regulation*: For example, in the United States, someone cannot just decide to build a nuclear power plant; nuclear power plants are regulated.
- *Knowledge*: Examples are patents, trademarks, copyrights, and other rights to key required elements of the industry.
- *High cost of entry*: For example, it takes someone with the billions of dollars of T. Boone Pickens to enter the field of wind farms.
- *Other cost/resource disadvantages for new entrants*: Examples are access to raw materials, favorable locations, subsidies, learning curve.

- *Expected retaliation by existing companies*: Retaliation can take the form of price wars and other tactics to keep customers from trying the new company's product.
- *Product differentiation*: A new entrant has to somehow differentiate its product from those of companies already in the industry.
- *Economies of scale*: The more one produces, the less it costs per unit; therefore, new entrants have to enter at a high level of production to succeed.

Threat of Substitutes

Substitutes are new products entering the industry that can replace the industry's key product. The most used example of a substitute is one we are familiar with: the introduction of sugar substitutes (first in pink, then in blue, and finally in yellow packets). In the early 2000s, the substitute being discussed most was the one for a gas-and-oil-using automobile engine. The availability of substitutes gives customers the option to switch products based on prices or other Business Environment factors (e.g., a sociocultural desire to diet or to be green). The CD served as a substitute for the vinyl record and put that industry out of business, as online music downloads are doing today to the CD industry.

Porter lists some factors that impact the availability of substitutes (1980, pp. 23–24; 1985, p. 6):

- *The attitude of the customer toward switching in the product area*: The authors, for example, still read print from books, not computer screens or Kindles.
- *The cost of switching to the substitute*: For example, most people have not yet switched to LCD or plasma TVs because it is expensive to substitute one for the conventional TV they already have, whereas many have switched to downloading music instead of buying CDs because it costs little (no new equipment is needed) to do so.
- *How well the substitute performs compared to the original product*: For example, movies shot on high-density video are still not the same quality as those shot on 35mm film.
- *Perceptions associated with switching to the substitute*: Is it "cooler" to switch to music downloads? Does a person's initial perception have to be that of being fat to switch to a sugar substitute?

What You Should Do

You should take two actions for this element of External Logic:

1. Find out what the Industry Structure looks like for the industry in which your organization creates, produces, or sells products and services. What are the five elements of the Industry Structure in which your organization operates?

2. Based on this Business Environment, what are the:
   a. Strengths/opportunities for your organization?
   b. Weaknesses/threats for your organization?

Measures for External Logic

There is no specific set of measures for External Logic for several reasons.

- First, given the interactive and dynamic nature of the forces in External Logic, merely counting the number of elements of the logic an organization has identified is meaningless.
- Second, since the forces are mostly beyond the control of the organization, you cannot measure:
  — What the organization has done to influence the forces (and, no, dollars spent lobbying Congress is not really a valid measure of understanding the Business Environment).
  — What the organization does about the External Logic issues is reflected in its Internal Logics, specifically Strategy Logic, Alignment.
- Third, measuring how well an organization is faring in a given set of External Logic factors may or may not be a function of understanding the logic, but merely being in the right place at the right time (sorry, but we are back to alcohol sales again).

Something can serve as both a measure of External Logic and a bridge between External and Internal Logics: understanding the threats and opportunities. We have asked you to identify those in the What You Should Do in each subsection of this chapter. If your organization has done (a) a complete and (b) an accurate job in identifying the threats and opportunities presented by the Business Environment and Industry Structure, that effort is a measure that the organization has been successful in applying External Logic.

Again, since External Logic is both complex and dynamic, the list of threats and opportunities may be more than a simple list. It is might be in the form of "if they stay as identified now, then the threats are. . . . But if the environment changes to this configuration, then the threats are. . . . " This shows that the organization is doing Type II and Deuterolearning (which is the last element of Structural Logic) and that this is anything but a linear process. Some organizations are using a form of this called Scenario Planning. They identify a few key factors that would be game changing, and then build alternative scenarios of what the business environment and the industry would be like and what the business should do if these changes come to pass.

Sample Worksheet for External Logic

In Chapter 2, we introduced the External Scan Worksheet. Table 3.4 shows it with the External Logic filled out for one of our clients. It is brief: just a few words summarizing each of the elements. This is the level of detail that we suggest you use to get the big picture without bogging yourself down in a major research project. Save your time and energy for more detailed analysis when you have a specific performance issue to investigate or when you are with an organization for the long term and want to develop a detailed understanding.

External Logic Job Aid

The job aid in Table 3.5 summarizes External logic with graphics, definitions, questions to be answered, and examples. Use it when you are trying to identify the External Logic for your own (or your client's) organization.

Your Turn

Use the External Logic job aid and the External Scan Worksheet to identify the Business Environment and Industry Structure in which your organization operates, as well as the opportunities and threats those present for your organization. (See Table 3.6.)

If you want an electronic version of worksheet, there is one on the Web site www.pfeiffer.com/go/kennethsilber. Copy it to your desktop and make any changes you feel appropriate before completing it. If it seems too constrained for your purposes, create your own in Excel before you get to work.

Summary

You are now in a position to identify the External Logic of an organization by scanning both the Business Environment and the Industry Structure. With this information you will be able to see where an organization is adapting to its environment and where it is out of touch. It will help you see partly why an organization is (or is not) doing well and predict some changes of direction the organization is likely to take in the near future. Next we will get into the Internal Logics of the organization, the first of which is Economic Logic.

TABLE 3.4. SAMPLE EXTERNAL SCAN FOR CREDIT CARD DIVISION OF A BANK

Do an environmental scan for the business you are targeting

BUSINESS ENVIRONMENT	KEY THREATS	INDUSTRY STRUCTURE
Economic? • American consumers have maxed out their credit.	• Competition for customers and employees • Interest rate changes (or any major economic shift)	The intensity of rivalry? CUTTHROAT
Demographic? • Huge influx of call centers in area makes it easy for workforce to find and switch jobs.	• Customer sophistication • Technological change too rapid to assimilate and exploit	Bargaining power of suppliers? • Key 5 Cost of funds. Company's strong equity position helps get good rates but money. Market is real driver
	KEY OPPORTUNITIES	Bargaining power of buyers? • High Credit card market saturated— buyers can go anywhere.
Political/legal? • Deregulation in banking, drive to ease state restrictions on home equity loans	• Innovative niche marketing • Exploit skills at collections/retrievals	
Technological? • Technology forcing rapid change to stay competitive	• Leverage technology to improve customer service through speed and access	Threat of new entrants? • High New credit cards being offered by growing number of organizations
Sociocultural? • Level of education in available labor pool is dropping	• Is the industry growing or shrinking? How fast? • Growing fast	Threat of substitutes? • Moderate • Possible electronic substitution for all credit services

• Considering your answers, what appear to be key threats and opportunities for this business?
• How can you test your assessment of the threats and opportunities?

TABLE 3.5. SUMMARY JOB AID—EXTERNAL LOGIC

From these, identify key threats and opportunities for this customer.

Business Environment
What current trends are/will be affecting this type of business?

Economic
What changes in the economy are impacting the business? Fluctuating interest rates? Availability of capital? Other?

Demographic
What changes in the population are affecting the business? Aging population? Labor market migrating? Other?

Political/legal
What changes in legislation, regulation or legal precedent is impacting this industry? Rise in lawsuits or awards? Changes in safety or environmental restrictions? Reductions in federal funding? Other?

Technological
What technological trends or innovations are affecting (or are likely to affect) this industry? Electronics? Biotech? Chemistry? What specific developments?

Sociocultural
What changes in people's habits, desires, actions, or beliefs are affecting the business? Changes in credit spending? Educational level? Other?

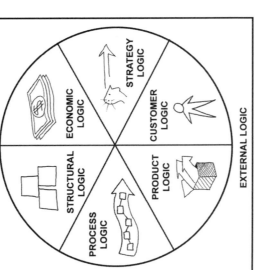

Industry Structure
For this type of industry, what is:

The intensity of the rivalry
How fiercely do firms in this industry compete with each other?

The bargaining power of suppliers?
Are key suppliers many or few? Are they tightly organized or fiercely competitive?

The bargaining power of buyers
Are there many sources of the customers' products/services, or are they a scarce resource?
The threat of new entrants
How easy is it for new competitors to enter the market?

The threat of new entrants?
How easy is it for new competitors to enter the market?

The threat of substitutes
How likely is it that the customer's product will be completely supplanted by something different (e.g., typewriters replaced by computers)?
Is the industry growing fast?

Based on Michael Porter's Competitive Strategy.

TABLE 3.6. EXTERNAL SCAN WORKSHEET

Do environmental scan for the business you are targeting: ■ Business Environment ■ Industry Structure

BUSINESS ENVIRONMENT	KEY THREATS		INDUSTRY STRUCTURE
Economic?			Competitors: what is intensity of rivalry?
Demographic?			Bargaining power of suppliers?
Political/Legal?	KEY OPPORTUNITIES		Bargaining power of buyers?
Technological?			Threat of new entrants?
Sociocultural?	Is the industry growing or shrinking? How fast?		Threat of substitutes?

- Considering your answers, what appear to be key threats and opportunities for this business?
- How can you test your assessment of the threats and opportunities?

CHAPTER FOUR

ECONOMIC LOGIC

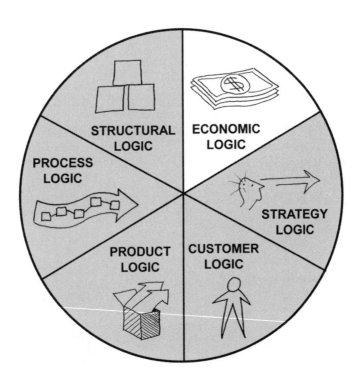

Economic Logic refers to things about the bottom line, an organization's financial picture. This logic is akin to the content people think about when they hear the phrase *finance for nonfinancial manager training*. However, *do not skip this section*. We promise that we have boiled down what you need to know to very small pieces of information that are easy to digest, and we will explain it in clear, simple English.

The purpose of the Model is to highlight and explain the key factors that an organization usually considers in making economic decisions and to clarify what those factors are for your target organization.

The three components of Economic Logic we will examine are as follows:

1. *Cost structure:* How the organization looks at and categorizes costs
2. *Financial focus:* How the organization values the two main categories of cost
3. *Profit source:* How the organization looks at where its profits come from

Finally, we will look into what measures the organization uses for its Economic Logic.

Why Economic Logic Is Important to You and the Organization

You may be asking yourself, why would you concern yourself with finance and Economic Logic? Isn't finance the province of the CFO and the accountants? And it is certainly not something that most HR, HPT, or other nonfinancial staff

TABLE 4.1. ELEMENTS OF ECONOMIC LOGIC

Cost structure	
Financial focus	
Profit source	
The financial picture: Measures	

specialists care about, study, or understand well. In fact, most of us in the kind of work we do deliberately avoid math, accounting, and any kind of financial statements.

We must step out of our comfort zone and learn to understand the Economic Logic of our organizations or clients for several reasons.

First, money is the basis of business. Ram Charan, the management consultant guru, says, in *What the CEO Wants You to Know*:

> When two businesspeople talk, whether or not they are in the same industry, whether or not they talk openly, they are always trying to gauge: Is her business making money? How is her business making money? How is the money making likely to change? (2001, p. 28)

So if you want to be able to talk intelligently to the other businesspeople in your organization, you have to understand how your company makes money. And if you want to understand some of those "incomprehensible" decisions management makes (like outsourcing the training or IT function to a consulting company), you have to be able to follow the money.

Second, many of those businesspeople, as well as many organizations in which they work, have adopted the balanced scorecard approach (Kaplan and Norton, 1996) or some variation of it. And the first perspective of the four in the scorecard is financial. This means there is a high probability that your organization or client has financial goals as part of its strategy and that all employees in the organization are judged on how they contribute to meeting those financial goals. It seems clear to us that it is crucial for HR, OD, training, and other staff specialists to be in the know about those goals, what they mean, how the organization plans to meet them, and how you contribute to meeting them.

Third, the Economic Logic of the organization will determine to a large extent how you can and cannot operate in the organization. Which organizational issues you are assigned or choose to address, how much analysis you can do, what solutions you can propose, and other decisions are all determined in part by the Economic Logic of the organization. For example, suppose you are called in to do training on a new computer system. And after analysis of the causes of poor performance using the system, you discover the problem involves the use of a poor system, poor work processes, lack of consequences for not using the system, and poor training. If the company is doing well financially, then fixes to or the replacement of the computer system might be an option. But if the company is facing hard times, that solution might not be an option.

This leads us to the fourth reason for understanding Economic Logic. In the preceding example, you might be able to make a rational case that replacing the computer system actually costs less than training everyone and redesigning the system. But Economic Logic will help you understand that all costs are not created equal. Some come out of one pocket, and some come out of another. The money for a system may come out of a pocket that has no more money in it—and would go out of the company if it did—whereas training comes out of another pocket that does have money in it, that is, "funny money" that stays within the company. This means you have to understand both what kind of money is in which pockets, and what money is real and what is not.

Fifth and finally—as you have probably heard by now from many sources—you are supposed to show how your HR, OD, or other staff function adds value to your company by showing its return on investment (ROI). And you have even seen formulas for calculating it. But Charan says, "money making in business has three basic parts: cash generation, return on assets . . . and growth" (pp. 28–29). So what happens if you start talking about ROI when everyone else is talking about return on assets (ROA) [or return on sales (ROS) or return on equity (ROE)]? And what happens if the way you calculate ROI is not the same as the way the organization calculates ROA? Might you feel just a little funny dueling formulas with a vice president of finance? So you have to know which financial measures the organization uses and how it calculates them.

Where Do I Get This Information, and How Do I Understand It?

Understanding Economic Logic is nowhere nearly as complicated as you think. Let's take a simple example. If the amount of your monthly paycheck you allocate to food is $600, and you spend $500, then you have an excess of income over expenditure of $100. And if you have to buy food on the sixteenth of the month, and you get paid on the fifteenth, then there is enough money in the bank to pay for the groceries. You understand that. In business, we have terms for those facts: profit and positive cash flow. And you also understand that if you pay $700 for groceries, and you get paid on the twenty-first of the month, you have a loss and negative cash flow.

We all understand that our annual income and expenses are more complicated than in this example and that an organization's certainly are as well. But the basic ideas do not change. So if you understand how to manage your own household, then you already understand all the concepts we are about to discuss. You just need to learn the fancy terms and forms accountants use to present some of this information.

Caveat: We are *not* accountants. We have learned this the same way you are learning it. You should check everything in this chapter with your friendly financial people. Yes, we said "your friendly financial people" because the answer to the question "How do I learn this?" is simple. We call it the *take-an-accountant-to-lunch* program. Do not sit through a finance for nonfinancial manager course (one of the authors has been very successful redesigning them because they are so ineffective). Instead, wander the halls and find a lonely accountant, surrounded by spreadsheets with lots of numbers. Say, "Excuse me, can I take you to lunch and ask you a few questions about our company's financial documents?" These lonely, people-deprived number gurus will be delighted to talk to you. And we have proof. On one day before our deadline for this manuscript, we ran into a question about whether some expenses went into COGS (cost of goods sold) or SG&A (selling, general, and administrative expenses). At 8:30 a.m., it was too early for lunch, so we sent out e-mails to five MBAs and PhDs in accounting whom we knew (plain old e-mails, not tweets, Facebook, Linked-In, text messages). By noon, we had five detailed responses to our question, all in understandable English. So we've done it and know whereof we speak.

TABLE 4.2. INCOME STATEMENT: PARTIAL INCOME STATEMENT FOR XYZ COMPANY (IN $,000)

	2008	2007	2006
Sales	410,000	400,000	350,000
Cost of goods sold (COGS)	140,000	105,000	80,000
Inputs	90,000	60,000	40,000
Production	50,000	45,000	40,000
Gross profit/margin	270,000	295,000	270,000
Selling, general, and administrative expenses (SG&A)	170,000	200,000	135,000
Sales expenses	20,000	25,000	15,000
Research and development (R&D)	60,000	75,000	50,000
Service	30,000	25,000	20,000
General and administrative	60,000	75,000	50,000
Net earnings (aka EBITDA, or earnings before interest, taxes, depreciation, and amortization)	100,000	95,000	135,000

One more explanation before we get into our explanation of Economic Logic. Of all the financial documents an organization uses—and there are many—the one we find the most telling about an organization, as well as the easiest to understand, is the income statement (sometimes called the profit and loss statement, or P&L).

The income statement in Table 4.2 usually contains financial data for three years (the years are the column headings). The rows show the company's income, broken down by various categories (e.g., product line or corporate function), the expenses associated with the income (e.g., cost of sales), and the net income (income less expenses).

Here are some financial picture items you can tell just by looking at the income statement itself or sometimes in the "notes accompanying financial statements" section of the 10K, which may contain some more of the detailed breakdowns below that are not in the statement itself:

- Over the last three years, which *income* items or geographical regions (e.g., U.S. versus foreign) have gone up and which have gone down?
- Over the last three years, which *expense* items have gone up and which have gone down?
- In the most recent year, which income categories showed a profit and which showed a loss?
  —Did certain products produce a greater or less percentage of the income than others?
  —Was more money or less spent on certain functions (e.g., sales, R&D, manufacturing)
- How does that picture compare with the picture over the two prior years?
- What numbers or trends strike you as good (e.g., sales doubled) or not so good (e.g., R&D expenses were cut in half)?
- Most importantly, which numbers or trends do you not understand or do not make sense to you? Which ones do you need to ask about at lunch?

From just this little portion of Table 4.2, we can see a lot about the organization and raise some questions to follow up on as we go through the rest of Economic Logic and all the rest of the logics. Reading the table line by line and comparing across years, we see that:

- Sales went up much less from 2007 to 2008 than they did the previous year (only a $10,000 increase instead of $50,000). Why?
- While COGS went up the from $25,000 to $35,000 from one period to another, there was a large and disproportional increase in the cost of inputs (by

50 percent, from $60,000 to $90,000), whereas production increased by only the same amount as the previous year. Why did input costs rise so much?

- R&D costs were increased from 2006 to 2007, but then scaled back again in 2008. Why were they increased, and why were they cut back?
- SG&A increased by $65,000 from 2006–2007 but then swung the other way and decreased by almost 50 percent of that increase from 2007–2008. What led to those sharp swings (hirings, layoffs, cutbacks of a certain type)?

Some companies even prepare income statements for different divisions, and some break down the numbers by product line, allowing us to see which products or divisions are responsible for increases and decreases. For example, pharmacies often show the numbers for the general merchandise sold in front separately from the numbers for prescription fulfillments, and some break down the prescription numbers by brand name and generic.

Some companies also provide numbers for items that affect operating costs, which enable you to see more clearly which areas are causing problems: higher pricing, higher input costs, lower volume, favorable mix, increased operating income from an acquisition, integration costs associated with an acquisition, higher marketing, administration or research costs, increased charges for legal matters, favorable foreign currency rates, and so on.

With that introduction and special section, it is time to look at the detailed elements and the measures of Economic Logic.

The Elements of Economic Logic

We have divided Economic Logic into three elements in addition to measures: cost structure, financial focus, and profit source. These three elements are not the only ones you could try to learn about your organization in addition to its measures, but they are three that we believe are key to understanding your organization's financial focus.

Cost Structure

Cost structure asks the question, "What is the balance in the organization between fixed cost and variable costs?" Let's look at what *fixed* and *variable* mean and their implications, and then talk about the balance.

Fixed Costs

If costs are *fixed*, then they are always incurred regardless of how much income the organization is bringing in. Your mortgage or rent is the same amount every

TABLE 4.3. COST STRUCTURE

	Definition	Examples
Cost structure	ASK: Which is more of an issue for you: fixed or variable costs? What are the key ones you focus on? What are you doing to manage these key costs?	
	Fixed = Costs that are always incurred regardless of what the business is doing.	Facilities, equipment, permanent staff
Fixed versus variable	Variable = Costs that change with the volume of business that is available.	Short-term rentals, raw materials, merchandise, temporary staff
	Organizations that have high fixed costs with relatively low variable costs:	Airlines, hospitals, refineries
	Organizations that have high variable costs, with relatively low fixed costs:	Retail stores, general contractors, small consulting firms
	Turbulence (rapid change) in the environment increases an organization's risk. Many businesses are trying to reduce risk by switching fixed costs to variable ones.	Downsizing, outsourcing, subcontracting, leasing

month no matter how much money you bring in or how much you want to spend; it is a fixed cost. An organization has fixed costs that usually fall into categories that are similar to your personal fixed costs, with a few additions. An illustrative list of fixed costs drawn from various discussions in Cooke (1993) includes the following:

- Personnel
  - Executive
  - Administrative
  - Salaried (versus commission) staff
- Taxes
  - Property
  - Payroll
- Insurance
  - Workman's compensation

- Health benefits
- Facilities
  —Mortgage/rent
  —Maintenance
- Utilities
  —Electric
  —Gas
  —Telephone
  —Computer
- Equipment
  —Lease
  —Maintenance
- Office supplies
- Debt interest

These costs occur and must be paid every month (or quarter or year), regardless of how much income the organization makes or how many products/services the organizations makes or sells.

Variable Costs

If costs are *variable*, then they are incurred in proportion to the amount of business the organization is doing, that is, the amount of products/services made and sold. Your clothing expenses at home, for example, may vary depending on what you are doing. If you are working during a week, then there may be expenses for buying or cleaning business clothes, whereas if you are not working that week and are sitting around the house in sweat pants and a T-shirt, your clothing expenses for that week may be less.

An organization has variable costs too, though you may find the list different from what you would consider variable at home. And Kotler (1991) points out that, in an organization, the *costs per unit* remain the same (fixed), but since the number of units vary, the costs vary. For example, the raw materials making a computer may cost $50. That cost remains constant, or fixed. But the total raw materials cost for a month or year varies because, to get the total cost, you multiply that $50 by the number of computers you actually make, and the number made varies. In addition, the total cost may vary even more based on quantity, because suppliers may give quantity discounts for larger purchases, which would lower even the cost per unit for purchases of large quantities.

An illustrative list of variable costs includes but is not limited to the following (again, consolidated from discussions in Cooke, 1993):

- Raw materials
- Shipping
- Personnel
  — Staff on commission
  — Temporary staff
- Advertising and marketing
- Research and development

Balance Dependent on Industry

No one is suggesting that either of these cost categories is better than the other or that it is better to have more costs in one of the two categories. Every organization has (and should have) some costs in each category. The question for the organization is, "What is the best balance between fixed and variable costs for our company, given our industry, our size, and the state of the economy?"

An industry that illustrates this balance issue was in the news in 2008–2009: the airline industry. This industry starts out with a high fixed cost: airplanes, gates at airports, pilot salaries, and the like; it has those costs regardless of the number of flights it makes or the number of people who fly. Historically, this industry has been a classic example of one with built-in high fixed costs and a balance of mostly fixed costs, with fewer variable costs.

But airlines also have variable costs, and one of those is fuel; this cost varies in two ways: with the number of flights and with the price of the fuel. In 2008 when the price of gasoline reached $4 per gallon in the United States, that variable cost rose significantly and changed the cost balance, increasing the proportion of total cost that was variable.

Shifting the Balance

In times of economic calm, when the External Logics are settled and favorable, most organizations are comfortable with relatively high fixed-cost structures. They still have U.S. plants, U.S. workers, health benefits, and other such expenses.

When economic times become difficult (as in 2008–2009, for example), companies try to both lower fixed costs and change the balance from more fixed to more variable costs. First, they try to find ways to lower the fixed costs. U.S. companies have sought to do this by moving facilities to and hiring workers in countries where the cost, while fixed, is lower than it is in the United States.

Second, they try to shift the balance to more variable costs. They move from full-time employees, whom they must pay regardless of sales, to contract employees (like external training vendors or designers), whom they have to pay only when they have the need and income to support the expense.

What You Should Do

You should identify three pieces of information for this element of Economic Logic.

1. What is the current set of fixed and variable costs for your organization?
2. What are the plans, if any, for changing the balance of fixed and variable costs in the organization over the next three years?
3. Does your department or consulting company (and you personally) fall into the fixed- or variable-cost category?

Financial Focus

Financial focus asks the question, "Which is more of a concern to the organization, cost of goods sold or sales, general, and administrative expenses or both. Let's look at what those terms mean, and their implications, and then talk about the balance.

Cost of Goods Sold (COGS)

This type of cost, also sometimes called cost of sales, is the direct costs "to produce or procure the products sold during the income statement period" Costales and Szurovy, 1994). These costs are directly tied to production: the materials used and the direct labor costs used to create the product.

According to the results of our send-an-accountant-an-e-mail-for-breakfast program, our financial experts (Cousineau, Durzo, Kirkey, Pavelka, and Schultz, see acknowledgments) say that COGS includes such items as the following:

- Purchased raw materials, kits, and assemblies used in manufacturing (e.g., purchased dashboard assemblies or wiring harnesses used in cars)
- Inbound freight and duties for those materials
- Rent/depreciation for the manufacturing facility allocated to manufacturing
- Labor applied to the making of the items (salaries, wages, and benefits of all manufacturing associates), as allocated in the bill of materials (BOM)
- Warranty returns and the like
- Information technology costs allocated to the manufacturing function directly related to production
- Warehouse expenses (sometimes included in SG&A, depending on the organization and the part of the process in which the warehouse plays a role)

COGS does *not* include indirect expenses such as:

- Distribution/shipping
- Marketing

TABLE 4.4. FINANCIAL FOCUS

	Possibilities	Definition	Examples
Financial focus	**ASK: Which is more of a cost issue for you, COGS or SG&A, or is it both?**		
	Cost of goods sold	The direct amount it costs to produce a product/service: Inbound freight Production costs Materials Manufacturing facilities Manufacturing labor	Companies that focus here are concerned with process and supply chain redesign for optimal efficiency and lowest cost. **Businesses** McDonald's Wal-Mart
	Sales, general, and administration expenses	The costs a company has that are not directly related to producing a product, including the costs of running the business as a whole, e.g.: Sales/marketing costs Distribution Management Human resources/ training	Companies that focus here are concerned with reducing fixed costs in administrative areas through outsourcing and downsizing. **Businesses** Just about all of them

- Sales force
- Accounting

Since businesses differ, the exact costs included in the COGS calculation vary from company to company. On the income statement, COGS helps a business determine which products are profitable and which are not. If you subtract the COGS from the sales revenue for that product, you have calculated the company's *gross* profit on the product.

Selling, General, and Administrative Expense (SG&A)

If you refer to the preceding list of things that COGS does *not* include, you have a pretty good idea of what *is* included in SG&A. This is the category of costs that are *not* linked directly to the production of goods but that are necessary for the running of the organization.

SG&A includes the following (Cousineau, Durzo, Kirkey, Pavelka, and Schultz, see Acknowledgements):

- Selling expenses:
    — Direct (linked to sale of a specific product)
        — Salespeople's salaries and commissions
        — Advertising and promotions
    — Indirect (not directly linked to a specific product, but allocated proportionally to all products sold; e.g., telephone, sales training, salespeople support, travel and entertainment)
- R&D expenses:
    — Salaries
    — Research activity costs
- Salaries of all nonproduction personnel, such as office personnel and executives
- Office mortgage/rent
- Utilities
- Legal
- Insurance
- Warehouses rent (sometimes included in COGS, depending on the part of the process)

SG&A is also found on the income statement, below (after) gross margin. It thus does not enter into the gross profit calculation. For this reason, SG&A expenses are sometimes called below-the-line costs.

Issues Relating to Financial Focus

High SG&A. Just as some industries have built-in high fixed costs, some have built-in high SG&A. But in difficult economic times, high SG&A expenses can be a serious problem for almost any business. The most common way to reduce SG&A is to turn fixed costs into variable costs and to reduce the size of the largest component of SG&A, personnel, through downsizing, offshoring, or outsourcing. Usually, there is little involvement of the HR/OD/training functions, beyond administrative and legal, in reducing SG&A, though frequently those functions are among those downsized or outsourced.

High COGS. Even without an MBA, we all know intuitively that the more it costs to produce something, the less profit you make on the sale. We'll deliberately keep the formulas out of this book, but from what we've said about COGS, there are two ways to increase the company's gross profit:

—Increase product sales revenue (by selling more or raising the price).

—Decrease cost of goods sold (by spending less on materials, making production processes more efficient, or giving people more skills so they cost less per unit produced).

Your process redesign, incentive plan development, and training skills can affect both these factors. If you are a training person and don't have incentive plan development skills, you can do this by partnering with a colleague in compensation who does. If you are an HR generalist and lack instructional design skills, you can partner with someone in training.

What You Should Do

You should identify five pieces of information for this element of Economic Logic:

1. What expenses does your organization include in COGS? And what is included in SG&A? (That should be anything not in COGS, but check to make sure.)
2. Is COGS high or increasing over the three-year period on the income statement, at a higher rate than sales? How does your organization's COGS compare to that of other companies in your industry?
3. How high is SG&A as a percentage of sales or net income? How does it compare to that of other companies in the same industry?
4. Which is more of a cost issue for your organization: COGS or SG&A? Which does senior management seem to spend a lot of time talking about?
5. If SG&A or COGS is high, what pieces of information do you want to focus on in the other Internal Logics to (a) better understand the sources of the problem and (b) be prepared to propose solutions to reduce costs?

Profit Source

Profit source asks the question, "How does the company segment where its profits come from, and which set of profits is most important?" The question makes the assumption that while, of course, the company wants a lot of profit and wants it from everywhere, some profits are more important than others. How can that be? Let's look at some examples:

- Although the retail industry wants to sell you clothes, toys, and electronics year-round, the profits it is most interested in are those that come between the day after Thanksgiving (called black Friday because that day is supposed to put the

TABLE 4.5. PROFIT SOURCE

	Definition	Examples
Profit source	ASK: How does the company analyze where its profits come from?	
	Profit margins by product sector: Which product in inventory (e.g., desktop computers, laptops, monitors, printers, or "extras") produces the greatest profits?	Apparel: Gap
		Electronics: Best Buy, Dell
	Profit margin by customer type: new versus return.	Retail: CostCo, Nordstroms
	Profit margin by market channel type: urban store versus suburban store versus Internet; large store versus smaller store.	Pharmacy chain: Walgreens, CVS
	Profit margin by geographical region	Retail: Target, McDonalds

company's books into the black) through the day after Christmas. So for the retail industry, the profits are divided (or to use the technical term, segmented) by month, and the month just described is the most important segment.

- The film industry segments its profits by the first weekend of U.S. receipts (the most important), total U.S. receipts thereafter, total international receipts, and total DVD receipts.
- Most TV advertisers segment by age, the most important segment being 18- to 30-year-old males. And the list goes on.

Caveat: This element of Economic Logic is related to and essentially uses the same market segmentation categories as the Market Strategy element of Customer Logic. This is not a typo or editing error. The two are different in this way:

- Profit source asks, "How does the organization segment profit margins, and which segment's profit margins are what the company cares about most?"
- Customer Logic, Market Strategy asks, "In your Market Strategy, in which of all the possible ways of segmenting the market does your company segment your customers, and which customers do you care about?"

The Segments

There are many different ways of segmenting profits and markets, but the one we find most useful and understandable comes from Kotler (1991), plus two we have added: product line and market channel. The original set of categories is shown in Table 4.6. In this discussion we will be focusing on some of these categories, plus the two categories we have added.

TABLE 4.6. MAJOR SEGMENTATION VARIABLES
FOR CONSUMER MARKETS

Variable	Typical Breakdown
Geographic	
Region	Pacific, Mountain, West North Central, West South Central, East North Central, East South Central, South Atlantic, Middle Atlantic, New England
County size	A, B, C, D
City or SMSA size	Under 5,000; 5,000–20,000; 20,000–50,000; 50,000–100,000; 100,000–250,000; 250,000–500,000; 500,000–1,000,000; 1,000,000–4,000,000; 4,000,000+
Density	Urban, suburban, rural
Climate	Northern, southern
Demographic	
Age	Under 6, 6–11, 12–19, 20–34, 35–49, 50–64, 65+
Sex	Male, female
Family size	1–2, 3–4, 5+
Family life cycle	Young, single; young, married, no children; young, married, youngest child under 6; young, married, youngest child 6 or over; older, married, with children; older, married, no children under 18; older, single; other
Income	Under $10,000; $10,000–$15,000; $15,000–$20,000; $20,000–$25,000; $25,000–$30,000; $30,000–$50,000; $50,000+
Occupation	Professional and technical; managers, officials, and proprietors; clerical, sales; craftspeople, foremen; operatives; farmers; retired; students; housewives; unemployed
Education	Grade school or less; some high school; high school graduate; some college; college graduate
Religion	Catholic, Protestant, Jewish, other
Race	White, black, Asian, Hispanic, etc.
Nationality	American, British, French, German, Scandinavian, Italian, Latin American, Middle Eastern, Japanese, etc.
Psychographic	
Social class	Lower lowers, upper lowers, working class, middle class, upper middles, lower uppers, upper uppers
Lifestyle	Straights, swingers, longhairs, etc.
Personality	Compulsive, gregarious, authoritarian, ambitious, etc.

Behavioral

Occasions	Regular occasion, special occasion
Benefits	Quality, service, economy
User status	Nonuser, ex-user, potential user, first-time user, regular user
Usage rate	Light user, medium user, heavy user
Loyalty status	None, medium, strong, absolute
Readiness stage	Unaware, aware, informed, interested, desirous, intending to buy
Attitude toward product	Enthusiastic, positive, indifferent, negative, hostile

Source: Used by permission from Prentice-Hall.

- *Product line:* A common practice is to track profits (as well as COGS) by product line. A computer company may track corporate systems, small business systems, home desktops, and laptops separately. A pharmaceutical company may track each medicine or each category of medicines separately. For companies that produce many different products, a decision about how to track the profits becomes strategic. This is because tracking profits for each stock keeping unit (SKU) might produce so much data that it becomes unusable, whereas lumping too many products together might obscure useful information.
- *Market channel:* A profit differentiator that has become more important since the late 1990s with the advent of online selling is the market channel. A company with both a physical and online presence (be it Borders or Eddie Bauer) is likely to track profits from online sales separately from in-store sales.
- *Geographic:* It has been a longtime practice in many industries to track profits by region. Going beyond the obvious and sometimes silly questions (do we sell more convertible cars in Southern California or Minnesota?), companies are interested in the profit differences for certain products based on the geographic region of the United States or now of the world (think about McDonald's and even Starbucks).
- *Demographic:* This category and the next two are ways to segment profits by customer type. The demographic category is the one we are all most familiar with in terms of understanding and application (e.g., beer sales to 21- to 30-year-old males and computer sales by level of education and race are two that have taken their turns in the news).
- *Psychographic:* This category is one we are more familiar with than the fancy name would allow us to think. We all have heard about the different ways Boomers, Gen X, Gen Y, and Millennials think, live, and work. And though these groups are age based, it is not age but the way of thinking about the world that shapes these groups' buying patterns and the profits that result from

them. So a cell phone company might want to track the profits from different services they offer (voice, photo, text, Internet access, etc.) based on the different lifestyle categories of its customers.

- *Behavioral:* This category is similar to psychographics but brings in some innovation theory (Rogers, 2003 and variables that address the relationship between the customer and company. Innovation theory talks about innovators, about early, middle, and late adopters, and about laggards as the way people react to change. Late in this first decade, two companies introduced products aimed at innovators: the Apple iPhone and the Toyota Prius. Now as those products roll out into the market to early and middle adopters, those companies might choose to compare profits among the different adopter categories. This category is also where a company would compare the profits from loyal (repeat) customers to those from new ones.

What You Should Do

You should identify three pieces of information for this element of Economic Logic:

1. Become familiar with the six types of profit sources just described, especially the four that might be new to you from Table 4.5.
2. Find out which way(s), if any, your organization uses to analyze where its profits come from.
3. If it seems to you that the organization is not doing some analysis that could help it better understand its Economic Logic, note it as something to ask questions about as you move in Customer and Product Logics. (Do *not*, at this stage, run around the company telling everyone what you have discovered or recommending a change; that is a premature and career-damaging move.)

Measures for Economic Logic

The measures for Economic Logic section asks the question, "What are the key financial numbers, or measures, your organization looks at to determine how its Economic Logic and all the other logics are working?"

In Table 4.7, you see a large number of possible measures of financial health listed. Since you will learn in detail what each of these means when you take an accountant to lunch, what we will do here is to make some observations about

TABLE 4.7. THE FINANCIAL PICTURE: MEASURES

The financial picture: Measures	ASK: What are the key metrics your organization looks at to determine how well its Customer Logic is working?	
	1. Profit (overall, by market segment, by customer, by product type) 2. Costs (per unit, versus competitors) 3. Cash flow (length of cash-to-cash cycle) 4. Reinvestment (percentage, where) 5. Return on investment (benefits/costs) 6. Return on capital employed [revenue/organization asset (employees, etc.)] 7. Earnings per share/price to earnings ratio	8. Profitability: Return on investment (return on assets, return on sales, and return on equity) Operating margin Gross margin Net margin 9. Solvency: Current ratio Total debt versus total assets Debt to equity ratio Efficiency Asset turnover (receivables turn, payables turn, and inventory turn) Collection period

some of the key measures, and give you some information to gather, as we have in the other sections in this chapter.

- *Measures related to profitability: margins:* Generally, two measures are used to measure profitability at the level we have been talking about:
  —Gross margin = Sales income – COGS
  —Net margin = Gross margin – SG&A
  —Again, remember our caveat that we are not accountants, so look at your company's income statement, and ask your accountant how your company calculates these measures, and which it is most concerned with.
- *Measures related to costs:* What are the COGS and SG&A values for your organization? What factors are included in each?
- *Measures related to cash flow:* Although we have not discussed cash flow explicitly in this chapter, your organization measures its cash flow. (Like you, if it does not have enough money at a given time to pay bills, it must pay them late, with interest.) What is the length of the cash-to-cash cycle? How does the company measure and control its cash flow?

- *Measures related to profitability: returns:* This is the measure with a hundred names and formulae, such as:
  — Return on investment (mostly by trainers)
  — Return on assets (on the income statement)
  — Return on sales (alternative to assets)
  — Return on equity (return on all of the equity the company has)
  — Return on capital employed (similar to ROE)
  — Return on XXXXX (yes, there are more)

These are all basically ratios, which divide something we receive (the top number, income) by something we spent or have to do to receive the income in (assets, equity, etc.). And, as Jack Philips (1997) has shown in his book on ROI (the result of that ratio differs depending on what you decide to include on the top and the bottom. The same is true with your accounting department. So find out the exact formula they use to calculate return and what they call it.

What You Should Do

You should answer the following questions about Economic Logic:

1. For which, of all the measures listed and of others we have not listed, does your organization collect and report data? Where is each one reported?
2. Where there are multiple names for the same measure (e.g., return on investment, assets, sales, equity, capital employed), which name does your organization use?
3. For the measures that can include different elements depending on the industry and company (e.g., COGS), what elements does your company include in the measure?
4. When it is explained to you, do you understand the formula for calculating the key measures (ROI/A/S/I/E/CE; gross margin/profit; net margin/profit)? If not, what more can you do to understand it?
5. As you look at the measures and income statement, what questions do you have that you want to try to answer as you gather data about the other logics? For example:
   a. If there is a very high COGS, you might want to be especially vigilant when you do your analysis of the Process Logic to see if any costly problems jump out at you.
   b. If there is a very high profit for one region, customer, or product segment, and very low ones for others, you might want to be especially vigilant when

you do your analysis of Strategy, Customer, and Product Logics to see if any possible reasons jump out at you.

Sample Worksheets for Economic Logic

In Chapter 2, we introduced the Internal Scan Worksheet. Table 4.8 shows this worksheet with the column for Economic Logic filled out for one of our clients. It is brief: just a few words summarizing each of the elements. This is the level of detail that we suggest you use to get the big picture without bogging yourself down in a major research project. Save your time and energy for more detailed analysis when you have a specific performance issue to investigate.

In Table 4.9 is the Measures Worksheet that we also introduced in Chapter 2, filled out for the same client. Notice we added some rows within the box so that we could capture a few key financial measures and keep them straight, but we didn't add a lot of space: We kept it simple.

Economic Logic Job Aid

This job aid summarizes Economic Logic with graphics, definitions, questions to be answered, and examples. Use it when you are trying to identify the Economic Logic for your own (or your client's) organization.

Your Turn

Use the Economic Logic job aid (see Table 4.10) and the Internal Scan Worksheet (see Table 4.11) to identify the Economic Logic and measures operating in your organization or your client's. Ways to find out:

- Organization's Web site
- Annual report
- 10-K report
- Hoover's, Mergent (most public libraries have a subscription), or other investors' publications
- Members of the organization, particularly managers, strategic planning office, and finance

If you want a reproducible version of worksheet, there is one on the Web site at www.Pfeiffer.com/go/kennethsilber. Copy it to your desktop, and either use it as is or modify it for the level of detail you need to work with. Consider creating an Excel spreadsheet.

TABLE 4.8. SAMPLE INTERNAL SCAN FOR CREDIT CARD DIVISION OF A BANK

Assess and fill in the logic the business appears to be using.

ECONOMIC LOGIC	STRATEGY LOGIC	CUSTOMER LOGIC	PRODUCT LOGIC	PROCESS LOGIC	STRUCTURAL LOGIC
Cost Structure • Variable: cost of funds and delinquencies • To manage: self-fund, control delinquencies Financial Focus • Cost of goods sold Profit Source • Channel: Direct versus oil company cards versus Sears, etc.					

- Do the logics in the six columns support each other or are they contradictory?
- If they are contradictory, does this have some bearing on the problem you were asked to solve?
- How can you test your assessment that these are the business logic(s) the company is using?
- Now review the logic in the light of your environmental scan. Do the six logics seem to be consistent with external realities?

TABLE 4.9. SAMPLE MEASURES WORKSHEET FOR CREDIT CARD DIVISION OF A BANK

Logic	Sample Measures	Target	Current	Gap	Performance Problems	Interventions	Measured Results
Economic	% Variable	85%	5%	80%			
	COGS	$5/card	$20/card	$15/card			
	Profit source	50% from lowest income demographic	95% from lowest income demographic	45%			
	Return on equity	10%	3%	7%			
	Cash flow	30 days late	120 days late	90 days			
Strategy							
Customer							
Product							
Process							
Internal							

- What specific measures does the organization use for each logic? Write them in column 2.
- What is the target for each measure? Write it in column 3.
- What is the current number for each measure? Write it in column 4.
- What is the gap between target and current number for each measure? Write it in column 5.
- Those measures with the greatest, and most critical, gaps are the focus of the Performance Problem Analysis and Intervention Selection that take place next in the Performance Improvement process.

TABLE 4.10. SUMMARY JOB AID—ECONOMIC LOGIC

How the organization gets profit and growth

	Definition	Examples
Cost Structure	Ask: Which is more of an issue for you: fixed or variable costs? What are the key ones you focus on? What are you doing to manage these key costs?	
Fixed vs. Variable	**Fixed** = Costs that are always incurred regardless of what the business is doing.	Facilities, equipment, permanent staff
	Variable = Costs that change with the volume of business that is available.	Short-term rentals, raw materials, merchandise, temporary staff
	Organizations that have high fixed costs with relatively low variable costs:	Airlines, hospitals, refineries
	Organizations that have high variable costs, with relatively low fixed costs:	Retail stores, general contractors, small consulting firms
	Turbulence (rapid change) in the environment increases an organization's risk. Many businesses are trying to reduce risk by switching fixed costs to variable ones.	Downsizing, outsourcing, subcontracting, leasing

TABLE 4.10. SUMMARY JOB AID—ECONOMIC LOGIC (Continued)

Financial Focus	Possibilities	Definition	Examples	Businesses
	Ask: Which is more of a cost issue for you: COGS or SG&A, or it is both?			
	Cost of goods sold	The direct amount it costs to produce a product/service: Inbound freight Production costs Materials Manufacturing facilities Manufacturing labor	Companies that focus here are concerned with process and supply chain redesign for optimal efficiency and lowest cost.	McDonald's Wal-Mart
	Sales, general, and administration expenses	The costs a company has that are not directly related to producing a product, including the costs of running the business as a whole, e.g.: Sales/marketing costs Distribution Management Human resources/ training	Companies that focus here are concerned with reducing fixed costs in administrative areas through outsourcing and downsizing.	Just about all of them

(Continued)

TABLE 4.10. SUMMARY JOB AID—ECONOMIC LOGIC (Continued)

	Definition	Examples	Businesses
Profit Source	**Ask: How does the company analyze where its profits come from?**		
	Profit margins by product sector: Which product in inventory (e.g., desktop computers or laptops or monitors or printers or "extras") produces greatest profits?	Apparel Electronics	Gap Best Buy Dell
	Profit margin by customer type: new versus return	Retail	Best Buy Nordstroms
	Profit margin by market channel type: urban store versus suburban store versus Internet; large store versus smaller store	Pharmacy chainRetail	Walgreens
	Profit margin by geographical region		Target McDonalds
The Financial Picture: Measures	**Ask: What are the key metrics your organization looks at to determine how well its Customer Logic is working?**		
	1. Profit (overall, by market segment, by customer, by product type)		8. Profitability: Return on investment (return on assets, return on sales, and return on equity) Operating margin Gross margin Net margin
	2. Costs (per unit versus competitors)		
	3. Cash flow (length of "cash-to-cash" cycle)		
	4. Reinvestment (percentage, where)		9. Solvency: Current ratio Total debt versus total assets Debt to equity ratio Efficiency Asset turnover (receivables turn, payables turn, and inventory turn) Collection period
	5. Return on investment (benefits/costs)		
	6. Return on capital employed [revenue/organization asset (employees, etc.)]		
	7. Earnings per share/price to earnings ratio		

© Lynn Kearny 2009. Reprinted with permission of Lynn Kearny.

Summary

You are now in possession of the passwords and the secret handshake used by decision makers in your organization. You hold the map that shows where the money is hidden. You know (if you didn't know before) how to look at an Income Statement and extract information from it. You don't have all the information, but you have enough to recognize big shifts in your organization's economic picture, see some implications, and ask intelligent questions about them. You have a better way of understanding why otherwise strange decisions are made, like cancelling a highly successful customer service training program (which affects SG&A) just at a time when customers are leaving in droves (driving down income and squeezing cash flow). In the following chapters, we will tackle other numbers and other lines of reasoning, specifically ways of deciding first for yourself whether that training program is aligned with strategy and will really boost income, then making a persuasive case using different kinds of numbers.

The next chapter addresses this very topic: Strategy Logic.

TABLE 4.11. INTERNAL SCAN WORKSHEET

Assess and fill in the logic the business appears to be using.

ECONOMIC LOGIC	STRATEGY LOGIC	CUSTOMER LOGIC	PRODUCT LOGIC	PROCESS LOGIC	STRUCTURAL LOGIC

- Do the logics in the six columns support each other or are they contradictory?
- If they are contradictory, does this have some bearing on the problem you were asked to solve?
- How can you test your assessment that these are the business logic(s) the company is using?
- Now review the logic in the light of your environmental scan. Do the six logics seem to be consistent with external realities?

CHAPTER FIVE

STRATEGY LOGIC

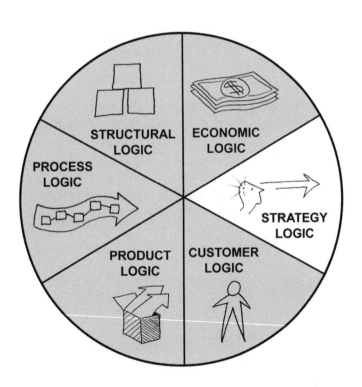

Strategy Logic refers to how the organization views itself, its purpose, its direction, its unique skills, its growth, and how well all these factors are aligned. It includes how strategy is measured. This logic is akin to what business people call strategic planning or business alignment. The purpose of the model is to highlight the key factors that an organization usually considers in its strategy and to clarify what those factors are for your target organization.

The seven components of strategy logic we will examine are:

- Mission and vision: The purpose and overall direction of the organization.
- Objectives and initiatives/projects: Current plans for getting there.
- Culture: How members of the organization conduct themselves.
- Core competencies: The unique talents and skills the organization has to offer.
- Growth strategy: How the organization grows itself and its business.
- Pricing strategy: How the organization prices its goods and services.
- Alignment: Whether all the elements of the organization's strategy are in harmony with each other.

Finally, we will look into measures: how well the strategy logic has been developed and how successful the organization is at implementing and achieving its strategy.

TABLE 5.1. ELEMENTS OF STRATEGY LOGIC

Mission and vision		Growth strategy	
Objectives		Pricing strategy	
Culture		Alignment	
Core competencies	MARKETING / R&D / PRODUCTION / DISTRIBUTION / POINT OF SALE	Measures	

Why Strategy Logic Is Important to You and the Organization

You may be asking yourself, "Why would I concern yourself with strategy? Isn't it the province of the strategic planning office, something that the executives direct, refine, and announce?" In most large organizations, a strategic planning office does develop strategy, with input from leaders and functional groups throughout the organization. And in a perfect world, you would have a place at that table. But it isn't a perfect world, and you want at least to know what the strategy is and who developed it. If you want your expertise used to help the organization get where it is going—if you want to have an impact—your efforts must be linked to and aligned with strategy.

Skilled individuals in staff positions spend a lot of time expressing their desire to have a seat at the table in top-level organizational planning and decision making. And we should. We are smart people with highly developed skills and expertise that are rarely used. Instead, we are used as organizational janitors, patching up problems that could have been avoided if we had been brought in and listened to when objectives were set and initiatives started. We often know whether the organization has the current capacity (skills, manpower, information technology, facilities, processes) to meet the objectives. We often recognize whole elements of an initiative that have been omitted from the planning and resourcing process. We want to help our organizations do things right the first time. We want to do our best work, to be part of our organization's success, to be effective, and to make a difference. We want to get in at the front end and apply our expertise to do things right, rather than being brought in at the back end to clean up messes that could have been avoided. And we want the dignity and respect that come with that level of contribution.

The key to getting in at the front end is to be proactive. We need to propose what needs to be done in a compelling way at the front end, rather than reacting to what is handed down. To do that, we first must understand the organization's purpose, direction, and other strategic issues as well as anyone else does in the organization. We can't leave it up to executives and the strategic planning office. If they haven't called you yet, they won't call you tomorrow—unless you do something different.

To find opportunities:

- Identify the real mission/purpose of the organization.
- Know the objectives and how they are measured.
- Know what strategic commitments (objectives) are being met and which are in trouble.
- Know the initiatives and how they are doing.

- Know if these are in conflict with earlier initiatives or if the initiatives of one division or department are in conflict with those of another.
- Know the culture and whether it supports the organization's purpose, direction, and objectives.
- Know the organization's key competencies and whether they support its strategy (purpose, direction, and objectives).
- Know the growth and pricing strategies of the organization.
- Know how well and comprehensively the organization is planning and aligning all these.

When you know all this, you will be more knowledgeable about the organization than most people in it. You will be able to see opportunities for your specialty to contribute significantly to the organization's goals, and you can then prepare short talks or presentations about the benefits you can offer, using the leaders' own strategic language and target measures. When you encounter organizational leaders in the elevator or hallway, you'll be able to ask relevant questions about the business and make comments that may pique their interest about what you have to offer. All these occasions are opportunities to gain visibility, credibility, and influence in your organization. The price of admission is acquiring a working understanding of your organization's strategy and staying up-to-date as things change.

The Elements of Strategy Logic

Strategy Logic has eight elements. Seven are defined here, illustrated with examples, and discussed. The eighth element is measures: how to assess the comprehensiveness and coherence of the strategy. We will deal with measures at the end of this chapter.

Mission and Vision

Mission and vision are important to you and to the organization because they provide specific direction to the organization and the people in it. A good mission helps clarify the purpose of the organization whenever people are updating strategy and making plans, as well as providing guidance while they are caught up in day-to-day operations throughout the year. A vision points the way into the future: It provides direction and a sense of excitement about what members of the organization can achieve beyond their current tasks and responsibilities. A good vision can engage people's hearts and minds. The authors believe that an idea unites people in a common effort, not just the charisma of a leader. Together, a vision and an effective leader provide a common purpose and focus for the organization. Mission and vision help people make decisions about what to do or not to do, and can help them figure out the priorities in situations where clear priorities have not been communicated by leadership.

Everybody has an individual definition of mission and vision and his or her own impassioned beliefs about what each "really" is. We will give you three or four ideas about each. We are not selling them to you; you will have to find out what your or your client's organization thinks those words mean. From our perspective, here are some definitions and some examples.

What Mission Is

A mission should answer the question, "Why does this organization exist?" The vision should answer the question "What will that look like?" See Table 5.2.

TABLE 5.2. MISSION AND VISION

	Definition	Examples
Mission and Vision	**ASK:** **Why does this company exist?** A mission is a statement of the specific purpose of the organization. A vision is a more affective, future-oriented statement of what the organization means. Missions and visions provide specific direction to the organization and people in it: • Mission statements should be specific and clear about the organization's industry, products/services and customers, and they should be measurable. • Vision statements should express what a *Harvard Business Review* article called a BHAG (big hairy audacious goal) for the future, and they should talk about the affective side of the business.	**Mission:** "ComputerGeeks.com, is a leading direct-to-consumer eCommerce site specializing in providing computer-related excess inventory, manufacturer-closeouts, high-demand and unusual computer components and peripherals at highly-discounted prices to tech-savvy, 'Geeky' consumers." **Vision:** "ComputerGeeks.com is committed to offering tremendous savings on computer products, and hosting a Web site providing a depth of value-added content. Our aim is to amuse, inform, and entertain you—while providing amazing values—and to push the envelope of interactive Web functionality and secure online shopping ease. . . ."

The mission is a statement of the specific purpose of the organization. Mission statements should be specific and clear about the organization's industry, products/services, and customers, and they should be measurable.

Here is how some leading experts in strategy management describe mission statements.

According to Henry Mintzberg (1994), a mission statement describes the company's basic role in the business world and in society, expressed in terms of who its customers are and the products and services it produces for them. A business mission should include four elements

- *Purpose:* Why the business exists
- *Strategy and scope:* What business does and how it does it
- *Values:* What management believes in
- *Standards and behaviors:* The rules that guide how the business operates

Mintzberg sees the mission as describing the business as it is today and the vision as describing its future state

Hamel and Prahalad (1990) address mission and vision under the heading of strategic intent. They define strategic intent as an ambitious and compelling dream that energizes; which provides the emotional and intellectual energy for the journey to the future. They break it down into three components: (1) sense of direction, (2) a sense of discovery (similar to mission), (3) a sense of destiny (similar to vision, discussed later in the chapter). The message of strategic intent is to set ambitious goals and a compelling vision of the future, then to figure out how to acquire or leverage existing resources to achieve it. This was ground-breaking at a time when most organizations were shaping their goals to fit their existing resources.

Some Web sites give guidelines for writing exemplary mission statements:

- http://www.missionstatements.com/
- http://www.shrm.org/hrtools/mission_published/
- http://www.stfrancis.edu/ba/ghkickul/stuWebs/btopics/works/mission.htm
- http://www.jou.ufl.edu/people/faculty/chanolmsted/mission.htm
- http://management.about.com/cs/generalmanagement/ht/Mission Statemen.htm

A good mission should do the following:

- Explain the purpose of the organization.
- Identify the products and/or services it provides.
- Identify its customers and/or primary stakeholders.

It may also state the organization's responsibilities toward its stakeholders, particularly in the case of governmental, human services, and not-for-profit organizations.

Good Examples

- *ComputerGeeks.com:* ComputerGeeks.com is a leading direct-to-consumer eCommerce site specializing in providing computer-related excess inventory, manufacturer-closeouts, high-demand and unusual computer components and peripherals at highly discounted prices to tech-savvy, "Geeky" consumers. (http://www.geeks.com/aboutus.asp as of November 8, 2008)
- *CARE International:* Our mission is to serve individuals and families in the poorest communities in the world. Drawing strength from our global diversity, resources and experience, we promote innovative solutions and are advocates for global responsibility. We facilitate lasting change by:
  —Strengthening capacity for self-help
  —Providing economic opportunity
  —Delivering relief in emergencies
  —Influencing policy decisions at all levels
  —Addressing discrimination in all its forms
  —(http://www.care.org/about/index.asp as of November 8, 2008)
- *Advance Auto Parts:* It is the mission of Advance Auto Parts to provide personal vehicle owners and enthusiasts with the vehicle-related products and knowledge that fulfill their wants and needs at the right price. Our friendly, knowledgeable and professional staff will help inspire, educate and problem-solve for our customers.
  —(http://www.missionstatements.com/fortune_500_mission_statements.html as of November 8, 2008)
- *Ameren:* Ameren's mission is to generate electricity, deliver electricity and distribute natural gas in a safe, reliable, efficient and environmentally sound manner. Our vision is to be the recognized performance leader of the U.S. electric and gas utility industry. Being a performance leader means we will achieve operational excellence, industry-leading customer satisfaction and superior financial performance. (http://www.missionstatements.com/fortune_500_mission_statements.html as of November 8, 2008)
- *Brannigans Restaurant:* To ensure that each guest receives prompt, professional, friendly and courteous service. To maintain a clean, comfortable and well maintained premises for our guests and staff. To provide at a fair price—nutritional, well-prepared meals—using only quality ingredients. To ensure that all guests and staff are treated with the respect and dignity they deserve.

To thank each guest for the opportunity to serve them. By maintaining these objectives we shall be assured of a fair profit that will allow us to contribute to the community we serve. (http://www.missionstatements.com/restaurant_mission_statements.html as of November 8, 2008)

- *The Viking Child Care Center:* The mission of the Viking Child Care Center is to provide safe, affordable, high quality child care for the students of Hudson Valley Community College and the community. In doing so, we support families in their efforts to reach their goals. The Viking Child Care Center provides a cognitively based program for children ages six weeks to five years. We provide a homelike environment where children are encouraged to develop at their own pace. The Viking staff is committed to the families we serve, providing support and encouragement. (http://www.missionstatements.com/day-care_mission_statements.html as of November 8, 2008)

A mission statement can still be good and useful even if it does not meet all four of Mintzberg's criteria. Here are some examples that lack two or more of the criteria and do *not* name the stakeholders, which are pretty much understood:

- *San Diego Zoo:* The Zoological Society of San Diego is a conservation, education, and recreation organization dedicated to the reproduction, protection, and exhibition of animals, plants, and their habitats. (http://www.sandiegozoo.org/kids/readaboutit_build_a_zoo.html)
- *San Francisco Opera:* To present opera performances of the highest international quality available to the widest possible audiences.
  — To perpetuate and enrich the operatic art form.
  — To be creative and innovative in all aspects of opera.
  — To take a leadership role in training, arts education and audience development
  — (http://sfopera.com/p/?mID=114 as of November 8, 2008)

Weak Examples of Mission Statements

- *Computer hardware company mission:* Delight our customers, employees, and shareholders by relentlessly delivering the platform and technology advancements that become essential to the way we work and live. (This doesn't clarify the purpose of the organization and provides little guidance for making decisions about what to do.)
- *Real estate company mission:* To be the leading real estate and homeowner service company from Manhattan to Montauk, always exceeding our customers'

expectations. (This gives only a general idea of who the customers are, making it difficult to exceed their expectations. It says nothing about what aspect of real estate or business it wants to lead in, again offering little guidance for deciding or taking action.)

- *Software company mission:* Our company strives to support improvements in education and make a positive difference in students' lives by providing software tools that help students learn to think. (It is unclear who the customer is, although it does identify one stakeholder: the end user. It provides no clarity about what characterizes software that helps students learn to think.)

Short and Sweet Mission Statements That Work. Some mission statements serve their organizations well by being so brief, clear, well-known, and well understood that they serve to guide daily decisions at all levels of the organization, even though they don't have all of Mintzberg's elements.

Examples

- *Starbucks:* To inspire and nurture the human spirit—one person, one cup, and one neighborhood at a time. (http://www.starbucks.com/mission/default.asp as of November 8, 2008)
- *Google:* Google's mission is to organize the world's information and make it universally accessible and useful. (http://www.google.com/corporate/)
- *Wal-Mart:* To help people save money so they can live better. (http://walmartstores.com/Investors/7614.aspx as of November 8, 2008)

Recently Wal-Mart buyers found a vendor who was able to offer a much better price for a product they sell a lot of. Although the merchandisers could have passed the savings to increase the bottom line, the mission was so integral to associates' thinking that they passed the savings on to the customer with no hesitation. (J. Swinney, see acknowledgments)

What Vision Is

A *vision* is a more affective, future-oriented statement of what the organization means. A vision should express what a *Harvard Business Review* article called a BHAG (big hairy audacious goal) for the future, and it should talk about the affective side of the business (Collins and Porras, 1996). It may express values, feelings, and beliefs. Above all, it must be clear, avid, and compelling. A vision statement describes what the organization wants to be. It projects the organization into the future and provides a source of inspiration for people. Most importantly, it provides members of the organization with clear criteria for making decisions and resolving dilemmas. A good vision statement should include:

- A description of a bright future
- A clear and vivid picture
- Emotional appeal
- Exciting and memorable wording
- Both challenge and achievability

It must also harmonize with the organization's values and culture.

Good Examples

- *Martin Luther King's speech "I Have a Dream":* This is perhaps the quintessential example of a vision that meets all of these criteria.
- *John F. Kennedy's vision for the nation:* By the end of the decade, we will land a man on the moon and return him safely to earth. (This is another example of a compelling vision that galvanized an entire nation to achieve that vision.)
- *Yahoo Search:* To enable people to find, use, share, and expand all human knowledge. (http://battellemedia.com/archives/001473.php as of November 8, 2008)
- *McCaw Cellular Communications:* To develop a reliable wireless network that empowers people with the freedom to travel anywhere—across the hall or across the continent—and communicate effortlessly. (http://www.csuchico. edu/mgmt/strategy/module1/tsld014.htm)
- *Long John Silver's:* To be America's best quick service restaurant chain. We will provide each guest great tasting, healthful, reasonably priced fish, seafood, and chicken in a fast, friendly manner on every visit. (http://www.csuchico. edu/mgmt/strategy/module1/tsld014.htm as of November 8, 2008)
- *ComputerGeeks.com:* ComputerGeeks.com is committed to offering tremendous savings on computer products, and hosting a Web site providing a depth of value-added content. Our aim is to amuse, inform, and entertain you—while providing amazing values—and to push the envelope of interactive Web functionality and secure online shopping ease.... (http://www.geeks.com/aboutus. asp as of November 8, 2008)
- *Southwest Airlines:* The Freedom to Fly for our customers: a safe and high-quality operation, exceptional service to customers, a great place to work and the most profitable airline. (Southwest Airlines Co. Annual Report 1999)
- *CARE International:* We seek a world of hope, tolerance and social justice, where poverty has been overcome and people live in dignity and security. CARE International will be a global force and a partner of choice within a

worldwide movement dedicated to ending poverty. We will be known every-where for our unshakeable commitment to the dignity of people. (http://www.care.org/about/index.asp?s_src=170920500000&s_subsrc=as of November 8, 2008) (*Note:* This statement serves as both a mission and vision for this organization, a not uncommon occurrence for values-based, not-for-profit organizations.)

Weak Examples

- *Vision of a city zoo:* To become a world leader at connecting people to wildlife and conservation. (This is weak because it doesn't create a clear destination, nor does it communicate emotional intensity.)
- *Vision of a beverage manufacturer:* To achieve sustainable growth, we have estab-lished a vision with clear goals.
  — *Profit:* Maximizing return to shareowners while being mindful of our overall responsibilities.
  — *People:* Being a great place to work where people are inspired to be the best they can be.
  — *Portfolio:* Bringing to the world a portfolio of beverage brands that anticipate and satisfy people's desires and needs.
  — *Partners:* Nurturing a winning network of partners and building mutual loyalty.
  — *Planet:* Being a responsible global citizen that makes a difference. (http://www.samples-help.org.uk/mission-statements/sample-vision-state-ments.htm as of November 8, 2008)
  (This is weak because it is a mission, rather than a vision. As a vision it is not emotional or galvanizing.)
- *Vision of a heavy equipment manufacturing firm:* Be the global leader in customer value. (This is weak because it violates every rule: It is generic, uninspiring, and does nothing to paint a picture of where the organization could be in the future.)

Issue Relating to Vision Statements

Word Salad. Most organizations publish their mission statements: They appear in Web sites, annual reports, posters, and newsletters. Vision statements are not as commonly published, but they are starting to appear in organizational materials.

Despite their publication, unfortunately, many existing missions and visions do not provide clarity or direction. We have all encountered mission and vision statements that appear to have been assembled by a committee. In fact, they often have been crafted through a series of meetings, agreements, and compromises. In the interest of getting everyone's buy-in, they end up full of buzzwords, and they lack clarity or passion. This characteristic is so widespread that until recently there was a popular Web page called Dilbert's Mission Statement Generator, where users could choose between current business buzz phrases to produce an absurd and meaningless mission statement. As of this writing the generator is no longer available.

What You Should Do

When you read a mission or vision statement that is unclear, wordy, and dull, do not take it at face value. Do what you can to figure out the actual purpose of the organization, and draft a workable mission that will help you understand the organization. You don't have to call it mission; just call it the organization's purpose anytime you discuss it with your client. Use the same approach with a muddy vision: Instead of worrying about it, ask knowledgeable members of the organization to describe what direction the organization is moving in. Call it direction and pass over the obscure vision in silence.

Objectives

Objectives should answer the questions, "How will we get there from here? What are some mileposts along the way?" Look also for initiatives or projects that answer the question, "What are some specific actions we will take right away?"

What Objectives Do

Objectives provide a clear, unambiguous target for the organization to work toward its vision and keep fulfilling its purpose. Mission and vision are very abstract: It's

TABLE 5.3. OBJECTIVES

	Definition
Objectives	**ASK: How do we get from here to there?**
	Objectives are specific, measurable, year-to-year goals that are steps in reaching the mission/vision. *Initiatives* or *projects* are the specific actions the organization is going to take to reach the objectives and therefore accomplish the mission/vision.
	Objectives should: • Be specific and measurable. • Be attainable and implementable. • Be consistent from year to year (unless other elements of total strategy change). • Provide a line-of-sight at all levels of the organization.

difficult for people to determine what to do to achieve them. Continually pursuing an abstract vision is a bit like being in a race with no finish line; people need a sense of progress and accomplishment. Objectives break the mission and vision down into worthwhile, achievable goals. They also serve as a mechanism for the organization to keep growing and developing (see Table 5.3).

What Objectives Are

Objectives are specific, measurable, year-to-year goals that are steps in reaching the mission/vision. Objectives should be:

- Specific and measurable.
- Attainable and implementable.
- Consistent from year to year (unless other elements of total strategy change).

The most commonly used method for writing objectives is SMART:

- *Specific:* Clearly defined, exact, not open to differing interpretations
- *Measurable*: Observable, countable, quantifiable
- *Attainable but challenging:* Can be done, but will take a stretch
- *Realistic:* Takes realities into account, such as available resources and allowable time
- *Time-bound:* Has a completion date by which it must be achieved

Good Examples

Objective from a service provider: Increase ABC Services' market share from 18% to 23% by end of fiscal year 20XX. (If ABC Services had multiple products and services with different target markets, the objective would have to be more detailed, such as increase which market shares by how much each?)
Objective from a supplier of bulk paper products: Increase sales to 75% of existing customers by an average of 5% by the end of the next fiscal year.

Weak Examples

- *For an ocean drilling contracting firm:* Recognized subsea Oil and Gas business provider within 2010
- *EPC contractor:* Acknowledged for providing high level of Product and System knowledge. Problem solver known for quick customer response and service-minded attitude

These business objectives are weak chiefly because they are not specific: How will management know that the company is a recognized subsea oil and gas business provider? They are also not measurable, and only one is time-bound.

- *From a computer company:*

   To expand the business aggressively and offer above-average returns to shareholders.

   To become the leading, innovative systems company within the *xx* market segments.

These objectives suffer from the same problems: They are even more vague than the first two and meet none of the SMART criteria. A member of these organizations would lack any guidance about what to do or when to do it. This sort of objective will probably result in internal disagreements and struggles over what course of action would best expand the business, offer better returns to shareholders, and so on.

Implementing Objectives

Objectives have to be translated into specific initiatives or projects in order to be implemented. It may take several initiatives to achieve a single objective. For example, an objective might be to increase market share by 5 percent by a specific year. There might be several initiatives to achieve this: one to identify a new market niche, one to bring three new products to market, and one to develop two new channels for delivering products/services. The first one could be done in less than a year; the third might take a couple of years to achieve. Or, one big initiative might cover several years, and it can be broken down into many interrelated projects.

As a case in point, one of our clients has an objective to increase the number of skilled jobs that are filled from within the organization while reducing the time and cost of filling vacancies. To accomplish this, the client has undertaken an initiative to integrate talent management. This means building or buying a fully integrated human resource information system (HRIS), standardizing HR processes, and creating Web-enabled self-service forms to support those processes. This will include recruitment, hiring, placement, performance management, compensation, training/development, and succession planning. This is an example of a multiyear initiative that is built up of many projects.

Issues with Objectives

Watch for two issues with objectives: dangling initiatives and hairsplitting over definitions.

Dangling Initiatives. These are a product of the process of setting strategy. Strategy is usually established at the executive level of organizations, which hands off direction and high-level objectives to the next level for more specific planning: they are turned into projects, often called initiatives. These initiatives are assigned resources and handed off to the next level down as projects for development and implementation. Having handed off the strategic objectives, executives may or may not track things for a while. Then their attention is drawn away by other demands: changes in the marketplace or economy, new technology, developing legislation, or a legal precedent may all demand attention and sudden action at the senior level. By the time a new year comes around, there is a whole new set of issues and opportunities to be woven into the strategic plan.

Not all organizations are disciplined about continuing to track the initiatives throughout the course of the year. If priorities and targets have shifted, the people executing the initiatives are not always told. New sets of objectives and initiatives may be handed down each year without the executive levels specifically deciding which of the old ones to modify or abandon. Resources are allocated to new initiatives without noting that the same resources are already tied up dealing with last year's priorities. In an organizational culture that discourages two-way communication about initiatives, resources, and priorities, this problem compounds itself. Nobody gives the people down the line permission to abandon one line of effort in order to pursue another; so capacity is exceeded and projects flounder. People become cynical about initiatives, giving mostly lip service and waiting for them to go away in the next round of strategic planning. Ultimately the organization underperforms.

Dangling initiatives are something to watch for. As you identify the organization's initiatives, try to connect them with the organization's current objectives. If you find initiatives that don't link to current objectives, take note. You have identified a performance improvement opportunity at the organizational level. Save this information to add to your performance analysis phase.

Hairsplitting over Definitions. When everyone has his or her own definition of objectives, hairsplitting can result. Terms such as *mission, vision, objectives,* and *initiatives* have been interpreted to mean many things. A person from corporate life is likely to talk about initiatives, while a person from the armed services is more likely to talk about tactics. Everyone in organizational life has a slightly different take on what objectives are. It is easy to get into a semantic battle over what each term "really" means. That is not our purpose here, and we caution you not to get into such a wrangle with clients, colleagues, or other members of your own organization. We have given our working definitions in this section: You may use them, your client's labels, or your own. The important thing is to identify your target organization's logic for each of these levels, regardless of what you call them.

What You Should Do

Once you have identified the organization's mission, vision, objectives, and key initiatives, do two things:

- Summarize the information in the Internal Scan Worksheet (see Table 5.11).
- Think about how any performance problems the client has brought you (or opportunities you or a client see for the organization) tie to the *mission, vision, and i*nitiatives you have identified.

For example, if your organization has already stated an objective to "increase sales of thingamobobs in each region by 10 percent in the next 12 months," then the business case for your performance analysis is already made. Your intervention selection and design have specific targets, and most importantly your evaluation will show how *you* contributed directly to an organizational (as opposed to a training or HPT) initiative.

Culture

What Culture Is

Culture is a set of social norms and agreements that govern how a group of people behaves with each other. It deals less with what people decide to do and more with how they do it. The simplest and clearest definition of culture is "the way we do things around here" (Burke and Litwin, 1989). Another is "knowing what to do and how to behave without a rule book" (Stumpf, 2009, p. C6).

What Culture Does for an Organization

Culture makes it safe and predictable to interact with a known group of people. When a group of complete strangers come together for the first time, there is a long initial period of risk and social discomfort until they work out how to behave with each other. What is acceptable and unacceptable behavior? What actions will make you accepted and admired, and what might expose you to others' anger or even risk your being ostracized from the group? When a large group (such as an organization) has a clear and well-defined culture, members know what to expect from each other and what is expected of them. This level of comfort makes it possible for employees to focus on daily life and the work of the organization, without having to continually negotiate everything—from who speaks first in a meeting to how to request resources. Culture helps stabilize the organization, creating continuity over time. For example, if an organization has a culture that promotes helping each other, it can weather rapid change and suddenly increased demands for a long time, even with staff turnover and disruptions in the economy. The downside is that unhelpful norms and behaviors are also perpetuated over time. If an organization has a culture that uses blame and punishment as a form of control, it is hard to change when the organization needs to become more collaborative and flexible.

Culture helps an organization by enabling interaction among individuals, groups, roles, and levels of authority. People know what is and is not appropriate in the organizational setting, a criterion that varies greatly from one organization to another. It stabilizes the organization and provides guidelines for how to handle daily problems and dilemmas. Because it influences behavior, culture is a major driver of organizational performance and results. "Many key organizational issues relating to effectiveness—quality, customer satisfaction, team work, innovation, decision making, and flexibility, to name a few, are primarily driven by the organization's culture. Therefore, organizational culture is a critical aspect of organizational survival and success" (Carlton and Lineberry, 2004, p. 19). See Table 5.4.

TABLE 5.4. CULTURE

	Definition	Businesses
Culture	**ASK: What does the organization stand for both internally and externally?**	
	The study of corporate culture can include many things depending on whom you read. Most definitions include three key elements that can be our focus:	Companies known (for better or worse) for their unique cultures are:
	• **Values:** What does this organization believe in, in terms of how it treats investors, employees, and customers and how it conducts business with other companies?	• Enron • Microsoft • Wal-Mart • Google • Sony • Gap • Disney
	• **Beliefs/stories:** How does an organization see itself, in terms of the beliefs it has about role and destiny in the marketplace and the stories it tells about how it got started, what success is, the good it does, and what employees should do?	
	• **Behaviors rewarded:** How does an organization operationalize the culture by rewarding behavior consistent with the culture and punishing behavior not consistent?	

Characteristics of Culture

Even if the short, practical definition of culture is "the way we do things around here," Edgar Schein (1999) warns us not to be superficial in our assessment. We should be aware of three levels of culture:

- Artifacts
- Espoused values
- Shared tacit assumptions

On the surface are the *artifacts:* easily observable differences between different cultures. For example, entering a national department store offering premium goods, you may see well dressed and attentive clerks approaching customers and offering help or directions. Clerks and managers address each other in quiet and polite voices. Merchandise is attractively displayed, and staff members are constantly neatening up tables and racks of goods so that everything looks orderly and fresh. Classical music or subdued jazz plays in the background. On the surface at least, this is a culture of ladies and gentlemen.

If you enter a big-box store of discounted clothing and general merchandise, you may have to look a long time to find a clerk. If you see a clerk in an aisle (usually pushing a large load of goods to be shelved), she may even duck into another aisle or change direction to avoid you. Clerks and supervisors address each other in shouts across large spaces. Most are dressed in sweats or polyester slacks and smocks with running shoes. Huge piles of merchandise are spilling out of tubs and off tables where customers have rummaged through them. The sound system plays rock or rap music and is frequently interrupted by announcements of specials in various parts of the store. On the surface, this is a culture of "the streets": everyone for himself and survival of the fittest. Although this gives us an initial sense of how to expect people to behave in each culture, we really don't know what the behaviors we are seeing mean. To learn the meaning, we must ask members of the organization things like why clerks approach (or avoid) customers and why the music played has been chosen.

This brings us to the second level of culture, the level of *espoused values,* which tell us what management thinks is important. In the first store, we are told that customer service is very important; clerks approach customers as soon as they enter the store to serve them. The music is playing because people love music, which makes employees and customers happy to be in the store. This means customers will come more often, stay longer, and buy more. But when you ask the same questions of people in the big-box store, they surprisingly have the same answers. Customer service is the most important thing and what customers want most is lots of choices and good prices. Everyone's first responsibility is to get merchandise stocked and tagged out on the floor where customers can find it. Tumbled merchandise is picked up and shoved back into the bins when clerks can get to it, but refolding takes time away from the more critical job of stocking. Once all that is done, the clerks can answer questions and give directions. The choice of music has the same rationale: popular music keeps employees and customers happy, brings them in, and keeps them in the store longer. At this point we realize that we don't yet have a clear understanding of both cultures. We need to dig deeper to the third layer, the layer of tacit shared assumptions. For this, we need to look at the history of the organization.

Tacit assumptions are values, beliefs, and assumptions that are taken for granted. Most originate with the founders of the organization, whose assumptions about how the world works are learned by new members as they join. When an organization is successful over time, these assumptions appear to be valid and become so ingrained they are out of individuals' awareness. Examples are:

- Market competition is a form of warfare.
- You reap what you sow.
- Teamwork is key to creating and launching successful products.
- Innovation requires individual creativity and autonomy.

As you can see, a culture that incorporates one of these assumptions will clash with a culture that operates on a very different one. Such clashes are at the core of some spectacular failures in mergers and acquisitions, and they are often the reason for the total failure of high-profile talent recruited from different organizations.

One of the authors worked with a West Coast organic food company that sold high-quality organic juices that were delivered fresh to stores every day. The company had been very successful since the 1960s, and its tacit assumptions were right out of that time period, influenced by pacifism, back-to-the earth values, a smattering of Eastern philosophy, and an intense commitment to well-being through natural foods. Interested in expanding their market, they hired a hard-charging director of marketing from New York. The author overheard an exchange between the new marketing director and one of the most senior distribution managers. The marketing man was trying to engage the distribution manager, saying, "You and your guys are our shock troops. You're out there in the field every day. You can move our product to the front of the shelves and shove the competition's to the back. With your help, we can really slaughter them!" The distribution manager stared at him for several seconds, then drawled, "That's bad juice karma, man!" and strolled away.

The important thing to keep in mind about this root level of culture is that it is learned and based on the organization's early experience of success. This makes it very hard to change. According to Schein, "culture is so stable and difficult to change because it represents the accumulated learning of a group—the ways of thinking, feeling and perceiving the world that have made the group successful" (1999). It is changed only by shared learning experiences that support a different assumption or set of assumptions.

Issues with Culture

One size doesn't fit all. Watch out for the assumption that there is an ideal culture or even a right or a wrong one. A culture is appropriate to the extent *that* it supports the mission of the organization and the business environment the organization is operating in. At the time of this writing, most organizations are interested in what cultural changes will make them more innovative. An open, innovative culture may not be the best match for an organization that needs to maintain tight control and discipline, such as a nuclear power plant or a munitions manufacturer. And we are currently experiencing severe economic fallout from an open, innovative culture in banking and investments.

Avoid stereotyping. Although you can identify the culture of an organization and make some generalizations about how members will behave as a whole, never make the mistake of expecting any one individual to conform exactly to those norms. Culture is a group phenomenon, but each individual is different.

You can't turn the battleship on a dime. Don't try to shift an organization's culture through a one-shot event, like a meeting or a training program. Remember that culture is a shared learning experience and takes time. Members of the organization will need to have more than one success experience with new behaviors and norms before they revise an assumption. This is where a systems approach is absolutely critical.

What You Should Do

When you are trying to understand an organization, assessing the culture is at least as important as any other information you might gather. Understanding the culture lets you know how members of the organization are likely to behave and why. You should do three things:

1. Look for cultural artifacts, the first level of easily observable behaviors. This is immediately useful and will help you understand how people will expect you to behave. At very least it will help you to avoid offending people or looking clueless.
2. As soon as possible, start asking organization members why they do things a certain way. That will lead you to the second level, espoused values. These,

once identified, are very helpful because you can use the same values (e.g., "customer service is our highest priority") to frame your ideas and communicate with organization members on a values level; this approach is always more persuasive than facts. It will help you present your diagnosis of problems/opportunities (e.g., "this policy is really hurting customer service") so that they care about what you are saying. It can also help you communicate your recommendations for change in a way that will engage them.

3. Learn what you can about the early history of the organization, to help in identifying the shared learning and assumptions that make up the third, deepest layer of the culture. It may circulate in the form of stories. Many organizations tell stories about the early days to socialize new members or to confirm an important assumption about how the world works for the organization. Build your own private map of the culture's core assumptions and how they drive the daily actions and decisions in the organization.

Following these steps will help you identify problems that stem from an organization's culture that is out of alignment with its strategy or with the external realities of its business environment. It will also help you predict what solutions will and won't be successful before you commit to one. Finally, it will help you identify elements of the culture that must shift in order for a strategy or solution to succeed. Then you can work with your client to plan the experiences that will start building new, shared learning in the organization, learning that will allow new assumptions to form and old ones to go away.

Core Competencies

What Core Competencies Are

According to Hamel and Prahalad (1990), core competencies are the unique combination of skills and abilities behind an organization's core products and services. These include the ability to integrate complex technical skills and to coordinate a wide range of production skills to deliver end products that are valued by the customer. (In this section we will use *products* to refer to both products and services.)

Why Core Competencies Are Important
for the Organization and for You

Core competencies are an organization's source of sustainable competitive advantage. They allow the organization to keep developing a wide range of new products and services and enter new markets. According to Michael E. Porter (1985), competitive advantage depends on balancing two things: costs and differentiation.

TABLE 5.5. CORE COMPETENCIES

	Definition	Businesses
Core competencies	**ASK: What are we uniquely good at?**	
MARKETING R&D PRODUCTION DISTRIBUTION POINT OF SALE	Core competencies are the organizational skills and knowledge without which the organization could not exist, that the organization does better than anyone else, and that make the organization unique. Frequently, the things the company is known for are not obvious.	Nike: Marketing and R&D McDonald's: Supply chain and marketing Amazon: Tracking customer preferences and adjusting recommendations

Core competencies allow an organization to differentiate its products in ways that customers value, and to control costs through expertise and efficiency. An organization that understands its core competencies and has a plan for continuing to develop them as a portfolio is able to make strategic decisions about both developing and divesting lines of business. For example, it can build desired competencies relatively inexpensively through seeking partnerships, alliances, and licenses that will expand its expertise in the right direction. It can also judiciously divest itself of products and lines of business that aren't in line with what Prahalad (1993) calls its strategic architecture. Organizations that lack this insight lose core competencies by selling off units to achieve short term cost savings. As Prahalad says, without core competencies, an organization is just a bunch of business units.

If you follow the career of your favorite sports figure or star athlete, you can probably say specifically what he does that makes him stand out among all other players. He may have greater reach, a longer stride, or an uncanny knack for always being where the ball is about to arrive. That is the athlete's core competency and his competitive advantage. Core competencies are the same thing for an organization. If you know what they are, you know what makes your client organization competitive. This will enable you to look for risks and opportunities that are of the greatest value to your customer: the organization.

Characteristics of Core Competencies

To understand core competencies, you have to first understand two underlying concepts: value chain and core products.

The *value chain* was identified by Porter in his influential book *Competitive Advantage* (1985). Each organization has a set of activities by which it designs, markets, and delivers its products. Each of these activities must add value for its stakeholders, especially customers. Porter identified five primary activities:

- *Inbound logistics:* Receiving, storing, and deploying materials used to produce products
- *Operations:* Creating and producing the product
- *Outbound logistics:* Getting the product to the customer and billing for it
- *Marketing and sales:* Getting information and incentives that create desire for the product in the customer
- *Service:* Ensuring that the customer gets value after the sale

He also identified four support activities the organization needs to perform its five primary activities successfully:

1. Infrastructure management (governance)
2. HR management
3. Technology development (R&D, not information technology)
4. Procurement (obtaining materials used to produce products)

Successful activities require competence; core competences will be the ones the organization does supremely well—the source of their differentiation. An organization may not excel in all aspects of the value chain; it may focus on one or two parts that it does supremely well and outsource other parts that are not strengths. For example, Nike excels at R&D, design, and marketing. It outsources much of its operations (manufacturing shoes and garments) and distribution, or outbound logistics. This allows them to focus on building and capitalizing on their core competencies.

Core products are not the end products or services delivered to the customer. Instead, they are products used to create end products. For example, some of 3M's core products include surfaces such as plastic films, coatings, and adhesives. These core products are used to create many end products that are useful to customers: office products; films that brighten displays on electronic devices like flat screen computers, PDAs, and cell phones; insulating layers for sports clothing, air filters, transdermal drug delivery systems; and so on. A visit to the 3M Web site is very instructive. Similarly, Black and Decker's core products are small electric motors. This lets the company keep producing new end products like power tools for home building and repair, for automotive diagnostics and care, for cleaning, for home appliances, and for yard work. Developing this core product has allowed the firm to branch out into related products that draw on the same highly developed skills and knowledge: power monitoring and power storage.

In some cases, an organization may sell its core products directly to other organizations for their own end products. For example, Intel sells semiconductor chips, its core product, to many manufacturers of electronic equipment: computers, cell phones, PDAs, and the like. 3M sells its films directly to manufacturers as well.

Hamel and Prahalad (1990) explain that core competencies are developed over time as an organization creates its core products. Core competencies are developed over time, often from the start of the organization. They are the result of continual learning and experience built by creating core products and constantly developing, testing, and refining them into different end products, and fine-tuning them to provide what their customers value. They do not involve just the engineering and design skills involved in creating a product; they also involve coordinating the efforts of different technical experts to create products and then mobilizing effort and expertise throughout the organization to produce them efficiently, deliver them at a price that customers feel equals their value, and provide any postsales service required to maintain that value.

Hamel and Prahalad identify three criteria for identifying a core competency:

1. It must make a very large contribution to benefits the customer values.
2. It must open doors to a wide range of markets.
3. It must be difficult for competitors to reproduce or imitate.

As staff people and professionals, we have to keep an eye on the future and keep developing our own skills and experience so that we remain competitive in the markets we serve. Because our market is in the support part of the value chain rather than the primary part, we have to be very good at identifying what our customers really value and being able to deliver it. We also need to keep an eye on the future, to some degree predicting where we think customer needs and our own technologies will go, and look for ways to build the competencies we think will be required. Sometimes this means taking workshops or courses. But for newly developing areas, there may not be any textbooks, courses, or workshops yet. Or the cost in time and money of going back to school may be more than we can afford. In both cases, we may develop skills by working in partnership with people who already have them or who are pioneering in the direction we think things will go. We may form alliances with clients who use a technology we want to learn, leveraging our existing skills and modifying our own rates in order to extend our core competencies in new directions.

It is the same for any organization that wants to build and maintain a competitive advantage. It must first identify its core competencies. Next it must assess where it thinks customer needs and developing technologies will go. Then it must create what Hamel and Prahalad (1996) call a strategic architecture: a multiyear plan for developing its core competencies (along with its core products) so that it can enter developing and future markets with products that deliver the value customers care about. This does not mean outspending the competition in R&D, nor does it necessarily require purchasing organizations that already have a needed competence: competencies can be developed less expensively through partnerships and alliances between businesses. For example, during the 1980s NEC had an R&D budget that was less than IBM. During that same time period they grew 23 percent per year, a much higher level than other organizations that were spending substantially more. It leveraged its R&D investment by many carefully chosen alliances based on its strategic architecture. It was constantly building broader competencies in computer development (from central to distributed processing, from vacuum tubes to chips, etc.) and communications (from analog transmission to digitalization and networks). NEC is now one of the largest producers of semiconductors—a core product—in the world. It provides end products that range from computers to broadcasting equipment to home appliances, and it serves a host of industries.

Hamel and Prahalad liken competitive advantage to a large tree: The roots are core competencies that feed the main trunk, which is the organization's core products. The branches are lines of businesses within the organization that draw on the core products to produce fruit, the end products valued by customers.

Good Examples

- Honda's core products include gasoline engines and power trains. It is able to mobilize core technologies and production expertise across the organization to produce these products and incorporate them into a wide variety of end products. The core competencies Honda has developed around engines and power trains allow it to compete successfully in markets that include automobiles, motorcycles, watercraft, lawnmowers, pumps, and generators and to maintain a competitive advantage in each.
- On the service side, Amazon has developed core competencies in Web-based retail sales. To deliver what customers value—selection, price, and convenience—they developed expertise in negotiating large volume, deep discount deals with producers (e.g., publishers), and providing a secure, user-friendly Web store. This includes tracking individuals' buying patterns and matching them up with products that appeal to them. They started with books, then branched out to other physical items like films and music, then appliances, clothing, beauty supplies, and more. They next expanded their competence into offering books, films, and music that can be downloaded directly to users'

personal electronic devices, eliminating physical objects that need to be mailed. They expanded into offering secure Web sales services to smaller vendors, creating a link for buyers and handling only the exchange of money. As of the writing of this book, Amazon is expanding into offering Web service and storage to other businesses. This is a good example of a service business that made a long-term investment in developing core competencies that gave it access to a wide variety of markets.

Weak Example

Some large U.S. automobile manufacturers have outsourced most of the components of the cars they assemble, keeping mainly the large facilities and heavy machinery for putting their products together. This leaves them with large fixed costs but few core products and core competencies that they can turn into new products as technology, the competitive landscape, and the economy change. Once a company is in trouble, it is doubly difficult to find the time and the money to invest in redeveloping competencies they once led in.

Issues with Core Competencies

Throwing the baby out with the bathwater. Organizations can hurt themselves by cost cutting without a strategic architecture. Organizations that don't have a clear, well articulated plan for developing their core competencies often respond to short-term profitability goals by cutting products and people that will be needed to sustain their competitive edge in the future. Prahalad and Hamel (1996) provide the example of U.S. market leaders who divested their color TV businesses along with the people, because sales were flattening and it was considered to be a mature (not growing) industry. By doing so, they gave up their video competencies just before video became digital. It was too late (or at least it would be very slow and expensive) for them to redevelop that competency and get back into a competitive position as HDTV took off. Sony has done the opposite, giving up their failed BetaMax videotape product but not relinquishing the people and the video competencies that produced it. They are now one of the global leaders in small camcorders.

Mistaking the trees for the forest. Some organizations think of core competencies in terms of technical skills alone, failing to recognize the production and support skills needed to deliver value to customers, as well as the management skills needed to coordinate all of them across the organization. Executive teams often miss the importance of people-handling skills: the ability to coordinate different groups across the organization in service of delivering value at an acceptable price.

Feudal camps. Business fiefdoms can make the development and deployment of core competencies impossible to achieve. If an organization treats lines of business as autonomous units that cannot be interfered with, it will never succeed in meshing technologies, putting the key talents where they're most needed, and coordinating the development and delivery of products across the whole organization. An organization that operates this way is a collection of businesses, not a strategic enterprise. In "The Role of Core Competencies in the Corporation," Prahalad (1993) describes the obstacles: secrecy, the failure to share competencies, the hoarding of key talent, reward systems that penalize a manager who releases key people if the business unit falls short of goals predicated on having those talents on hand, and peer-to-peer competition for resources at the expense of the larger organization. We have all seen the destructive impact of running businesses this way, but the model persists.

What You Should Do

You should do five things to understand core competencies for your organization:

1. First find out whether the organization has defined its core competencies.

   If it has, ask to see them. Before taking them at face value, look for some of the issues just discussed: an organization may be talking only about the technical skills involved (such as the science and engineering that go into a semiconductor) without considering the production and governance skills required to deliver customer value. Apply the three criteria as a test to determine whether these are really core competencies or just ordinary business skills and practices. The three criteria of a core competency are, again, as follows:

   > It must make a very large contribution to benefits the customer values.
   > It must open doors to a wide range of markets.
   > It must be difficult for competitors to reproduce or imitate.

   If the core competencies presented to you don't meet these criteria, there is no need to embarrass the client. Simply continue your search for the true core competencies to gain a deeper understanding of their competitive advantage. Use the following guidelines:

2. Identify the core products that the organization assembles into the end products sold to their customers or that it sells to other providers for assembly.

3. Identify the core competencies behind the core products. What are the organization's skills and abilities that meet the three criteria? Remember to consider production and coordination skills as well as technical ones.

4. Assess whether the organization has a long-range plan for developing its core competencies in a sustainable way. This is not the same as a corporate university or a training plan: It is a map of changing customer needs, types of core products needed to meet them, and the competencies the organization will need (both technical and production) to keep developing and delivering those core products.

5. Assess whether the organization views itself primarily as a portfolio of competencies or as a portfolio of businesses. A test is to talk with people to find out whether talented individuals are borrowed from different parts of the organization to build new products and services. Are product creation, delivery, and service seen as the purpose of the organization as a whole? Do sharing and learning move across lines of business? Or does each line of business operate as a separate organization, neither sharing talent nor coordinating with others?

If the core competencies are identified and there is a plan for sustaining their development into the future, the organization has a good chance of being able to execute its strategy and maintain competitive advantage. If not, this is an area to address when you consult with your client.

Growth Strategy

What Growth Strategy Is

A *growth strategy* is how an organization intends to create and sustain growth. There are two levels to a growth strategy. The first level is what it intends to do to grow, such as increasing the type of products or services it offers or expanding into new technologies. The second level is how it plans to do that, such as growing from within or through mergers and acquisitions. As you can see, growth strategy is closely linked to core competencies. See Table 5.6.

Why Growth Strategy Is Important for You and for the Organization

"Grow or die" has been a principle of organizational thinking for a long time. Examples of this are all around us: from small retail businesses that have been displaced by big-box stores with bigger selection and lower prices to large corporations that failed to develop a capability to reach rapidly expanding markets and were overtaken (literally) by competitors. In the period running from the 1950s through the early 1980s, many organizations were able to keep growing just by doing the same things on a larger scale. In the 1990s, as globalization and technological advances picked up speed, successful growth for the average organization was no longer a matter of doing more of the same thing. Organizations needed

TABLE 5.6. GROWTH STRATEGY

	Possibilities	Definition	Examples
Growth strategy	ASK: How are you growing the company?		
	ACQUISITIONS	Buying other businesses: • To increase market share by buying a competitor • To acquire expertise, distribution channels, other resources	• Big banks • Automotive (credit and insurance) • Software developers • Pharmaceuticals
	INTERNAL GROWTH	Adding "growth rings" to the business: • Grow by building facilities, hiring people to expand capacity • Acquire needed resources and expertise by developing them in-house or hiring to expand capabilities	• Retail stores • Manufacturers
	ALLIANCES	Expanding business by joint ventures and strategic alliances to reduce risk.	• High-Tech • Transportation • Banks • Grocery stores • Convenience retailers • Fast food

to analyze new markets, develop new strategies, adapt to new environments, and keep up with accelerating changes in technology.

To keep changing and growing, organizations need a strategy and a source of capital. One of the first things investment capital looks for is a plan for growing the organization's business and thus the value of the investment. A well thought-out growth strategy allows an organization to ensure that it keeps growing. It also encourages investors to provide capital. It helps the organization determine in what directions to grow and how best to achieve that growth. It is an integral part of the overall business strategy from year to year.

It's important for you to know the overall growth strategy at a high level, so that you understand where the business is headed. You also want to know if the organization is more likely to be engaged in widespread hiring and training to build its workforce internally, to acquire other organizations whose operations and culture will have to be assimilated, or to engage in partnerships with other organizations where coordination and project management will be major issues. Depending on the markets and technologies targeted by the growth plan, you may need to expect some combination of the three.

Characteristics of a Growth Strategy

Any healthy organization, whether a for-profit enterprise, a not-for-profit service organization, or even a city or county, has a growth plan. There should be two levels of information addressed in the plan: the what and the how.

The first level is what it intends to do to grow, such as increasing the number and type of products or services it offers, reaching a broader market for its existing business, breaking into new technologies so that it can broaden its offerings, or perhaps some new and innovative approach. Some possibilities include continually opening more locations (like Wal-Mart), finding new markets (like Amazon), offering new products (like Black & Decker), continually innovating with technology (like Intel), working closely with customers to develop and fine-tune products/ services that offer increasing value, and so on.

The second level is how it plans to grow, whether by growing from within or through mergers and acquisitions, or perhaps through franchises, partnerships, alliances, and joint ventures. Since we discussed expanding service offerings and new technologies in Core Competencies, here we will focus more on the how level.

- *Internal growth:* The organization builds itself from within, hiring and developing people, building new facilities, learning and applying new technologies through judicious planning, and hiring experts. Some organizations build growth by constantly increasing the amount of business it does through each location. For example, Wal-Mart constantly works to reduce processing time and accelerate the turnover of merchandise in its stores, enabling more sales in the same number of square feet (Herbold, 2004). Wal-Mart is well-known for taking an internal growth approach. This growth strategy takes constant investment, patience, and a long-term focus.
- *Mergers and acquisitions:* The organization buys other organizations to obtain market share, products, technologies, and other forms of expertise quickly. This form of growth takes big capital investments and then an often long and painful period of assimilation as the purchased organization is incorporated into the acquiring business. This has been the growth strategy of choice for large organizations in the 1990s and 2000s. It has proved to be a high-risk strategy that often costs far more than the purchase price and yields less than the projected value (Carleton and Lineberry, 2004).

- *Partnerships, alliances, and joint ventures:* Two or more independent organizations can work together on an initiative to achieve some kind of growth: to reach new markets, to expand products/services, and sometimes to acquire new expertise. All share the risks, the costs, and the benefits. For example, Starbucks has built alliances with grocery stores all over the country, setting up kiosks where customers can buy their favorite drinks, and grocery carts have sprouted cupholders. We are all familiar with alliances between travel providers: Airlines, hotels, and car rental companies offer package deals and recognize each other's customer incentive plans. Silicon Valley in California is full of technology companies that work mostly on joint ventures: Most large projects are sold and developed by a group of firms, each with a different technical specialty. This is the most economical growth strategy because it doesn't require the same level of capital investment, it is usually not long term, and it doesn't leave any one organization holding all the risk.

Issues with Growth Strategies

Mergers and acquisitions. These are very high risk and have a low success rate. The first risk is that costs can far exceed the initial cost projections when the sale was made. In addition, although some turnover is expected, top talent with desired expertise often leaves early and in unanticipated numbers. Also, as mentioned in Culture, little effort is made in most merger situations to assess the compatibility of the two cultures or to mesh them successfully. Some organizations maintain two separate and incompatible cultures for years after a merger. One of the authors was present at a meeting just after one computer company acquired another. When the engineers from the acquired company were asked to introduce themselves and their history, one said, "Before all of the mergers we've been through, we were Tandem Engineering. And as far as I'm concerned, we're still Tandem Engineering." This was 10 years after Tandem had been acquired. Finally, stock prices typically drop, productivity drops, and the valuation of the acquiring company drops (Carleton and Lineberry, 2004). Most studies of mergers and acquisitions report a less than 50 percent success rate on any dimension measured (profitability, net worth, market share, innovation, and the like).

Organizations that grow from within. These organizations can have problems if they treat human resource development as a last-minute logistic issue rather than as a long-term strategic one. When a new big-box store or plant is under construction, the organization turns to HR to obtain staff. If the right skills aren't readily available in the new area (when initial analysis chooses a location based chiefly on customer markets with little regard for the labor market), the organization often has to compromise several locations. For example, key people may have to be taken away from existing facilities to staff key positions in the new one, and most of the facility may have to be staffed with poor hiring choices due to shortages or stiff competition for qualified people. One particularly challenging skill set to grow internally is leadership: Organizations have a difficult time approaching this in a long-term, systemic fashion and look for quick, sheep dip programs that will produce leaders in short order.

Partnerships and alliances. These can run into problems if they focus only on the shared opportunity, finance, and the technology, without carefully considering how compatible the partner organizations are. Things to work out before a joint venture begins, not after, are deciding how conflicts over timing, resources, and credit will be resolved, where project management will reside, and what clout the project managers will have.

What You Should Do

Although you don't need to know all the ins and outs of your organization's growth strategy, you do want to collect two pieces of information:

1. What does the organization intend to do to grow? Will it offer more products, broaden its market, do some combination of these options, or do something else entirely?
2. How does it plan to make that happen? Will it build from within, build through mergers and acquisitions, or use alliances, partnerships, and joint ventures? Or will it devise some other means?

Some organizations publish this information. SAP posts the what part of its growth strategy on its Web site. Many cities publish their growth strategies; for example, Albuquerque New Mexico, puts its strategy on the city's Web site. If you can't find the information publically, find it by talking to your client and other people in the organization. You can ask things like, "In what directions do you see the business growing over the next five years?" "How will the organization do that?" It may be helpful to prompt your source with some of the possibilities like acquisitions versus partnerships.

Pricing Strategy

Pricing strategy consists of the objective your organization determines and the method it uses to set rices for the products and services it sells, and how that price relates to those of competitors. Pricing strategy is one of the 4 P's of marketing and a basic corporate strategy decision (Kotler, 1991). See Table 5.7.

TABLE 5.7. PRICING STRATEGY

	Possibilities	Definition	Examples
Pricing strategy	**ASK: How are you pricing your product/service? What variables determine your price?**		
	TOP OF MARKET	Charging highest prices and competing on prestige, uniqueness, perceived quality	Luxury cars Designer clothing Exclusive privilege
	MID-RANGE	Minimizing focus on price by staying in the middle of the pack	Internet service Providers Most airlines
	LOW END OF MARKET	Competing to be the low-cost provider	Superstores Commuter airlines

Why Pricing Strategy Is Important for You and Your Organization

Pricing is one way a company operationalizes and communicates to the public the value of its mission, vision, objectives, and core competencies. If the strategy is right, it can produce appropriately high profits for the organization. If it is wrong, it can cause an uproar. When Apple first introduced its iPhone, it set a price that it felt reflected the uniqueness of the product and the demand for it. After an initial surge, sales fell. Apple then reduced the price of the iPhone to increase sales. But instead it produced an outcry from those who purchased it at the initial price. This resulted in a public relations nightmare and the need to send rebates to all initial customers.

Pricing, then, is not a trivial matter. As you will see, there are many possible pricing objectives and methods, and there is a complex process for deriving price. But understanding that process and the options is an easy way for you to understand how the company sees the value of its strategy and products, as well as the kinds of customers it has.

In addition, though we are not in the Economic Logic chapter, there is simple formula involving price that impacts *your* budget:

$$(\text{Selling price per unit} - \text{Cost per unit}) \times \text{Number of units sold} = \text{Total Profit}$$

As we discussed in Chapter 4, much of the work we do and our budget, fall into the costs category (either as COGS or SG&A). And according to the formula, price has a direct impact on costs in order reach an acceptable profit for the organization.

So knowing how the organization sets price can help you understand how costs have to be managed and therefore how your budget is set or limited. See table 5.7.

Characteristics and Examples of Pricing

The six-step process for determining price is (Kotler, 1991):

1. Select the pricing objective
2. Determine demand
3. Estimate costs
4. Analyze competitors' prices and offers
5. Select a pricing method
6. Select the final price

To avoid turning this section into a marketing course, we will focus only on pricing objectives and pricing methods.

Select the Pricing Objective. Just when we thought we were done with strategic objectives, we see there is another set to be looked at. Kotler (1991, pp. 476–478) says there are six different pricing objectives a company can choose from in deciding what it wants to accomplish with its price for a product:

1. *Survival:* This objective involves covering all variables costs and some fixed costs. It is typically used when the company is faced with a poor economy (as in 2008–2009), with intense competition, or with overcapacity (as automobile manufacturers were in 2008–2009). This is, as the name implies, only a short-term strategy. At the time of writing, some auto companies were trying this pricing objective.
2. *Maximum current profit:* This objective assumes the company knows both its costs and demand. The company applies a formula that produces a price that maximizes the profit or ROI at the present time. Again, in addition to other problems, this strategy focuses on short-term rather than long-term financial performance. If this strategy is necessary, it tells you something about the financial position of the company today. Again, at the time of writing, some auto companies were trying this pricing objective.
3. *Maximum current revenue:* This objective, which can be used when the company knows only its demand, is focused on maximizing its current sales revenue. Some believe that this objective will lead to long-term profits and growth of market share. Print media (newspaper, magazines, and other periodicals) are using this strategy as they attempt not only to stay afloat, but to increase circulation, thus allowing them to increase ad rates for long-term growth.

4. *Maximum sales growth:* Also known as market-penetration pricing, this objective involves setting the lowest possible price, which leads to a higher volume of sales, which in turn leads to lower unit costs, which in turn leads to higher long-term profit. Fast-food giants use this strategy in economically hard times, with 99-cent items playing a major role in their menus.

5. *Maximum market skimming:* This objective involves setting high prices to skim the cream of the market several times. First, the organization sets the highest possible price for the value of its product for some market segment (as discussed in Chapter 4) that will pay it. Then, when sales slow down, it lowers the price to entice the next layer of market segment. And it repeats this until all market segments have been addressed. Cell phone companies aim for this objective with new cell phones, charging early adopter customers more for the new models, then gradually lowering the price for different market segments, and starting the cycle anew as newer models become available.

6. *Product quality leadership:* This objective, in partnership with the Company Image element of Product Logic, involves creating an image of the highest-quality product on the market, thereby justifying the highest price on the market. Apple's computers, phones, and MP3 players all are priced in line with this objective, as are some high-end automobiles.

Select the Pricing Method. Armed with the objective, and some cost and competitor data, the company is now ready to choose a pricing method. Kotler (1991, pp. 482–488) says there are four pricing methods a company can choose from in determining what to charge for a product:

1. *Markup pricing:* This method involves determining the cost of a product and then adding a standard markup to the cost. The markup is determined by the pricing objective: the percentage profit the company wants to receive on the product. Construction companies frequently use this method, as do retail stores (e.g., the markup price on clothing is between 50 and 100 percent of what the store paid).

2. *Target return pricing:* This method involves determining the desired return-on-investment on a product or service, and then, applying a formula involving the ROI and estimated sales, determining what price will produce that desired ROI. Pharmaceutical companies frequently use this pricing method, because they have a huge R&D investment in new medicine development, and want to see an ROI for that high investment.

3. *Perceived value pricing:* This method involves focusing not on the costs of the product, but rather on the value the target market attaches to the product. One may immediately think of luxury cars and the inauguration ball or Versace gowns, where "looking good" trumps all other qualities in the eyes of

the target market, or of leadership in product quality", where the safest car trumps all other attributes for that target market. But one can also think of big-box stores, where some chains focus on the lowest price like Wal-Mart, but others do not, focusing on higher (though not the highest) prices for higher-quality everyday goods, like Target and Costco.

4. *Going rate pricing:* This method involves focusing on the prices that competitors are charging and determining the company's price based on staying within a certain percentage of those prices. In this method, less attention is paid to the company's own costs. Instead, the company decides to charge the same as the competitors, less than they do, or more than they do, based on the pricing objective. Gasoline prices are an excellent example of this pricing method.

Issues with Pricing Strategy

Watch out for two main issues as you learn about your company's pricing strategy:

Too much information. Remember that our purpose is help you understand overall corporate strategy, not to become marketing experts. Thus we have to avoid discussing everything there is to know about pricing. So we have omitted from the preceding discussion other pricing issues such as geographical pricing, price discounting, promotional pricing, discriminatory pricing, product-mix pricing, initiating price increases and decreases, and responding to customer responses to price changes (Kotler, 1991). These will fascinate the marketing people you talk to in order to learn about your company's pricing strategy, but they are more than you need to know about.

Formulas and graphs. A related issue comes from the enthusiastic, newly minted MBAs who want to show you the slide presentations they gave to management just last week, with all the formulas and graphs they used to derive the exact price—to the penny. This will cause you to get lost in the weeds and to be unable even to see the trees, let alone the forest. All you want is the pricing objective and the method. No more.

What You Should Do

You should take five actions for this element of Strategy Logic.

1. Find out who in the organization knows about how prices are set.
2. Armed with what you just read (or even with the book itself, open to these pages) visit that person.
3. Find out what pricing objective and method the company uses (and there may be more than one, perhaps even a different one for each product line).

4. Ask yourself how this pricing strategy fits in with the Profit Source in Economic Logic and with the other elements of Strategy Logic. Does it support or contradict them?
5. Ask yourself how this pricing strategy might affect you, your department, your budget, and any projects you are considering working on. Does it constrain you, or does it give you some leverage, something you can tie to your approach to the project? For example, if the pricing objective is maximum current value, then arguing for long-term ROI is not going to get you far, but showing how to immediately reduce COGS will.

Alignment

What Alignment Is

An organization is in *alignment* when it has a set of goals, strategies, plans, values, practices and behaviors that all units (divisions, departments, lines of business, etc.) support and are part of. Each unit has a subset of the larger plan, and all are synchronized with each other so that their goals and strategies do not compete or interfere with each other. Leadership manages the culture of the organization to support the strategy, articulating values, defining management practices, and modeling behaviors that clearly align with the goals, processes, and tasks identified in the plan (Tosti and Jackson, 1994). See Table 5.8.

Why Alignment Is Important for You and for the Organization

Alignment enables organizations to execute their strategies effectively. Once an enterprise-level strategy is developed, different parts of the organization develop their own goals and detailed plans for supporting them. If there is an organized

TABLE 5.8. ALIGNMENT

Alignment	ASK: Are all the elements of strategy logic in alignment with one another and with other logics?	
	Ask, "Are all the elements consistent with one another?" "Is it clear how each element is derived from the preceding elements and guides the following ones?"	If the mission/vision is to be the low-cost leader, then are the prices the lowest, are the processes designed to minimize COGS and SGA, and are stores located in the correct areas? If the vision is to push the envelope of interactive Web functionality, does the organization have the core competencies, culture, financial metrics, processes, and technology to do so?

process for aligning goals, strategies, and initiatives among all these parts of the organization, leaders and employees can focus their efforts on implementing the strategy efficiently. Without this step, effort is duplicated, there is unproductive competition for resources, and initiatives started in one area obstruct initiatives created in another. When management practices and daily behaviors of the workforce are in alignment with the organization's goals and strategies, the organization has a much better chance of achieving its goals. For example, consider an organization whose strategy is to offer new products and to gain competencies by acquiring smaller companies that already have them. When members of the organization treat members of an acquired company with interest and respect, the strategy is likely to bear fruit. However, if they treat newly acquired members as second-class citizens who are on probation, a successful transfer of new skills is unlikely and the strategy will probably fail. Alignment skills correlate with strategic positioning as key sources of competitive advantage (Powell, 1992).

Alignment is important to you for the same reason that it's important to anyone else in the organization who wants to support the strategy, achieve its goals, and complete its objectives. Working without alignment is like trying to drive a cart hitched to several horses, each pulling in a different direction. It's hard to improve performance or to provide HR support to an organization that isn't clear on where it's going or how. If you identify areas where the organization is out of alignment and if you can both show how it's preventing the enterprise from reaching its goals and propose ways to fix it, you will be adding more value than you could by revising the performance appraisal form or designing a training program.

Characteristics of Alignment

We will look at two aspects of alignment:

- *Strategic:* What the organization is doing
- *Cultural:* How it is doing it

We will use Tosti and Jackson's organizational alignment model, as adapted by Addison, Haig, and Kearny (2009). See Figure 5.1. This model shows two aspects of organizational governance: strategy and culture. You are already familiar with the strategy, or operational, side. We have also discussed how the strategy side must be aligned vertically and across the organization. If the organization is aligned, all unit plans and strategies support and are subordinate to those at the enterprise level. This means the organization's strategy and the resources for achieving it are not split up among fiefdoms of independent lines of business, each with its own internal turf, processes, and strategies to protect (Herbold, 2004).

FIGURE 5.1

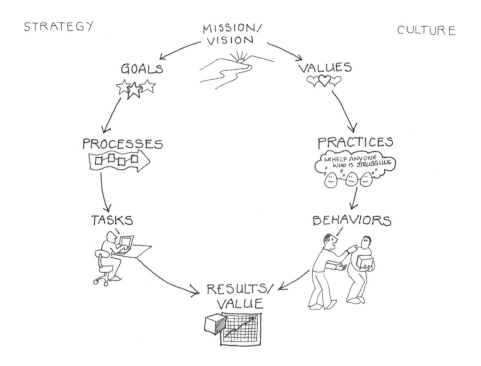

The levels on the culture side correspond with the levels on the strategy side: Both sides must be aligned with each other. Since the culture side is less familiar, we will look at it in more detail. It includes values, practices, and behaviors.

Values. Values are often articulated when leadership develops or updates the vision and mission of the organization. Values created at that time often represent the personal values and beliefs of the senior leaders, or at least the values they would like the organization to have. Tosti calls these aspirational values. To achieve alignment, values at this level should be operational values, derived from the results the organization wants to achieve with its strategy. It must be perfectly clear how these values (e.g., integrity, inclusiveness, etc.) relate to the organization's goals (Tosti, 2007). The values must provide unambiguous guidance to employees at all levels, not leave people guessing how to interpret them.

Practices. Practices are replicable patterns of behavior. *Merriam-Webster* defines a practice as "to do something customarily." In the present context, it means a set of actions that have become habitual to people in the organization. We are particularly interested in management practices, since they set a model that the rest of the organization is likely to follow. Remember our earlier definition of culture as "the way we do things around here." Senior management practices are the most influential of all. To achieve alignment, practices must describe how members of the organization should behave when carrying out an objective, not how they habitually do things. For example, an organization has a goal to fill 60 percent of all skilled positions from within, and it has set several objectives to make that happen. One objective is to complete performance reviews and developmental plans for all employees during the first six months of the year. Actual management practice has been to put this unpopular task off until the last possible minute, then complete the required form and e-mail it to the employee with a note to contact the reviewer with any questions. If leadership wants to develop skilled people to fill positions from within, they will have to realign management practice to match the goal. They must identify the practices needed to support the objective, make them public, model the practices themselves, and hold others accountable. This is alignment.

Behaviors. Behaviors are simply individual actions. When we are talking about behaviors in this context, we mean how individual members of the organization carry out their daily tasks. Customer service supervisors instinctively understand the importance of behaviors: Answering the phone is not enough; it's how you answer the phone. It's not just a technically correct greeting or accurate information; it's the tone of voice, pace, the presence or absence of a smile in the voice. It's whether an assignment is received with a smile and nod or a roll of the eyes. This is obvious in customer service work, but it is often overlooked where boundaries are crossed: between groups, jobs, or authority levels. People in jobs with higher prestige or higher authority levels can become careless and hold people lower on the totem pole to a higher standard of behavior than they hold themselves.

When planning gets down to the task level, management needs to ask not only what specific tasks need to be done, but what behaviors will be important to make it work—especially when the work is new or different or when the organization needs to change old, negative forms of behavior. Management must state what is expected, model the behaviors themselves, and only then hold people accountable. This represents alignment between the task side (strategy/operational) side and the behavior side (cultural) of the organization.

When leadership identifies the values, practices, and behaviors required to carry out strategies and then manages them, the organization can implement the strategy effectively.

Issues with Alignment

Feudal camps. You cannot get alignment when independent fiefdoms fragment the organization, hoarding resources and information, duplicating effort, driving up costs, and creating a partisan planning process. This is not an unusual state of affairs in business organizations today (Herbold, 2004).

Vacuum-packed plans. A strategic planning exercise is done every year, then the plans are sealed away and everyone goes back to business as usual. The plans are rarely reviewed or discussed, nor are they changed as the business environment changes. At the end of the year a new strategic planning process starts. If plans are created and kept in a vacuum like this, they can't be aligned because they aren't real.

"It's all about them". Leadership creates a high-level plan and hands it off with fanfare but no follow-through. It's left up to the remaining layers to figure out what it means and what to do to achieve it. The hand-off behavior being modeled by the leadership often gets repeated on down the organization, finally leaving it up to the front-line employees to figure out what objectives like "greater customer intimacy" mean and what to do about it. The leadership frets that it doesn't have the right kind of people to implement strategy. This cannot be aligned because not enough of the work has been done. Another version of this issue is the assumption by senior leadership that the specified practices and behaviors are for their direct reports and everyone below: They make the mistake of not taking it seriously enough to change their own behavior. Continuing our example, senior leaders must conduct a performance review and developmental plan for their own direct reports before they can expect the same action from their followers. The rest of the organization determines what is important by watching what senior leaders actually do.

What You Should Do

1. *Diagnose:* You have already determined the organization's mission, vision, and goals/objectives/initiatives. The elements of a strategic plan are there, and you know (at least generally) what they are. The following questions should help you determine how aligned the organization is for achieving its goals. You won't be able to find the answers to all of them, but you'll be able to find out enough to get a good sense of where things stand.
   - How is the strategy created? Is it strictly handed down from the top, or is there an iterative process involving the divisions and departments? As the divisions and departments build and refine their plans, do they meet with each other to coordinate and align, or does each group complete its own plan independently?

- When conflicts arise, how are they handled? Are they ignored in hopes that things will work themselves out? Does the senior team resolve issues around strategic priorities or leave subordinates to slug it out? If senior team members get involved, do they resolve issues for the good of the organization as a whole, or do they take a partisan stance and fight to ensure that their team wins?

- How far down does the operational side of the plan go? Are there processes for carrying out the objectives? Have the needed core competencies been identified, and are they in place? Has the planning been taken down to the task level, so that it can be implemented? Are the tasks being done, or do they mostly wait for people to get around to them?

- Are cultural factors (values, practices, behaviors) addressed as part of the strategic plan? Are operational values articulated? Do they relate to the strategy, goals, and desired end results? Are practices and behaviors consistent with the values? Do practices and behaviors support the end results that the strategy is trying to achieve? Is leadership modeling the practices and behaviors they need employees to adopt?

2. *Apply:* When you have answers to these questions, or at least a general sense of the answers, you will know how aligned the organization is. If alignment is poor, consider what bearing that has on the project your client has asked you to take on.

    - If you were asked to solve a problem, is a lack of alignment a root cause? What specific kind of alignment is at stake? As you can see, poor alignment can cause anything from poor communication to low productivity, high costs, facilities snafus, and accounting problems. Whatever your area of expertise, you know you will have to address alignment as part of the solution.

    - If you have been asked to help realize an opportunity (such as building technical skills to enter a new market), where is alignment missing relative to this initiative? Is the organization out of alignment about goals, ownership, processes, practices, and behavior? Part of your work will be to partner with your client and build some alignment around the necessary actions.

Measures for Strategy Logic

Let's begin this section with a clear statement of what will soon become obvious: Measuring strategy is not the same as measuring ROA or COGS. There are no numbers in Strategy Logic, not even in pricing. So you cannot go to the accountant or production supervisor and have her print out reports with numbers in them.

TABLE 5.9 MEASURES

	Possibilities
Measures	**ASK: How can we measure how well Strategy Logic has been developed?**
	Identified (yes, sort of, no)
	Stated/documented
	Clearly understood by all
	Specific
	Measurable
	Consistent with other elements of Strategy Logic and with External and Economic Logics
	Supported by the organization
	Agreed to by people in the organization

But that does not mean there are no measures of an organization's strategy. If you've been reading closely, you've seen that we've been planting hints about such measures. First, let's talk about what they are *not*. They are not things like how much money the company made last year or the market share. Although those measures are important, they are not measures of the strategy or even of the result of the strategy alone. They are measures of the success of the whole organization, including all six Internal Logics and the whims of the External Logic. Also, these measures are *not* always numbers, though we could turn them into numbers if someone asked us to. An obvious example relates to something we already know. If good objectives are SMART, then the simplest way to measure this is by asking whether the objectives are SMART—yes or no? For a computer, that's a 1 or 0. That question is a good measure because it tells you what you need to know simply, quickly, and meaningfully.

Now, your question might be, "How do we score objectives that have only three or four of those characteristics?" You can take four approaches.

1. One is the quantitative. We can rate objectives on a 0-to-5 scale, based on how many parts of SMART the objective has. Using this approach, the measure for objectives could be a 3 or 4 if it is good but not perfect.

2. The second one is even more precise: "Some parts of SMART are more important than others, so one that is missing the *T* but has a good *S* actually should be scored 4.5."

3. The third one is the absolutist. Either objectives are SMART or they are not; the equipment in an operating room cannot be half sterile, it is either sterile or it is not.

4. The fourth approach—the one we recommend—is based on the fact that we have lives as HR practitioners and cannot spend our entire lives parsing points and decimal portions of points for things that do not require them. And we accept the fact that the world is not a perfect place and will not be even after you apply everything in this book. So we recommend that in this logic, you use as the measure the following three-point scale for measuring each element of the logic:

—Meets *all* the criteria.

—Meets *most* of the criteria.

—Meets *none or few* of the criteria.

This last measure will tell you exactly what you need to know about how well the organization is doing on the element of Strategy Logic, without spending time you don't have.

The criteria for the measures for each element of Strategy Logic are presented in Table 5.10.

Sample Worksheets for Strategy Logic

In Chapter 2, we introduced the Internal Scan and Measures Worksheets. Here they are with the column for Strategy Logic filled out for one of our clients. It is brief: just a few words summarizing each of the elements. This is the level of detail that we suggest you use to get the big picture without bogging yourself down in a major research project. Save your time and energy for more detailed analysis when you have a specific performance issue to investigate. Table 5.11 shows the Internal Scan Worksheet, and Table 5.12 shows a sample set of strategy measures for the same client, done using the criteria listed.

Strategy Logic Job Aid

This job aid summarizes strategy logic with graphics, definitions, questions to be answered, and examples. Use it when you are trying to identify the strategy logic for your own (or your client's) organization. The Strategy Logic Summary Job Aid is in Table 5.13.

TABLE 5.10. STRATEGY CRITERIA

	Strategy Logic element	Measures criteria (each is rated: all, most, or none or few)

	Mission and vision	Mission:
		    Purpose
		    Products and/or services
		    Customers and/or primary stakeholders
		
		Vision:
		    A description of a bright future
		    A clear and vivid picture
		    Emotional appeal
		    Exciting and memorable wording
		    Both challenging and achievable

	Objectives	Specific (concrete, detailed, well-defined) Measurable (numbers, quantity, comparison) Attainable but challenging (feasible, actionable) Realistic (considering resources) Time-bound (a definite time line)
	Culture	Artifacts visible Espoused values articulated Tacit assumptions shared
	Core competencies	Make a very large contribution to benefits the customer values Open doors to a wide range of markets Difficult for competitors to reproduce or imitate
	Growth strategy	Articulated Meets growth objective Consistent or inconsistent by design
	Pricing strategy	Pricing objective Articulated Met Consistent or inconsistent by design Pricing method Articulated Meets objective Consistent or inconsistent by design
	Alignment	Mission/vision, objectives, core competencies, growth strategy, and pricing Strategy: Articulated Practiced Consistent with each other Consistent with values side Values, practices, behaviors Articulated Practiced Consistent with each other Consistent with mission side

TABLE 5.11. SAMPLE INTERNAL SCAN FOR CREDIT CARD DIVISION OF A BANK

Assess and fill in the logic the business appears to be using.

ECONOMIC LOGIC	STRATEGY LOGIC	CUSTOMER LOGIC	PRODUCT LOGIC	PROCESS LOGIC	STRUCTURAL LOGIC
Cost Structure • *Variable: cost of funds and delinquencies* • *To manage: self-fund, control delinquencies* **Financial Focus** • *Cost of goods sold* **Profit Source** • *Channel: Direct versus oil company cards versus Sears, etc.*	**Mission and vision** • *Provide profitable credit services to higher-risk market* **Initiatives/tactics** • *Seek new customer-facing partners* • *Manage delinquencies tightly* **Culture** • *Do it now, ask forgiveness later* **Core competency** • *Collections* **Growth Strategy** • *Alliances: Oil company, large retailer credit* • *Purchase: Other banks' delinquent portfolios* **Pricing Strategy** • *High end of middle*				

- Do the logics in the six columns support each other or are they contradictory?
- If they are contradictory, does this have some bearing on the problem you were asked to solve?
- How can you test your assessment that these are the business logic(s) the company is using?
- Now review the logic in the light of your environmental scan. Do the six logics seem to be consistent with external realities?

Reprinted with permission of Lynn Kearny, 2009

TABLE 5.12. SAMPLE MEASURES WORKSHEET FOR CREDIT CARD DIVISION OF A BANK

Logic	Measures	Target	Current	Gap	Performance Problems	Interventions	Measured Results
Economic							
	Mission/vision, objectives	Meet all criteria	Meet all criteria	None			
	Culture	Meet all criteria	Meet all criteria	None			
	Core Competencies	Meet all criteria	Meet all criteria	None			
	Growth Strategy	Meet all criteria	Meet all criteria	None			
Strategy	Pricing strategy	Meet all criteria	Meet all criteria	None			
	Alignment	Meet all criteria now, and with addition of new customers and products	Meet all criteria now	Evaluate strategy with addition of new customers and products; revise strategy or customer/ product to keep aligned			
Customer							
Product							
Process							
Structural							

- What specific measures does the organization use for each type of logic? Write them in column 2.
- What is the target for each measure? Write it in column 3.
- What is the current number for each measure? Write it in column 4.
- What is the gap between target and current number for each measure? Write it in column 5.
- Those measures with the greatest, and most critical, gaps are the focus of the Performance Problem Analysis and Intervention Selection that take place next in the Performance Improvement process.

Reprinted with permission of Lynn Kearny, 2009

TABLE 5.13. SUMMARY JOB AID—STRATEGY LOGIC

How the organization finds a strategy

	Definition	Examples
Mission and vision 	**ASK: Why does this company exist?** A mission is a statement of the specific purpose of the organization. A vision is a more affective, future-oriented statement of what the organization means. Missions and visions provide specific direction to the organization and people in it: Mission statements should be specific and clear about the organization's industry, products/services and customers, and they should be measurable. Vision statements should express what a *Harvard Business Review* article called a BHAG (big hairy audacious goal) for the future, and they should talk about the affective side of the business.	**Mission** "ComputerGeeks.com, is a leading direct-to-consumer eCommerce site specializing in providing computer-related excess inventory, manufacturer-closeouts, high-demand and unusual computer components and peripherals at highly-discounted prices to tech-savvy, 'Geeky' consumers." **Vision** "ComputerGeeks.com is committed to offering tremendous savings on computer products, and hosting a Web site providing a depth of value-added content. Our aim is to amuse, inform, and entertain you—while providing amazing values—and to push the envelope of interactive Web functionality and secure online shopping ease…"
Objectives	**ASK: How do we get from here to there?** Objectives are specific, measurable, year-to-year goals that are steps in reaching the mission/vision. Initiatives or tactics (sometimes mislabeled strategies) are the specific actions the organization is going to take to reach the objectives and thus the mission/vision. Objectives and initiatives should: Be specific and measurable. Be attainable and implementable. Be consistent from year to year (unless other elements of total strategy change). Provide a line of sight at all levels of the organization.	Objectives and initiatives should be steps in reaching the mission/vision. Initiatives are the specific actions the organization is going to take to reach the objectives and thus the mission/vision (unless other elements of total strategy change).

TABLE 5.13. SUMMARY JOB AID—STRATEGY LOGIC (Continued)

	Definition	Businesses
Culture	**ASK: What does the organization stand for both internally and externally?**	Companies known (for better or worse) for their unique cultures are:
	The study of corporate culture can include many things depending on whom you read. Most definitions include three key elements that can be our focus:	Enron
		Microsoft
	Values: What does this organization believe in, in terms of how it treats investors, employees, and customers and how it conducts business with other companies?	Wal-Mart
		Google
		Sony
	Beliefs/stories: How does an organization see itself, in terms of the beliefs it has about role and destiny in the marketplace and the stories it tells about how it got started, what success is, the good it does, and what employees should do?	Gap
		Disney
	Behaviors rewarded: How does an organization operationalize the culture by rewarding behavior consistent with the culture and punishing behavior not consistent?	
Core competencies MARKETING R&D PRODUCTION DISTRIBUTION POINT OF SALE	**ASK: What are we uniquely good at?**	Nike = Marketing and R&D
	Core competencies are the organizational skills and knowledge without which the organization cannot exist, that the organization does better than anyone else, and that make the organization unique.	McDonald's = Supply chain and marketing
		Amazon = Tracking customer preferences and adjusting recommendations
	Frequently, the core competencies the company is known for are not obvious.	

TABLE 5.13. SUMMARY JOB AID—STRATEGY LOGIC (*Continued*)

	Possibilities	Definition	Examples	Businesses
Growth strategy	**ASK: How are you growing the company?**			
	ACQUISITIONS	Buying other businesses:	Big banks	Wells Fargo
		To increase market share by buying a competitor	Automotive (credit and insurance)	Ford
		To acquire expertise, distribution channels, other resources	Software developers	Microsoft and AOL
			Pharmaceuticals	Merck (Med 6)
	INTERNAL GROWTH	Adding "growth rings" to the business:		
		Grow by building facilities, hiring people to expand capacity	Retail stores	Wal-Mart
		Acquire needed resources and expertise by developing them in-house or hiring to expand capabilities	Manufacturers	Intel
	ALLIANCES	Expanding business by joint ventures and strategic alliances to reduce risk	High-tech	Apple Partners
			Transportation	Airlines, hotels, and car rentals
			Banks	Wells Fargo
			Grocery stores	Safeway
			Convenience retailers	Amoco
			Fast food	McDonald's

TABLE 5.13. SUMMARY JOB AID—STRATEGY LOGIC (Continued)

	Possibilities	Definition	Examples	Businesses
Pricing strategy	ASK: How are you pricing your product/service? What variables determine your price?			
	TOP OF MARKET	Charging highest prices and competing on prestige, uniqueness, perceived quality	Luxury cars Designer clothing Exclusive privilege	Lexus Armani First-class air travel
	MID-RANGE	Minimizing focus on price by staying in the middle of the pack	Internet service providers Most airlines	AOL, AT&T Worldnet United
	LOW END OF MARKET	Competing to be the low-cost provider	Superstores Commuter airlines	Wal-Mart Southwest Air
Alignment	ASK: Are all the elements of Strategy Logic in alignment with one another and with other Logics?			
	Ask, "Are all the elements consistent with one another?" "Is it clear how each element is derived from the preceding elements and guides the following ones?"	If the mission/vision is to be the low-cost leader, then are the prices the lowest, are the processes designed to minimize COGS and SGA, and are stores located in the correct areas? If the vision is to push the envelope of interactive Web functionality, does the organization have the core competencies, culture, financial metrics, processes, and technology to do so?		
Measures	ASK: How do we measure how well Strategy Logic has been developed?			
	Identified (yes, sort of, no) Stated/documented Clearly understood by all Specific Measurable Consistent with other elements of Strategy Logic and with External and Economic Logics Supported by the organization Agreed to by people in the organization			

© 2009. Reprinted with permission of Lynn Kearny.

Your Turn

Use the Strategy Logic Job Aid and the Internal Scan Worksheet (Table 5.14) to identify the Strategy Logic and measures operating in your organization or your client's. Here are sources of information:

- Organization's Web site
- Annual report
- 10-K report
- Hoover or Mergent (Most public libraries have a subscription.)
- Members of the organization, particularly managers, the strategic planning office, and finance
- Any other sources suggested in this chapter

If you want a reproducible version of worksheet, there is one on the Web site at (www.Pfeiffer.com/go/kennethsilber). Copy it to your desktop, and either use it as is or modify it for the level of detail you need to work with. Consider creating an Excel spreadsheet.

Summary

You now know how to identify the Economic and Strategy Logics of an organization. You are now armed with the most important terms, ideas, and information you need to understand what leadership is trying to do and assess the completeness and coherence of the plan. You can also talk with business leaders about problems and opportunities that your expertise can help with. Next we will get into the logics that support strategy and help the organization achieve its purpose in specific ways. The first of those is Customer Logic.

TABLE 5.14. INTERNAL SCAN WORKSHEET

Assess and fill in the logic the business appears to be using.

ECONOMIC LOGIC	STRATEGY LOGIC	CUSTOMER LOGIC	PRODUCT LOGIC	PROCESS LOGIC	STRUCTURAL LOGIC

- Do the logics in the six columns support each other or are they contradictory?
- If they are contradictory, does this have some bearing on the problem you were asked to solve?
- How can you test your assessment that these are the business logic(s) the company is using?
- Now review the logic in the light of your environmental scan. Do the six logics seem to be consistent with external realities?

CHAPTER SIX

CUSTOMER LOGIC

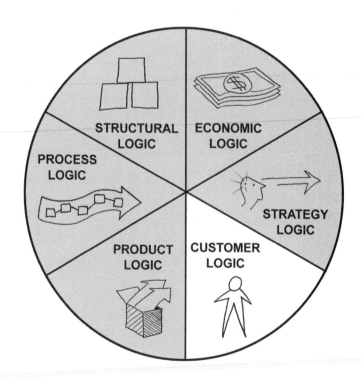

Customer Logic refers to how the organization thinks about, creates, and keeps customers. Part of this logic will sound familiar to you because we have already discussed it in the profit source element of Economic Logic in Chapter 4. The logic will also begin to sound more familiar to you than the last two logics because we have all heard some of the concepts marketers use to segment customers. Finally, it will intuitively make sense because we are, after all, all customers, and we think of ourselves in many of the ways that we will be talking about in Customer Logic.

Why Customer Logic Is Important to You and the Organization

Customer Logic is important to your organization for several reasons we have already discussed. In External Logic, we discussed the importance of demographics in the Business Environment and the bargaining power of buyers in the Industry Structure. In Economic Logic, we discussed profit source. And in Strategy Logic, the kind of mission and vision statements we championed were clear about who the customers were. So understanding Customer Logic is a must for success for the organization.

Customer Logic is important to you because it impacts how you do your job. The kinds of customers your organization has affect the kinds of people you hire. (Do Wal-Mart and Nordstrom's hire the same type of staff?). The kinds of customers also influence the kinds of performance improvement interventions you do, the kinds of examples you use in training classes, and so on.

The Elements of Customer Logic

We have divided Customer Logic into two elements in addition to measures: market strategy and customer needs satisfaction strategy. See Table 6.1.

TABLE 6.1. ELEMENTS OF CUSTOMER LOGIC

Market strategy	
Customer needs satisfaction	
Measures	

TABLE 6.2. MARKET STRATEGY

		Possibilities	Examples
Market strategy	**ASK: How are you segmenting the market?**		
		Geographic	Pacific, Mountain, Mid Atlantic, New England, etc.
		Demographic	Age, sex, family life cycle, etc.
		Psychographic	Social class, lifestyle, personality
		Behavioral	Occasions, benefits, readiness, etc.
	ASK: Which segment(s) are you going after? Why?		
		Pacific region	Coast and islands
		Age	Families with young children
		Lifestyle	Upwardly mobile young urbanites
		Benefits	Quality, service, reliability

Market Strategy

Market strategy asks several questions (see Table 6.2):

- How does your organization segment the market?
- Which segments are you going after?
- And, of course, why those segments?

Market segmentation is a relatively straightforward proposition (after the nuanced complexities of Chapters 4 and 5). It is something marketing professionals have down to a science. A good introduction to those possible segments is found in Table 6.3, taken from one of the gurus of marketing, Philip Kotler at Northwestern University.

As Table 6.3 shows, marketers divide the bases for segmenting consumer markets into four categories:

- Geographic
- Demographic
- Psychographic
- Behavioral

Geographic and demographic are the most familiar to all of us.

TABLE 6.3. MAJOR SEGMENTATION VARIABLES
FOR CONSUMER MARKETS

Variable	Typical Breakdown
Geographic	
Region	Pacific, Mountain, West North Central, West South Central, East North Central, East South Central, South Atlantic, Middle Atlantic, New England
County size	A, B, C, D
City or SMSA size	Under 5,000; 5,000–20,000; 20,000–50,000; 50,000–100,000; 100,000250,000; 250,000–500,000; 500,000–1,000,000; 1,000,000–4,000,000; 4,000,000+
Density	Urban, suburban, rural
Climate	Northern, southern
Demographic	
Age	Under 6, 6–11, 12–19,20–34,35–49, 50–64, 65+
Sex	Male, female
Family size	1–2, 3–4, 5+
Family life cycle	Young, single; young, married, no children; young, married, youngest child under 6; young, married, youngest child 6 or over; older, married, with children; older, married, no children under 18; older, single; other
Income	Under $10,000; $10,000–$15,000; $15,000–$20,000; $20,000–$25,000; $25,000–$30,000; $30,000–$50,000; $50,000 and over
Occupation	Professional and technical; managers, officials, and proprietors; clerical, sales; craftspeople, foremen; operatives; farmers; retired; students; housewives; unemployed
Education	Grade school or less; some high school; high school graduate; some college; college graduate
Religion	Catholic, Protestant, Jewish, other
Race	White, Black, Asian, Hispanic, etc.
Nationality	American, British, French, German, Scandinavian, Italian, Latin American, Middle Eastern, Japanese
Psychographic	
Social class	Lower lowers, upper lowers, working class, middle class, upper middles, lower uppers, upper uppers
Lifestyle	Straights, swingers, longhairs, etc.
Personality	Compulsive, gregarious, authoritarian, ambitious

(Continued)

TABLE 6.3. CONTINUED

Behavioral

Occasions	Regular occasion, special occasion
Benefits	Quality, service, economy
User status	Nonuser, ex-user, potential user, first-time user, regular user
Usage rate	Light user, medium user, heavy user
Loyalty status	None, medium, strong, absolute
Readiness stage	Unaware, aware, informed, interested, desirous, intending to buy
Attitude toward product	Enthusiastic, positive, indifferent, negative, hostile

Source: Used by permission from Prentice-Hall.

Geographic

This category not only covers the region of the country (or the world) that consumers live in (New England, Pacific Northwest, etc.) but also goes deeper to get:

- The size of the county and city in which they live (based on U.S. census data for domestic areas).
- The population density (urban, suburban, or rural).
- The climate (sunny hot dry Arizona vs. cold and snowy Minnesota for example).

This information gives the organization an easy way to select one or more market segments to focus on or, perhaps more importantly, an idea about which products to market in which locations (e.g., sun hats in Arizona and fur hats in Minnesota).

Demographic

This category covers age and gender (for example, the 18- to 35-year-old males coveted by TV advertisers), family size and where in the family cycle a customer is, income, occupation, education, religion, race, and nationality.

This is another easy way for the organization to focus on certain market segments or to have different products for different segments. Nordstrom's and Wal-Mart clearly are after difference income levels, for example, whereas Gap has a special division, GapKids, to address one age group. And if you live in a city like Chicago, with one of the most ethnically diverse populations in the United States, you see different food selections in the same supermarket chain to match the preferences of the ethnic groups that live in that section of the city. Kotler points out that now even dog food is segmented by a demographic: age.

But geographic and demographic segmentation are not really enough to help a company determine market strategy. Variables interact, and many of the demographic variables are no longer as predictive in the marketplace as they once were, such as male versus female or senior behavior. And some variables do not result in intuitive behavior; for example, the greatest percentage of high-density TV purchasers is of lower- rather than higher-income consumers with large families because it is actually cheaper to stay home and watch films than it is to go out to the movies with the whole family. Therefore, market strategy is also determined by more sophisticated measures, called psychographic and behavioral.

Psychographic

These variables divide markets by social class, by lifestyle, and/or by personality. They are concerned, for example, not with demographic age, but with the psychographic, lifestyle variable of how one thinks about age. Pharmaceutical companies' commercials aimed at illnesses of an aging population, for example, clearly are aimed at showing "a better quality of life" (lifestyle) as a result of their medicines (for everything from arthritis to fibromyalgia, from high cholesterol to erectile dysfunction).

One way of viewing the lifestyle and personality variables is to think of the more popular and well-known characterizations of the generations: Boomers, Gen X, Gen Y, Millenials. Each generation has a different view of life, a different belief about success, and different takes on self-worth, work style, play style, and way of relating to others.

It is not surprising, therefore, that Blackberrys are marketed to Boomers, whereas iPhones are marketed to Millenials. Each group has a different belief about the product's purpose and about the variety of applications such a tool can and should be used for. For example, Boomers use their machines to send e-mails or to make telephone calls, while Millenials uses phones to text each other.

It is also not surprising that the professional networking site, LinkedIn, addresses a different lifestyle and personality from those addressed by Facebook or MySpace. Each company is clear on how it segments the market based on the psychographics of its users.

Behavioral

Finally, markets can be segmented based on the knowledge, attitude, use, or response of consumers. Of all the segments listed in Table 6.3, two are worthy of more discussion here.

The first, benefits, we will see come into play again in Product Logic. This type of market segmentation or strategy calls for identifying the major benefits people could look for in a product/service, then either targeting one or more of those or relating each benefit segment to other market segment characteristics.

For example, a restaurant might segment the market based on the perceived benefits of speed, quality, location convenience, coolness, "organicness," and price. Then it might decide either to focus on the market segment that wants coolness, or it might note that, although the segment that sees the benefit of coolness is made up of 21–30, single, urban, fickle, and occasional users, a second segment that sees the benefit of organicness consists of 30–45, married, urban, loyal, and frequent users. That distinction could lead to a market strategy decision, reflected in Product Logic, to go after the two market segments by being cool and by being organic.

The other element of behavioral segmentation worthy of more discussion is the buyer readiness stage. The stage is based on the work of Rogers (2003) on the theory of diffusion of innovations. He divides people into several categories:

- *Innovators:* The people who sign up to beta test the latest software program or who wait in line all night to get the latest technology gadget or game.
- *Early adopters:* Those who want to be on the cutting edge of the innovation, whether it be food, fashion, or electronics.
- *Middle adopters:* The vast majority of people who adopt an innovation after some period of time, when the bugs have been removed and some agency like Consumer Reports has tested it.
- *Late adopters:* Those who will adopt the innovation, but not before everyone else has it and not having it becomes an inconvenience.
- *Laggards:* Those who will be the last to adopt an innovation; one of the authors of this book, for example, still uses a paper day-timer and a separate cell phone that only makes phone calls.

Each of these groups of buyers needs a different market strategy, and the organization may decide to focus its market strategy on a particular segment of the market. For example, Apple tends to target the innovator and early adopter market segments, in combination with the other behavioral factors of attitude (enthusiastic), loyalty (high), usage (frequent), benefit (coolness, functionality, and adaptability), in combination with the psychographic factors of lifestyle (Millennials and Gen Y), social class (middle to upper), in combination with the relevant demographic factors.

Putting together a market strategy for an organization or for a product/service of an organization involves addressing all these market segment variables in an aligned manner.

What You Should Do

You should do five things for this element of Customer Logic:

1. Become familiar with the four categories of market segmentation variables and the specific variables in each, as described here and shown in Table 6.3.
2. Find out your organization's market strategy.
3. Analyze the market strategy using the variables presented here.
4. Determine if, in your mind, the strategy has addressed all the market strategy variables *and* done so in an aligned, coherent way.
5. If it seems to you that some analysis that could help the organization better understand, articulate, complete, or align its market strategy logic is not being done, note it down as something to ask questions about as you move into Customer and Product Logics.

Satisfying Customer Needs

We will look at two large topics under satisfying customer needs. The first of these is niche focus versus wide product range, in which we will consider the product or service itself. The second is relationship versus transaction selling, where we will focus on how the organization interacts with customers to make a sale. See Table 6.4.

Niche Focus Versus Wide Product Range

First, let us provide a little background in niche thinking. The traditional approach in mass marketing is losing ground because potential buyers are overwhelmed with more marketing messages than they can possibly attend to. Taking its place is niche marketing. A *niche* is an opening or space specifically adapted to its contents. Niche marketing gains buyers' attention by offering a product or service targeted directly to one of their specific needs. Daljik (2005) defines a niche market as a

TABLE 6.4. CUSTOMER NEEDS SATISFACTION

		Definition	Examples
Customer needs satisfaction	**ASK: How are you satisfying customer needs?**		
	NICHE FOCUS	Narrowly focus on customers that have a specific need under specific circumstances.	People who love to go on cruises People who want analyses of companies before investing in them
	WIDE PRODUCT RANGE	Try to do more business with the same customers by providing a variety of goods/ services that meet a wide variety of needs.	Dot-com retailers Department stores Software General contractors
	ASK: How do you sell to the customer?		
	RELATIONSHIP	Uncover and sell exactly what the customer needs and seek repeat business.	Medical providers Consulting firms Organizations that track individual buying patterns
	TRANSACTION	Sell as many items to the customer as possible and seek repeat business.	Big-box stores Large-volume niche retailers

small market of relatively few customers with similar needs and qualities. It is a small part of a market segment whose needs are not being fulfilled. Daljik draws parallels between market niches and ecological niches.

What Niche Focus Versus Wide Product Range Are

Springboarding off the niche marketing concept, the authors take a related but slightly different perspective. We are looking from the angle of the products and services the business is providing to satisfy customer needs. Niche focus businesses provide products that meet a very specific need under specific circumstances. A personal trainer is a niche-focused business. Wide-product-range businesses offer an assortment of products that the same customer could use to meet many different needs. Amazon.com is a wide-product-range business.

Why Niche Focus Versus Wide Product Range Is Important to You and to the Business

If you are working with a niche-focused business, any solutions you propose will have to be aligned with the niche. For example, if you are working with an eco-tourism organization and you are trying to fix a booking and tracking process that is hamstrung by their current communication equipment, the solution you propose will have to be compatible with their ecotourism niche. It will have to be ecologically responsible, i.e., green, and will have to work in remote parts of the world with little telecommunications infrastructure. It may also have to be secure against hacking and pfishing (or phishing). Otherwise your proposed solution will not only be rejected members of your client organization, it may actually hurt their business. The same is true for a wide-product-range organization: Any changes you propose should be aligned with the broad market they are serving. It should also probably offer them some options to choose from and include several elements. For example, instead of packaging an intervention as a training program, you could present it as a knowledge management wiki, some job aids, a set of case studies, a learning board game, and a trainer's guide.

The way the organization is satisfying customers needs should be in alignment with the other logics. For example, if a bank is providing financial products to a few very wealthy account holders, the bank's processes and information technology must align with the expectations of that niche and deliver rapid, accurate, and convenient access to money and information. If a consulting organization offers a wide range of expert services to clients, their processes must allow for rapidly locating and deploying their experts. They must also be consistent and accurate about tracking, reporting, paying, and billing for their labor. Finally a manufacturer who produces a wide range of products must have production measures and reporting that allow floor managers to see their production data in ranges for manufacturing lines and equipment, not just high-level averages, in order to keep production and costs aligned with goals. Otherwise, even if customer needs are satisfied, it can't be done profitably.

Examples

- *Niche focus:* A niche-focused business offers products and services that address a specific and well-defined need. One example is a business that does data recovery from computer disks that have been damaged due to water, fire, or other physical accidents. Another is Lasik, a business that corrects one particular vision problem by doing a few very specific eye surgeries. The ecological tour company is an example of a niche provider that does repeat business with customers on an ongoing basis. These are all businesses with a niche focus. It enables them to cut through the babble of market offerings, provide something that exactly meets their customers' needs (instead of approximately satisfying them) and allows them to build secure and loyal customer relationships.

- *Wide product range:* Some organizations offer a broad range of related products and services in order to capture more business from the same customers. Home Depot offers everything for home construction, repair, and remodeling in one location, from lumber to wiring to plumbing and appliances. Black & Decker provides a wide array of tools for do-it-yourselfers and light construction. Oracle has a wide product range relating to databases and their uses. Kaiser Permanente offers a wide range of health-related services to individuals and families, all within one organization and often in one cluster of buildings. Physicians, hospital, labs, pharmacy, emergency medicine, specialized diagnostic and therapeutic equipment and operators, and even education are provided by one organization. Once customers are in the door, the business becomes a one-stop-shop, and there are endless opportunities for providing the same customer with more goods and services.
- *A continuum:* As marketing practice shifts from predominantly mass marketing to niche marketing, some organizations offer a wide range of products that serve a cluster of niche markets. For example, Procter & Gamble has been pointed out as a business of many, many product niches. As the concepts of customer-centric organizations and mass customization (such as Dell) continue to take hold, we will see organizations appear somewhere along a continuum between filling a niche and providing a wide range of products.

Issues with Niche Focus and Wide Product Range

Build it and they will come. An organization may offer a product or service that targets a niche without having done the initial research to determine what the niche market really needs and wants. We have all seen this in small storefront businesses that open and close within a year or less. One of the authors watched a shop selling hookahs open for a few months on a street of small shops near a residential neighborhood. The local population was Anglo, Hispanic, and African American with a very few East Asians stirred in. The proprietor was blinded to local realities by his own enthusiasm for his product. Larger businesses make the same mistake. If you are working with a niche-focused business, do what you can to learn what market research and testing were done before the product was offered.

I know what they want. Some organizations offer different products that were inspired by the interests and enthusiasms of owners or other senior people, with little or no market research. One major purpose of developing a wide range of products is to leverage existing customers by offering them more things they will buy. For this to pay off, the offerings should be related (as in tools for a shop, or productivity software) and must appeal to the same customer who showed up for the first product. If all the products appeal to different people, the organization is simply doing a messy and expensive form of niche selling. This requires the same discipline as niche focus: good market research and testing.

Silos. Both niche-focused and wide-product-range organizations suffer if they have not done the cross-functional work needed so that economic, product, process, and support activities are aligned to deliver what the customer requires. Some examples were given above, under "Why Niche Focus Versus Wide Product Range Is Important to You and to the Business".

Relationship Versus Transaction Selling

The second part of customer need satisfaction is relationship versus transaction selling. See Table 6.5. Again, we're going to provide a little background first.

- *Transaction marketing* is a label for traditional marketing as it existed before the digital age. Becker (2007) describes its goals as maximizing the number of sales transactions and the number of people buying, thereby capturing market share. It was very much a push strategy. Many organizations use transaction marketing today.
- *Relationship marketing* has the goal of developing long-term customer–provider relationships and is therefore centered on the customer. It is as concerned with what happens after the sale as before or during it. It therefore considers quality to be a marketing function, and front-line employees to be an important part of the marketing team. Many businesses have migrated to relationship marketing or are attempting to migrate.

Becker points out that transaction and relationship marketing are not necessarily mutually exclusive. In fact, transaction and relationship selling are similar in nature. Transaction selling is concerned with the sales transaction itself, so focus is on the products being offered and the selling process. Relationship selling is concerned with building a long-term relationship with customers and ultimately gaining their loyalty. There is a major focus on postsale satisfaction, follow-up, and support.

TABLE 6.5. RELATIONSHIP VERSUS TRANSACTION SELLING

	Definition	Examples	Businesses
Customer needs satisfaction	**ASK: How are you satisfying customer needs? How do you sell to the customer?**		
RELATIONSHIP	Uncover and sell exactly what the customer needs and seek repeat business.	Medical providers Consulting firms Organizations that track individual buying patterns	Physicians Site for Sore Eyes Amazon
TRANSACTION	Sell as many items to the customer as possible and seek repeat business.	Big-box stores Large-volume niche retailers	Target Home Depot Borders

What Transaction and Relationship Selling Are

Transaction selling is the traditional sales model we're all familiar with. The salesperson is well versed in product knowledge, features, and benefits, what the competition is offering, and how it compares to her products. She is good at delivering a sales script, can anticipate and handle objections, and knows when and how to ask for the sale. Her focus is on making sales, and she's incented and rewarded for high-volume or high-ticket item sales and for obtaining new customers. The transaction is the sale itself, and the person who sells the most for the month, quarter, and year is the best salesperson. The bulk of the sales transaction is over when she gets the order and moves on.

The advantages of the transaction selling approach are efficiency for both the buyer and the seller, high sales volume, and a relatively low SG&A (salespeople in this mode are paid less and spend less time per customer, lowering SG&A). The disadvantages can be customers made unhappy by feeling pressured or manipulated or by winding up with products that are not really a good match for their specific needs and constraints. All of us have heard about enterprise resource planning systems that were far more time-consuming and costly to implement than the customer was led to believe and that required more extensive changes to his organization's operations than he would have agreed to up front. These problems are not uncommon, and they are why most providers of large, complex systems and services struggle to find referenceable accounts.

You have probably encountered both appropriate and inappropriate uses of transaction selling in your life. When you go into a music store to get the latest CD by your favorite musician or stop in a shop to replace a sauté pan, you are not interested in a salesperson developing a deep understanding of your needs.

You just want to make your purchase and go home. If you have bought a car from a salesperson who is driven more by his need for a commission than his willingness to consider your needs and your budget, you have encountered inappropriate transaction selling. In the HR services world, the effort to persuade an executive team to support a new performance appraisal system, a diversity initiative, or process reengineering (any of which may be highly appropriate) is usually an example of transaction selling.

Relationship selling has to accomplish some of the same things as transactional selling and a great deal more. It goes about selling in a completely different way. The goal of relationship selling is to build a close, trusting, and loyal relationship between the salesperson and the customer. First and foremost, the salesperson has to understand the customer's business: its strategy, its goals and constraints, its competition, and its market. He must know a bit about its finances, its labor issues, and what's being said about it in the news. There is a lot of homework to be done before a sales call ever takes place. When the salesperson thoroughly understands the customers needs, he proposes not just a product but a solution to a problem the customer is dealing with. The proposed solution is tailored to the customer's exact situation. Relationship selling is also called solution selling or consultative selling.

When the sale has been made, the service part of the salesperson's job begins. He remains involved in what is delivered, how it works, and how it is integrated into the customer's business. If there are problems, he works on solutions. He stays with the customer until the customer's needs are met and the customer is satisfied. Often this means the salesperson must act as a coordinator and project manager for the people in his own organization that are providing (and troubleshooting) the products and services. Large enterprise-wide purchases and system changes always require relationship selling. IBM is noted for this. A more everyday example of relationship selling is the instance of a car salesperson who really did listen, who asked questions that helped you clarify your real needs, who followed up by calling after the sale to see how the car was working for you, and who later reminded you to take it in for its first servicing. If your car had any problems, he wouldn't just point to the service department and say, "Tell 'em I sent you." He would work with you to get the problems solved as quickly and as economically as possible. Good real estate agents also use relationship selling when they help you buy a house.

Why Relationship and Transaction Selling Matter to You and to the Organization

Johnson, Barksdale, and Boles (2001, p. 123) summarize theory (Reichfield, 1996) and research that suggest that "as little as a five percent increase in customer retention can increase profits by fifty percent or more." (Reichheld and Sasser 1990). In addition, "retaining customers through close, long-term, cooperative relationships can impart a competitive advantage to the supplier" (Weitz and Bradford, 1999). In their conclusion, Johnson et al. point out that their study supports the notion that "high levels of customer commitment to the salesperson (directly) and satisfaction with the salesperson (indirectly) are important in reducing customer defection." That is, "If satisfaction and commitment are high, it is unlikely that the buyer will determine that the benefits associated with leaving a supplier justify the costs involved in making such a move." (2001, p. 130) Conversely, they also suggest that lower commitment levels "make it more likely that the buyer will evaluate favorably the level of benefits obtained by leaving. Post-sales support and follow-up calls by the salesperson (as well as other personnel from the supplier) are one way to help build greater levels of satisfaction and commitment . . ." (2001, p. 131).

When you try to influence decision makers in your organization to listen to your advice and implement your solutions, you will have a much higher success rate if you use relationship selling. One major purpose of this book is to give you the tools to understand your client's business so that you can do relationship selling. It will equip you to target real needs that executives in your organization are struggling with and enable you to talk with them about it in their own terms.

Relationship selling is important to the organization for many reasons you are probably already familiar with: It costs less to sell to an existing customer than to find and cultivate a new one. Customers tend to buy more when they've been customers for a long time, and they require less attention when mutual systems of ordering, payment, and problem solving have been established. When problems do arise (and there will always be some problems), customers who have their problem fixed by someone they know and trust are even more likely to remain loyal, to keep buying, and to give referrals.

Issues with Transaction and Relationship Selling

Just do it my way. Some customers are not interested in having a long-term, trusting relationship. They do their own product research, like to negotiate, and are interested only in getting the most features for the lowest price. Transaction selling is appropriate with these customers; relationship selling is not.

I love you baby, but I gotta go. When the relationship is well established, a busy client may not want to spend time in face-to-face discussions unless she is dealing with a real problem. Sometimes it is better business for the salesperson to move into transaction selling mode for a while until the customer is ready for a close relationship again.

Not my job. A sales and marketing organization may change to relationship selling but find it difficult to engage the rest of the organization in the service- and
quality-oriented attitude and behavior needed to develop and maintain good customer relationships. Alignment issues may have to be worked out at the top of the
organization and imposed on the rest of the organization.

What You Should Do

You now know the two parts of Customer Needs Satisfaction: niche focus versus
wide product range, and transaction versus relationship selling. You should take
six actions for this element of Customer Logic:

1. Determine whether the business is satisfying customer needs by offering products or services with a niche focus or by offering a wide product range.
2. If it has a niche focus, identify the niche (or which, if there are several)
3. If it has a wide product range, identify the range (e.g., power tools, data bases,
   cooking equipment, business consulting services, etc.). Note whether the range
   is likely to attract more business from the same customers or the items are
   unrelated and will probably require different customers.
4. Identify which sales approach the organization uses and promotes: transaction
   selling or relationship selling?
5. Assess whether the selling approach is appropriate to the type of product/
   service and customers or something else would be more appropriate. If you think
   it should change, do not share this information yet. Doing so could be a career
   limiting move. Sales organizations must be handled with care and forethought.
6. Identify any disconnects you see between the Customer Logic and Economic
   or External Logic.

Measures for Customer Logic

There is good and bad news about the measures for Customer Logic.

The good news is that you can use actual measures to assess how the organization is doing on this logic. And the organization already collects these measures
on a regular basis because they are important to its success. See Table 6.6.

There is also some bad news. The number of possible measures is larger than
anyone can possibly track and make sense of. The next statement is very important, and we will repeat it in every chapter: Both Stack (1994) and Kaplan and
Norton (1996) caution *that an organization can keep its eyes on only four to six measures
at a time* and that having a list of 20 measures to track at once is confusing,

TABLE 6.6. MEASURES FOR CUSTOMER LOGIC

Measures	ASK: What are the key metrics your organization looks at to determine how well its Customer Logic is working?
	Size of market segment (absolute, growth)
	Share of market (absolute, growth, overall, in niche)
	New customers (number, percentage, overall, in niche)
	Current customer renewal (number, percentage)
	Complaints (number, percentage, decrease, versus competition)
	Net profit/customer (cost of sale/profit from sale)
	Value (perceived benefits versus cost)

dispiriting, and useless in performance improvement. We cannot help you narrow down which measures to focus on because that answer depends on which measures your organization uses to track its performance. You can, however, use the list in Table 6.6 as a starter menu. We encourage you first to go through the table and see if there are measures that you know right away match those that you should be tracking. Then talk to the numbers people in your organization to find out which measures they are actually tracking and which of those are most important to the organization this year.

Sample Worksheets for Customer Logic

In Chapter 2, we introduced the Internal Scan worksheet. Here it is with the columns through Customer Logic filled out for one of our clients (Table 6.7). It is still brief: just a few words summarizing each of the elements. This is the level of detail that we continue to suggest you use to get the big picture without bogging yourself down in a major research project. Save your time and energy for more detailed analysis when you have a specific performance issue to investigate or when you have decided to do a detailed overview of the business instead of a high-level one. If you are doing a detailed level overview, we suggest you use an Excel spreadsheet.

Table 6.8 is a Measures Worksheet filled out for the same customer.

Customer Logic Job Aid

This job aid summarizes Customer Logic with graphics, definitions, questions to be answered, and examples (Table 6.9). Use it when you are trying to identify the strategy logic for your own (or your client's) organization.

TABLE 6.7. SAMPLE INTERNAL SCAN FOR CREDIT CARD DIVISION OF A BANK

Assess and fill in the logic the business appears to be using.

ECONOMIC LOGIC	STRATEGY LOGIC	CUSTOMER LOGIC	PRODUCT LOGIC	PROCESS LOGIC	STRUCTURAL LOGIC
Cost structure • *Variable: Cost of funds and delinquencies* • *To manage: Self-fund, control delinquencies* **Financial focus** • *Cost of goods sold* **Profit source** • *Channel: Direct versus oil company cards versus Sears, etc.*	**Mission and vision** • *Provide profitable credit services to higher risk market* **Initiatives/tactics** • *Seek new customer-facing partners* • *Manage delinquencies tightly* **Culture** • *Do it now, ask forgiveness later* **Core competency** • *Collections* **Growth strategy** • *Alliances: Oil company, large retailer credit* • *Purchase: Other banks' delinquent portfolios* **Pricing strategy** • *High end of middle*	**Market strategy** • *Segment by economic groups* • *Target: $20K-$45K/ year* • *Low white-collar, high blue-collar* • *Some high-risk credit* **Customer Need Satisfaction** • *Niche: Consumer Credit Card* **Relationship/ transaction strategy** • *High volume of transactions key to income (fee-based)*			

- Do the logics in the six columns support each other or are they contradictory?
- If they are contradictory, does this have some bearing on the problem you were asked to solve?
- How can you test your assessment that these are the business logic(s) the company is using?
- Now review the logic in the light of your environmental scan. Do the six logics seem to be consistent with external realities?

Reprinted with permission of Lynn Kearny, 2009

TABLE 6.8. SAMPLE MEASURES WORKSHEET FOR CREDIT CARD DIVISION OF A BANK

Logic	Measures	Target	Current	Gap	Performance Problems	Interventions	Measured Results
Economic							
Strategy							
Customer	Target market segmentation	Demographic and behavioral	Demographic	Add behavioral			
	Niche focus	3 niches (add 2 niches to improve cash flow with new product)	1 niche	2 new niches			
	New customers	100/week in existing niche; 1,000/week in 2 new niches	50/week in existing niche	50/week in existing niche; 1,000/ week in 2 new niches			
Product							
Process							
Structure							

- What specific measures does the organization use for each logic? Write them in column 2.
- What is the target for each measure? Write it in column 3.
- What is the current number for each measure? Write it in column 4.
- What is the gap between target and current number for each measure? Write it in column 5.
- Those measures with the greatest, and most critical, gaps are the focus of the Performance Problem Analysis and Intervention Selection that take place next in the Performance Improvement process.

Reprinted with permission of Lynn Kearny, 2009

TABLE 6.9. SUMMARY JOB AID—CUSTOMER LOGIC

How the organization finds and keeps customers

		Possiblities	Examples	Businesses
Market strategy				
	ASK: How are you segmenting the market?			
	SEGMENT	Geographic	Pacific, Mountain, Mid Atlantic, New England, etc.	Manufacturers and distributors, regional specialties
		Demographic	Age, sex, family life cycle, etc.	Health care, housing, big retailers
		Psychographic	Social class, lifestyle, personality	Entertainment, furniture, clothing
		Behavioral	Occasions, benefits, readiness, etc.	Bridal stores, retirement services, personal technology
	ASK: Which segment(s) are you going after? Why?			
	TARGET	Pacific region	Coast and islands	Channel Islands Surfboards
		Age	Families with young children	Target
		Lifestyle	Upwardly mobile young urbanites	Pottery Barn
		Benefits	People who care about quality, service, reliability	AAA Insurance

(Continued)

TABLE 6.9. SUMMARY JOB AID—CUSTOMER LOGIC (*Continued*)

	Definition	Examples	Businesses
Customer needs satisfaction	**ASK: How are you satisfying customer needs?**		
(NICHE FOCUS)	Narrowly focus on customers that have a specific need under specific circumstances.	People who love to go on cruises People who want analyses of companies before investing in them	Royal Caribbean Cruise Lines Hoovers.com
(WIDE PRODUCT RANGE)	Try to do more business with the same customers by providing a variety of goods/services that meet a wide variety of needs.	Dot-com retailers Department stores Software General contractors	Amazon Macy's Microsoft
	ASK: How do you sell to the customer?		
(RELATIONSHIP)	Uncover and sell exactly what the customer needs and seek repeat business.	Medical providers Consulting firms Organizations that track individual buying patterns	Physicians Site for Sore Eyes Amazon
(TRANSACTION)	Sell as many items to the customer as possible and seek repeat business.	Big box stores Large volume niche retailers	Target Home Depot Borders Books
Measures	**ASK: What are the key metrics your organization looks at to determine how well its Customer Logic is working?** Size of market segment (absolute, growth) Share of market (absolute, growth, overall, in niche) New customers (number, percentage, overall, in niche) Current customer (renewal (number, percentage) Complaints number, percentage,decrease, versus competition) Net profit/customer (Cost of sale/profit from sale) Value (perceived benefits versus cost)		

RELATIONSHIP vs TRANSACTION

Your Turn

Use the Customer Logic Job Aid and the Internal Scan Worksheet (see table 6.10) to identify the Customer Logic and measures operating in your organization or your client's. Here are some sources of information:

- Organization's Web site
- Annual report
- 10-K report
- Hoover's or Mergent (most public libraries have a subscription)
- Members of the organization, particularly managers, strategic planning office, and finance
- Any other sources suggested in this chapter

If you want a reproducible version of the worksheet, there is one on the Web site at www.Pfeiffer.com/go/kennethsilber. Copy it to your desktop, and either use it as is or modify it for the level of detail you need to work with. Consider creating an Excel spreadsheet.

Summary

Customer Logic sets the stage for the other logics, which must support the organization in finding, securing, and maintaining a customer base. This chapter has focused on how the market is analyzed and targeted and on how customer needs are satisfied by looking at whether the business is more niche focused or offers a range of related products. It also looked at how the organization asks customers to buy: through transaction selling or relationship selling. You now have a menu of measures that organizations use to assess how well their marketing and selling efforts are succeeding. Although analyzing Customer Logic may not lead you directly to problems and opportunities that your expertise can help with, it can help you identify where a problem exists. It will also help you be strategic about how you present your recommendations: by aligning your recommendations to the organization's preferred service mode—niche or wide product range—and by using a relationship selling approach.

Next we will get into the logic that specifies further how the organization meets customer needs: Product Logic.

TABLE 6.10. INTERNAL SCAN WORKSHEET

Assess and fill in the logic the business appears to be using.

ECONOMIC LOGIC	STRATEGY LOGIC	CUSTOMER LOGIC	PRODUCT LOGIC	PROCESS LOGIC	STRUCTURAL LOGIC

- Do the logics in the six columns support each other or are they contradictory?
- If they are contradictory, does this have some bearing on the problem you were asked to solve?
- How can you test your assessment that these are the business logic(s) the company is using?
- Now review the logic in the light of your environmental scan. Do the six logics seem to be consistent with external realities?

© Lynn Kearny 2009. Reprinted with permission of Lynn Kearny.

CHAPTER SEVEN

PRODUCT LOGIC

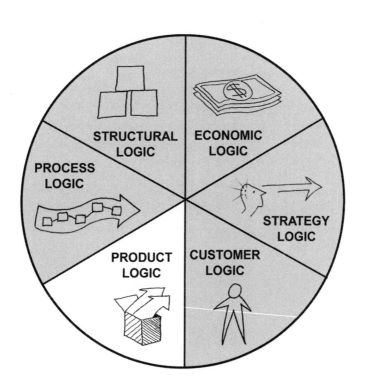

A product can be defined as "anything that can be offered to a market for attention, acquisition, use, or consumption that might satisfy a want or need" (Kotler, 1991, p. 429). *Product Logic* refers to the actual characteristics of the product or service the organization produces and distributes and to the organization itself as a product. See Table 7.1.

Our view of Product Logic is slightly different from the balanced scorecard view of customer perspective put forward by Kaplan and Norton (1996). They see the product as part of the customer value equation. We see it as a unique and distinct entity more along the lines of product in a marketing context (Kotler, 1991), referring to the product's "Quality, Design, Features, Brand Name, Packaging, Sizes, Services, Warranties, Returns" (p. 68).

Marketers acknowledge that customer value is made up of the perceived product, services, personnel, and image value (Kotler, 1991, p. 290). Similarly the balanced scorecard formula for value is made up of product/service attributes, image, and relationship (Kaplan and Norton, 1996, p. 74). Yet marketers still see the product itself as separate from the customer and its perceived value, as do we. Therefore Product Logic can be seen as a bridge between Customer Logic and Process Logic: the output of the system processes that go to the receiver of the system.

- First, Product Logic includes how the product differentiates itself from other products in the same market. This includes the features already mentioned and others, such as niche versus mass focus.

TABLE 7.1. ELEMENTS OF PRODUCT LOGIC

Differentiation	
Company image	
Measures	

- Second, it includes company image, or what today is called branding—how the company itself is seen by customers.
- Finally, we will look into measures of how well the Product Logic is doing.

Why Product Logic Is Important to You and the Organization

Your company has a strategy and customers. Now it has to deliver products/ services to them. Those products/services can be aligned with the strategy and customers or not. They can be targeted broadly (like Dora the Explorer dolls, aimed at every child) or narrowly (symphony concerts, aimed at the few remaining classical music lovers). They can be high quality, well designed, and expensive (a BMW auto) or lower quality, adequately designed, and inexpensive (the oft joked-about package of eight pairs of men's white tube socks for $1.99). And the company that produces and sells the products can be seen (rightly or wrongly when compared with facts) as community minded and green (like Target) or profit minded and nasty to workers.

Your company likely knows, by and large, which Product Logic it is following and how that relates to its Customer Logic. In cases where companies have produced products that did not match, such as Apple's Newton, introduced in the early 1990s, the product quickly sinks from sight. Customers (and software developers) were not yet ready for a small, hand-held computer of the type now known as a personal digital assistant (PDA). Results in many of these cases have spelled disaster for the company. Other examples include Gillette's shampoo named and boldly labeled For Oily Hair Only. Customers didn't want to be seen pushing shopping carts with this public announcement of a personal grooming problem on display. Or a toothpaste introduced by Listerine in 1979. Even though the toothpaste was labeled Cool Mint, it was marketed under the Listerine brand, which customers associated with a strong medicinal taste. Both of these grooming products were a flop, and they lost their organizations all the money invested in development and promotion (McMath and Forbes, 1998).

For you, understanding your organization's Product Logic is essential because it impacts how you solve every business problem you are called on to solve. In a manner related to corporate culture, the corporate image and market focus dictate the kind of solutions you can propose. If you are developing training for the Omega watch company, it should have the same feel of prestige and expense and exclusivity that the product has or it will not be accepted. If you are developing training for Apple Computers, it will have to have the same level of design and simplicity that its products have, or its employees will laugh at it (one of the authors knows this firsthand, having spent a week being "Apple-ized" before being allowed to begin work on a project). See Table 7.2.

The Elements of Product Logic

Product/Service Differentiation

We have divided Product Logic into two elements in addition to measures: product/service differentiation and company image.

What Product/Service Differentiation Is

Before delving into how organizations differentiate products, let's spend another few paragraphs being clear on how organizations look at products. It's not as simple as you might think. There is a seven-level product hierarchy that makes clearer what we mean when we say product. We will use General Motors (GM), circa 2008, as an example to help make these categories clearer (Kotler, 1991, p. 431).

- *Need family*: The need the product family fills—GM = personal transportation
- *Product family*: All the product classes that can satisfy the need—GM = automotive vehicles
- *Product class*: A group within a product family that has a similarity of function—GM = cars, trucks, etc.

TABLE 7.2. PRODUCT DIFFERENTIATION

	Options		Examples
Differentiation	**ASK: What is it about your product that makes it distinctive and unique? What are you doing to differentiate it?** Examples		
	Ordinary	**Unique**	
	Delivery service	Know exactly where your shipment is at any time	Federal Express
	Personal computer	Distinctive product styling	Apple Computers
	Personal productivity software	Most widely distributed, readable by more people	Microsoft

- *Product line*: A group within a product class that has a similar function or similar customers—GM = sedans, sports cars, vans, SUVs, etc.
- *Product type*: A group within a class that share one of several possible forms of the product—GM = full-size and minivans
- *Brand*: The name associated with several items in a product line—GM = Chevrolet, Cadillac, etc.
- *Item*: A distinct item within a brand or product line—GM = Malibu, Escalade

Thus, often when we use the term *product*, we may be referring to an item—a specific distinct item within a product line. Or we may be referring to a whole product line, a product type, or a brand. Since the kinds of performance problems we are called on to solve are frequently product specific, we need to be clear at which of the seven levels the problem is occurring. Be aware: You will not always encounter all seven levels. For a simpler business, or one with fewer products and services, the categories may collapse into each other a bit.

The GM example is for a product, but this applies to a service in much the same way. For example, here is a quick look at FedEx. FedEx consists of several lines of business: FedEx Express, FedEx Ground, FedEx Freight, FedEx Office, FedEx Custom Critical, FedEx Trade Networks, and FedEx Services. We will focus on one need family: to send, create, or receive documents and packages.

1. *Need family*: The need the product family fills—Sending, creating, or receiving documents and packages
2. *Product family*: All the product classes that can satisfy the need—Delivery services, document creation
3. *Product class*: A group within a product family that has a similarity of function— FedEx Express, FedEx Ground, FedEx Office
4. *Product line*: A group within a product class that has similar function or similar customers—Delivery service options within FedEx Express (before eight, before noon, next day, second day, Saturday); document creation/duplication options at FedEx Office (e.g., document duplication, document binding, chart creation)
5. *Product type*: A group within a class whose members share one of several possible forms of the product—The same as product line in this case
6. *Brand*: The name associated with several items in a product line—In this case, subsumed under the product class that carries the brand name
7. *Item*: One single item within product line and type—Priority Overnight package or duplicated documents

Products and services can be differentiated in several ways that repeat the general list at the beginning of the chapter: "Quality, Design, Features, Brand Name, Packaging, Sizes, Services, Warranties, Returns" (Kotler, 1991, p. 68). Some of these refer to products, some to services, and others to the company image (which we will discuss in the next section).

Product Differentiation

Products can be differentiated in the following ways according to Kotler (1991, pp. 294–297):

Features. The elements that the basic model has to perform the product's basic function, as well as additional features that allow the product to perform either the basic function better or more functions. For example, as of early 2009, the basic iPod (an "item") has the features of storing music, playing it back, moving from track to track (with no visual cues about what is on a track), volume control, and on/off switch. Other items in the same product line have additional features that allow for seeing what is on tracks, increasing memory, including video, and performing other functions.

Performance. How well a product's basic features allow it to perform. For example, computers with more memory and cable connections to the Internet can surf the Web faster than computers with less memory and dial-up connections.

Conformance. A term close to what we would call quality, how close a product's design and operation come to its specifications for performance. If, for example, you are paying your cable company for a 10 MGPS Internet connection, you expect your connection to conform to that standard, and if the connection only provides you 3 MGPS speed, the connection does not conform.

Durability. For what length of time will the product continue to function, and whether the product will conform for its whole life or begin to degrade at a certain point. Cell phone and computer batteries all come with stated lifetimes (anywhere from one to five years), but conformance begins to degrade over that time, and batteries need more frequent charging toward the end of the their lives.

Reliability. How likely a product is to fail or function improperly during its lifetime. Consumer Reports continues to rate Honda as the most reliable automobile sold in the United States based on its needing the fewest repairs throughout its lifespan.

Repairability. If a product does break or function improperly, how easy it is to fix the problem. One of the major complaints about computer hardware and software is that they are very hard to repair; hence the numerous helplines and Geek Squad-like companies that make a living repairing them.

Style. What are the look and feel of the product? Apple and Google are renowned for having vice presidents of design who can veto any hardware or software product based on how easily it looks, feels, and operates from the point of view of the customer.

Design. The integrating force. How do all the seven factors fit and work together in a product to achieve the goals of each, rather than focusing on one or two to the exclusion of others. If all seven are not optimized, what trade-offs are made to fit the Customer Logic of the company? For example, look at the different approaches of two high-tech companies that provide software to the same markets. Company A's products optimize all seven, so you can buy version 1.0 of a new software product and it will work very well. Version 1.5 will have more enhanced features, but verson 1.0 will work. Company B's products, on the other hand, are renowned in the industry for version 1.0 not working well because there are too many bugs and having to issue updates to patch the bugs. Many people do not like Company B's most recent large product release because of the many ways in which it doesn't work as expected. Some computer vendors even expect buyers to pay extra to get an older program installed when they purchase a new computer, along with a disk to install Company B's program later when they feel it has been fixed well enough.

Services Differentiation

Services, which are related to products, can be differentiated in the following ways, according to Kotler (1991, pp. 297–299). Although this list is not as detailed or exhaustive as the one for products, it is a helpful way to categorize the kinds of services an organization offers. The list can be seen as it was developed (as services that are related to specific products).

However, the authors are also using it, as the examples will illustrate, to categorize the varieties of strictly/mostly service companies that are prevalent in today's economy. Examples include FedEx, which delivers packages; Geeks.com, which repairs computers; and performance improvement consulting companies, which make recommendations on how to improve an organization. All these companies primarily deliver a service, and any products (from making copies to writing reports) are really tangential artifacts to the core business.

Delivery. How well the product or service is delivered to the customer. For product-based organizations, it includes criteria like accuracy, speed, reliability, and lack of breakage. For example, a rug company in Chicago promises next-day installation, and Amazon.com lets the customer make the delivery decision for themselves—for a price. Reliability ("when it absolutely has to be there overnight") is the criterion on which FedEx, UPS, and USPS Overnight compete. (Given the number of yellow and black "we could not deliver because you were not home" notices the authors have received, we see a definite difference between reliably delivering the package and reliably leaving a note saying one tried to deliver the package.) For service-based organizations, delivery includes additional criteria, including the fit between consultant and client personalities and styles, how feedback meetings are conducted (discussed in detail in Block, 2000), and how deliverables (reports, PowerPoint presentations, etc.) are designed and presented.

Installation. How the product is made to work in the customer's environment.

- For product-based organizations, the most familiar criterion to home consumers is the electronics slogan that everything is plug and play; for those involved in the installation of large-scale system applications, however, criteria may include number of years, number of data revisions, or number of complaints.
- For service-based organizations, installation is usually referred to as implementation and is widely recognized as the most difficult part of any consulting project (see Block [2000] and other authors he references). Criteria frequently used include amount of executive support, amount of change required, amount of support available to workers during the implementation, acceptability of the change to the majority of workers, and the like.

Customer training. How customers receive the skills and knowledge needed to operate the new product successfully. Since this is business many of us are in, we discuss this in more detail in Structural Logic.

Consulting service. How organizations offer advice to a customer. For product-based companies, this advice is usually focused on the optimal use of the product, and it may come packaged with the product or may be an add-on feature (see the Features item under Product Differentiation) available at an additional charge. For some product-based companies, this service may be more than just an add-on feature. The company may use the product sale as an entre into a customer company, and then try to sell additional and more profitable consulting services to solve additional problems the customer has. Information technology and training companies frequently use this sales strategy. Some service-based companies may provide consulting services as the major part of their business but have resulting or ancillary products. A training development company may provide consulting services in analyzing and defining the problem, for example, but also develop a training product as part of its solution to the problem (part of the same consulting project). A different strategy is used in some sales, information technology, and management consulting. The consulting company does the analysis and provides advice about the solution, but it just so happens that part of the solution is a product the company has developed and sells (a process, a system, a course, etc.)

Repair. Despite the reliability and repairability built into the product (see Product Differentiation), if it does fail, what is the speed, cost, and quality of the repair service available? This service is frequently offered as an add-on feature to some products (e.g., Dell Computers next-day on-site repair), or it is built into the price of the car (e.g., BMW and Mercedes 100,000-mile warranties).

Issues Related to Product/Service Differentiation

Two issues are related to product differentiation: the real product and proper balance.

What's Our Real Product? In trying to understand Product Logic, it is very easy both the organizations and its employees to get confused between (a) product class, line, type and item, and (b) product-focused and service focused organizations. Generally we see the first type of confusion when people in the organization come to us with some problem to solve, and we try to ascertain the scope of the problem. We have to do some digging to find to out if the problem is occurring in one item, in one product type, in one line, or across the whole product class. For example, if we are told there are too many defects in the electronic games our company is producing, we have to find out if it is all games, all games of one type, all games with certain functions, or just one specific game.

The second type of problem occurs when the organization we work for is unclear itself, or unclear to its customers, about the nature of its product/service mix. Is the company primarily a product company that offers some ancillary services? Is the company really a services company that offers products as entrees to the customer? Is the company really a product company that uses services as an enter to sell more products?

Improper Balance. This issue arises when the product differentiation factors and the service differentiation factors are not aligned in the Design: The Integrating factor. For example, as you add more Features, they may be designed correctly (an analogy would be that as you add more software and data to your home computer, you also add more memory) or incorrectly (you add more software and data, but not enough memory).

If designed incorrectly, while Features and Style may increase, the Performance, Conformance, Reliability and Repairability decrease to unacceptable levels – leading to decreases in Repair Service level. An example where features and repairability clash (at least in the minds of customers) is the non-replaceable battery in some Apple products. It is a Feature, and it Performs and Conforms. But it can only be repaired by shipping the product to Apple for battery replacement, which, in the minds of customers, makes the factor of Repairability unacceptable.

There are many other possible ways in which the differentiation elements can be out of balance (e.g., excellent features, performance etc., but ugly style). The key thing to remember is that, like the Project Management triangle (you can only have two out of the three variables [good, fast, cheap]), organizations have to compromise on one or more of these differentiators to produce a profitable product—unless they raise the price of the product, or charge extra for some of the differentiators (as Dell does for extended warranty service).

What You Should Do

You should take five actions for this element of Product Logic:

1. Identify all seven levels of the product hierarchy for your company so that you understand the product lines, classes, items, and whatever else is necessary.
2. For the product line or class with which you are most associated, and for all of them if you work for all of them, identify all seven elements of product differentiation.
3. For the service line or class with which you are most associated, or for all of them if appropriate, identify the five elements of service differentiation.
4. Given the elements of product and service differentiation, identify any disconnects you see within Product Logic itself (e.g., promised high reliability, but also frequently used repair service).
5. Identify any disconnects you see between the Product Logic and the Customer and Strategy Logics.

Company Image

Company image answers the question, "What is the image your company projects in order to appeal to customers?" It is the emotional message a company sends to its consumers (and employees) about what it is, why it is unique, and why it is the best. See Table 7.3.

Why Company Image Is Important to You and the Organization

Company image is important to the organization's customers and employees in general, and to you specifically, for several reasons.

Employees. Despite the poor economy of 2009 at the time of writing, what HR people know about the future is this: When the economy recovers and companies need workers, the demographics are clear; there will not be enough employees to fill all the positions and certainly not enough good ones. So companies want to attract the best possible employees who fit their corporate cultures. The best way to do that is to project a desirable company image. *Desirable* is a subjective term, and there is no one best image to project. So Google, for example, spends a great deal of time projecting its company image as an innovative, leading company at which it is fun to work, whereas the big three consulting firms (like Accenture) project company images of competence, vast experience, and global resources, as well as companies at which you have to work very hard and long hours. Neither image, as projected to prospective employees, is right or wrong, but applicants know which company they should apply to.

Customers. Customer purchases are influenced by the company image. The emotional part of a purchase is related to how people respond to an indelible, striking, emotional image that the company image projects. If we say, for example, that a book is published by Harvard Business School Press, customers have an automatic emotional response to that company image or brand: prestige, Harvard

TABLE 7.3 COMPANY IMAGE

Company Image	ASK: What is the image your company projects in order to appeal to customers?		
	The experience economy	Examples:	Image:
	Building customer loyalty through identity	Viacom	The experience of being in a movie
		Nordstroms	The ultimate customer service experience
		Southwest Airlines	The let-your-hair-down experience

professors, important, difficult, and the like. In reality, some books match that company image and some don't. According to Clifton, Simmons, and Ahmad (2004), only two companies of the top 10 brands in the world actually sell products based solely on their brand, or company image. The other eight are top brands that are top because they are backed by high-quality products and services. So, for customers, brand is important, but only as important as product.

You. Assuming that your job is to solve problems and help the organization function more effectively, it is important in two ways. First, it is important because any solutions you propose have to be in alignment with the company image. So if the company image is high quality, you cannot propose solutions that look cheap; and if the company image is to be the cheapest source for a product, you cannot propose solutions that look expensive. Disney is an organization that has a company image as fun and theatrical; clearly, text-based online training is not a solution that is aligned with that company image. Second, on the flip side of the coin, any solution you propose that is aligned with or that can enhance, the company image is more likely to be accepted. So (and this is pure speculation by the authors), an online game-based learning experience using Disney characters delivered through Second Life might be more sellable at Disney than at a staid insurance company.

What Company Image Is

Since the early part of this century, the notion of branding has swept corporate America as the newest, hottest, coolest business innovation to save organizations. It turns out that the notion of company image has been around much longer than that, and a staple of every marketing text and of earlier versions of this Product Logic. We will continue to use the term *company image* to avoid all the noise about branding.

Company image "must convey a *singular message* that establishes the . . . [company's] major virtue and positioning. It must convey the message in a *distinctive* way so it is not confused with similar messages from competitors. It must have *emotional power* so that it stirs the heart as well as the mind of the consumer" (Kotler, 1991, p. 300). For simplicity and coherence we have combined two of Kotler's categories into one and added elements of our own (based on Clifton, Simmons, and Ahmad, 2004). Company image differentiation is made up of the following factors:

Idea. What the organization is about, how it is unique, and how it will deliver a competitive advantage. This is the often forgotten beginning point of image (and branding, see Issues with Image). It is derived from Strategy Logic, especially the vision and core competencies). It says, in an emotional, powerful, memorable way, what this organization is about. It is the concept behind the visual symbol of the image. Some examples of ideas you are probably familiar with are:

- Old Navy's "shopping here is fun, cool and hip," where the shopping "experience" is the most important part.
- Apple's "simple to use, cool and for tech leaders."
- Starbuck's "coffee is prestigious, cool, socially responsible and socializing."
- Target's "upscale, socially responsible discount store that all consumers can afford and at which all are welcome."
- Nike's "athletic clothing for people who really are the best, who 'just do it.' "
- Disney's "magic kingdom."

Symbols. The set of visual elements (image, icon, logo, color), sounds, and feelings that both represent some aspect of the company (name, product, concept) and communicate it to the consumer. Although these are the first and most visible aspects of the company image that the consumer sees, they work only if they somehow represent the core idea of the company image. Although the corporate logos of all the companies mentioned listed in the Ideas entry are instantly recognized the world around—and that is an important part of corporate image—interestingly, most of those images do not communicate anything about the idea behind the symbol; only Disney's clearly does to the authors. When the idea is not expressed in symbols, it is expressed in other ways.

Atmosphere. What the physical space (or Web site) through which the product is delivered is like. Here is where we can begin to see the ideas behind many of companies mentioned under Ideas clearly flower. An Old Navy store truly is a unique experience, with music, visual design, and people portraying the notion that shopping is a fun, community experience. A Starbucks store, with its drink names and focused, skillful baristas, makes it clear that you are in a special world that exemplifies the idea of the image. An Apple store has clean design, lots of help available, hands-on try-it-out access to products, and it is a cool place to hang out.

Advertising. How the company is portrayed in print, television, and online ads. Target's designer products and upscale store design, as well as its community service activities, are emphasized in its ads. Apple ran a series of ads (in 2008–2009) showing a cool 20-something-year-old Mac user, for whom there are no problems, sympathizing with a nerdy, older man who is a Windows user with a myriad of problems. The ads clearly portrayed the easy-to-use, few problems idea of the brand.

Events and donations. The type of events an organization puts on or sponsors and the charities it contributes money to. Target sponsors many African-American events in Chicago and donates to charities in all minority communities. Accenture sponsors high-end charity events to raise large sums of money to fight diseases, and it contributes to the symphony, opera, and major theater companies in Chicago.

Personnel. The kind of people who work at the company, both in the back of the house where products are designed and produced and in the stores in which products are sold. We have already mentioned the important roles of the barristas in fostering Starbuck's image and of the salespeople in Old Navy's. It is so ingrained, we take for granted the integral role all the staff at Disney Parks, dressed and acting as Disney characters, play in fostering that image. Even the people who sweep the parks are recruited, trained, and managed as cast members. On the other hand, Google emphasizes the brainy creativity of its employees (whom customers never see) as a way of fostering its image. Personnel can demonstrate the following six characteristics that provide company image differentiation, according to Kotler (1991, p. 300):

- Competence
- Courtesy
- Credibility
- Reliability
- Responsiveness
- Communication

  To that list, we could add:

- Personality that matches the image and customers.
- Demographic and psychographic similarity to customer.

Issue with Image: External Flash Only

The biggest mistake organizations make in establishing corporate image, according to Clifton, Simmons, and Ahmad (2004) is to focus on the symbols and to forget that the image begins with the idea. Remember, as we said earlier, only two brands actually sell based on the image and symbol alone. The rest need both the idea and the product to back that symbol up. Clifton, Simmons, and Ahmad stress this point:

> If branding is treated as a cosmetic exercise only…it will have a superficial effect only. . . . If this cosmetic approach is applied in an effort to make a bad or confused business look more attractive, it is easy to see why such these so-called "rebranding" exercises encourage such cynicism. . . . Branding needs to start with a clear point of view of what the organization should be about. . . . (2004, p. 6).

What You Should Do

You should take three actions for this element of Product Logic:

1. Identify all the elements of company image differentiation for your organization.
2. Given the elements of product and service differentiation, identify any disconnects you see within Product Logic itself—disconnects with company image or between product/service differentiation and company image.
3. Identify any disconnects you see between the Product Logic and the Customer and Strategy Logics.

Measures for Product Logic

The good news is that more measures are consistently gathered and tracked for Product Logic than for any of the other logics. This is because products are easy to count and are directly linked to the organization's income and expense. The bad news is that services are typically not as well measured, tracked, and accounted for, no doubt because they aren't as easy to pin down and count.

Another problem is that there are more measures than anyone can possibly track and make sense of. As we are repeating in each chapter where we have a bounty of possible measures, both Stack (1994) and Kaplan and Norton (1996) caution that an organization can keep its eyes on only four to six measures at a time, and that having a list of 20 measures to track all at once is confusing, dispiriting, and useless in performance improvement. More good news is that you don't have to guess which ones to focus on; the production people in your organization will know which ones they are using and which are the ones that cause panic, overtime, and sometimes reorganization if they are not doing well. All you have to do is ask them. The same is true of service organizations: They will be measuring

Possible Product Measures

TABLE 7.4. PRODUCT MEASURES

Measures	ASK: What are the key measures your organization looks at to determine how well its product logic is working?	Services
	Products **Differentiation:** Features (number, novelty, time) Performance (number of days, percentage on time, percentage right address, percentage delivered first try) Conformance/durability/reliability (returns [number, percentage], defects [number, percentage] number of accidents) Repairability and repairs (number, time, repeats) Style (percentage customers rating 4 out 5, percentage favorable reviews by critics, novelty) Design (percentage alignment of other 5 elements according to customers, critics, internal design monitors, percentage returns for any of the other 5 elements) **Company image:** Knowledgeable (questions answered [number, percentage]) Innovative (sales, service, finance [number, novelty]) Confident (attitude conveyed) Store environment (pleasant/unpleasant) Proactive (number questions asked, number solutions generated, number problems avoided) **Relationship between company and customer:** Convenient (steps involved [number, complexity, hassle]) Responsive (problems solved [number, percentage, time]) Welcome given (customer feelings [number, percentage, degree]) Thanks given (percentage, timeliness) Guarantee (amount, ease) After-sale service (number of questions answered, loaners)	Delivery (speed, accuracy, reliability, fit, number of days, percentage on time, percentage right address, percentage delivered first try) Installation/implementation (time, cost, number of referenceable accts) Customer training (volume, number complaints/rework, number preventable repairs) Consulting service (percentage utilization, referenceable accounts) Helpful (number problems solved, number problems welcomed) Speedy service (cycle time, time OOS) Quality service (number revisions, number callbacks) Availability (percentage of time available when needed) Team rapport (number of arguments, problem-solving speed) Contracting (number of steps, hassles, arguments) Drive out costs (number innovative ideas presented)

something that helps them assess how well they are doing. Call centers measure calls answered, dropped, and handled. Consulting and software firms measure staff utilization and projects completed on time and on budget. Everyone has some numbers to keep an eye on. Table 7.4 provides you with an illustrative list of measures under the three broad Product Logic categories.

We suggest you first go through the table and identify any measures that you know right away match those that you should be tracking. Then, find someone in production (or whoever tracks and reports service delivery data) and identify the few most important product/service measures tracked by your organization.

Sample Worksheets for Product Logic

In Chapter 2, we introduced the Internal Scan Worksheet. Table 7.5 shows the columns through Product Logic filled out for one of our clients. It is still brief: just a few words summarizing each of the elements. This is the level of detail that we continue to suggest you use to get the big picture without bogging yourself down in a major research project. Save your time and energy for more detailed analysis when you have a specific performance issue to investigate or when you have decided to do a detailed overview of the business instead of a high-level one. If you are doing a detailed level overview, we suggest you use an Excel spreadsheet.

Table 7.6 shows the measures for the same client, the credit card division of a bank.

Product Logic Job Aid

This job aid summarizes Product Logic with graphics, definitions, questions to be answered, and examples. Use it when you are trying to identify the strategy logic for your own (or your client's) organization.

Your Turn

Use the Product Logic Job Aid (Table 7.7) and the Internal Scan Worksheet (Table 7.8) to identify the Product Logic and measures operating in your organization or your client's. Here are some sources of information (*text continues on page 188*):

TABLE 7.5. SAMPLE INTERNAL SCAN FOR CREDIT CARD DIVISION OF A BANK

Assess and fill in the logic the business appears to be using.

ECONOMIC LOGIC	STRATEGY LOGIC	CUSTOMER LOGIC	PRODUCT LOGIC	PROCESS LOGIC	STRUCTURAL LOGIC
Cost structure • Variable: Cost of funds and delinquencies • To manage: Self-fund, control delinquencies Financial focus • Cost of goods sold Profit source • Channel: Direct versus oil company cards versus Sears, etc.	Mission and vision • Provide profitable credit services to higher risk market Initiatives/tactics • Seek new customer-facing partners • Manage delinquencies tightly Culture • Do it now, ask forgiveness later Core competency • Collections Growth strategy • Alliances: Oil company, large retailer credit • Purchase: Other banks' delinquent portfolios Pricing strategy • High end of middle	Market strategy • Segment by economic groups • Target: $20K–$45K/year • Low white-collar, high blue-collar • Some high-risk credit Customer needs satisfaction • Niche: Consumer credit card Relationship/trans-action strategy • High volume of transactions key to income (fee-based)	Differentiation • Focus on needs of target group • Familiarity: Piggyback on oil company cards • Really good at controlling delinquencies (accept high-risk customers) Image • Familiar, reliable, "home folks"		

- Do the logics in the six columns support each other or are they contradictory?
- If they are contradictory, does this have some bearing on the problem you were asked to solve?
- How can you test your assessment that these are the business logic(s) the company is using?
- Now review the logic in the light of your environmental scan. Do the six logics seem to be consistent with external realities?

Reprinted with permission of Lynn Kearny, 2009

TABLE 7.6. SAMPLE MEASURES WORKSHEET FOR CREDIT CARD DIVISION OF A BANK

Logic	Measures	Target	Current	Gap	Performance Problems	Interventions	Measured Results
Economic							
Strategy							
Customer							
	Differentiation	Novel (focused on target group needs) + familiar for new customer	Novel (focused on target group needs)	Familiar for new customers			
Product	Price	Appropriate for current and new customers	Appropriate for current customers	Appropriate for new customers			
	Innovative	Only product for this market	Only product for this market	None			
	Responsive	97% satisfied	97% satisfied	None			
	After-sale service	Within 6 hours; cheery	Within 6 hours; cheery	None			
Process							
Internal							

- What specific measures does the organization use for each type of logic? Write them in column 2.
- What is the target for each measure? Write it in column 3.
- What is the current number for each measure? Write it in column 4.
- What is the gap between target and current number for each measure? Write it in column 5.
- Those measures with the greatest, and most critical, gaps are the focus of the Performance Problem Analysis and Intervention Selection that take place next in the Performance Improvement process.

TABLE 7.7. SUMMARY JOB AID—PRODUCT LOGIC

How the organization's product or services appeal to the customer, how they are differentiated and the company's image with its customers

	OPTIONS	EXAMPLES	BUSINESSES
Differentiation	**Ask: What is it about your product that makes it distinctive, unique? What are you doing to differentiate it?**		
	Examples		
	Ordinary	**Unique**	
	Delivery service	Know exactly where your shipment is at any time	Federal Express
	Personal computer	Distinctive product styling	Apple Computers
	Personal productivity software	Most widely distributed, readable by more people	Microsoft
Company Image	**ASK: What is the image your company projects in order to appeal to customers?**		
	The experience economy by building customer loyalty through identity	**Examples**	**Image**
		Viacom	The experience of being in a movie
		Nordstroms	The ultimate customer service experience
		Southwest Airlines	The let-your-hair-down experience

TABLE 7.7. SUMMARY JOB AID—PRODUCT LOGIC (Continued)

	POSSIBILITIES	EXAMPLES	BUSINESSES
Measures	Ask, what are the key measures your organization looks at to determine how well its Product Logic is working?		
	Products	Differentiation,	Services
		Features (number; novelty; time)	Delivery (speed, accuracy, reliability, "fit", number of days, percentage on time, percentage right address, percentage delivered first try)
		Performance (number of days, percentage on time, percentage right address, percentage delivered first try)	Installation/implementation (time, cost, number of referenceable accounts)
		Conformance/durability/reliability (returns [number; percentage]; defects [number; percentage] number accidents)	Customer training (volume, number of complaints/rework, number of preventable repairs)
		Repair ability and repairs [number, time, repeats]	Consulting service (percentage utilization, referenceable accts)
		Style (percentage customers' rating 4 out 5, percentage favorable reviews by critics; novelty)	
		Design (percentage alignment of other 5 elements according to customers, critics, internal design monitors; percentage returns for any of the other 5 elements)	
		Company image	
		Knowledgeable (questions answered [number; percentage])	Helpful (number of problems solved; number of problems welcomed)
		Innovative (sales, service, finance [number; novelty])	Speedy service (cycle time; time [OOS])
		Confident (attitude conveyed)	Quality service (number of revisions; number of callbacks)
		Store environment (pleasant/unpleasant)	
		Proactive (number of questions asked, number solutions generated; number of problems avoided)	
		Relationship between company and customer	
		Convenient (steps involved [number; complexity; hassle])	Availability (percentage of time available when needed)
		Responsive (problems solved [number; percentage; time])	Team rapport (number of arguments, problem-solving speed)
		Welcome given (customer feelings [number; percentage; degree])	Contracting (number of steps, hassles, arguments)
		Thanks given (percentage; timeliness)	Drive-out costs (number of innovative ideas presented)
		Guarantee (amount; ease)	
		After-sale service (number of questions answered; loaners)	

- Organization's Web site
- Annual report
- 10-K report
- Hoover's or Mergent (Most public libraries have a subscription.)
- Talk to members of the organization, particularly line managers, production people, quality control, accounting, and finance
- Any other sources suggested in this chapter

If you want a reproducible version of the worksheet (Table 7.8), there is one on the Web site at (www.Pfeiffer.com/go/kennethsilber). Copy it to your desktop, and either use it as is, or modify it for the level of detail you need to work with. Consider creating an Excel spreadsheet.

Summary

Product Logic is the bridge between Customer Logic, where the focus is on the customer, and Process Logic, where the focus is on how products and services are developed and provided. This chapter has focused on the products and services themselves, explaining how products/services are differentiated and outlining the factors involved in company image or brand. You now have a menu of measures that organizations use to assess how well their differentiation and branding efforts are succeeding. Although that menu may not lead you directly to problems and opportunities that your expertise can help with, it can help you pinpoint where a problem exists (which level of product or product line). It will also help you be strategic about how you present your recommendations: by aligning your approach to the organization's image. Next we will get into the logic that gets products and services to the customers: Process Logic.

TABLE 7.8. INTERNAL SCAN WORKSHEET

Assess and fill in the logic the business appears to be using.

ECONOMIC LOGIC	STRATEGY LOGIC	CUSTOMER LOGIC	PRODUCT LOGIC	PROCESS LOGIC	STRUCTURAL LOGIC

- Do the logics in the six columns support each other or are they contradictory?
- If they are contradictory, does this have some bearing on the problem you were asked to solve?
- How can you test your assessment that these are the business logic(s) the company is using?
- Now review the logic in the light of your environmental scan. Do the six logics seem to be consistent with external realities?

CHAPTER EIGHT

PROCESS LOGIC

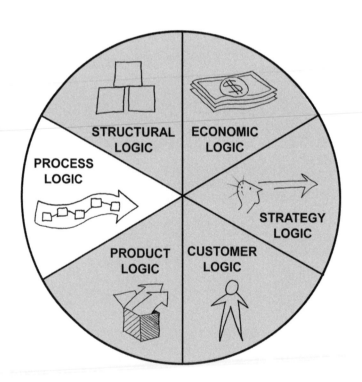

There are many definitions of business process, though, interestingly, there are more definitions of "business process redesign." The one we find most useful is from Rummler and Brache:

> A business process is a series of steps designed to produce a product or service. Most processes . . . are cross-functional, spanning the 'white space' between the boxes on the organization chart.
>
> Some processes result in a product or service that is received by an organization's external customer. We call these *customer processes* [called external processes in the 1995 edition]. Other processes produce products that are invisible to the external customer but essential to the effective management of the business. We call these *administrative processes* . . . , [called internal processes in the 1995 edition]
>
> Another category of processes—*management processes*—includes actions mangers should take to support the business processes. . . . (1990, p. 45)

Our view of Process Logic is similar to not only the balanced scorecard view, but also the views of CMM (capability maturity model), Porter, the quality movement, and information technology. The only differences among all these sources is how the numerous processes in an organization are grouped. The grouping we use is reflected in the three categories of this chapter. See Table 8.1.

- First, we discuss research and development processes.
- Second, we discuss production and/or logistic processes, which include much of the value chain.
- Third we discuss postsale processes, which map very closely with some elements of service and company image in Product Logic.

TABLE 8.1. ELEMENTS OF PROCESS LOGIC

R&D process (product development)	
Production and/or logistic processes	
Postsale processes	
Measures	

Finally, we will look into measures—how the organization determines how well their Process Logic is doing—with a series of very metrical measures.

Why Process Logic Is Important to You and the Organization

"We have found the Process Level to be the least understood and least managed level of performance," say Rummler and Brache (1990, p. 44). And despite all the business process reengineering and redesign (Hammer and Champy, 1993) and quality improvements that have been going on by Six Sigma black belts since the 1980s (Harmon, 2003), most business processes are still in that state in the authors' experience. For the organization, this is a problem because, according to Rummler and Brache (1990, pp. 45–47):

- It is cross-functional processes, not hierarchical, siloed organization structures, that actually produce products/services
- Organizations are only as good at producing and delivering products/services as their processes are
- Individual performers' ability to work, or to improve work, is limited by the work processes
- A good performer cannot overcome poor, weak, confused processes
- Automating processes (including information technology) is waste of money if it is used to facilitate poor processes.

For you, Process Logic is important because it enables you to think and work at one level higher than the individual or team level at which most of us work. Taking a higher-level perspective enables you to both see and solve problems that simply are not visible from the level of people engaged in the day-to-day work of the organization. To paraphrase Albert Einstein, the significant problems we face cannot be solved at the same level of thinking we were at when we created them. Working with Process Logic enables us to have much a larger impact on organizations and to use more of the tools in our tool kits than most of us are currently using.

What Processes Are in General and Issues Related to Processes

 Before delving into the categories of processes, this chapter will make more sense if we talk first about what processes are in general, then about some issues with processes across the board.

Fields of Study in Processes

Harmon (2003 p. 36) points out that processes have been the subject of study in many different fields since the 1980s. He identified the following fields, dates, and authors/subfields and the nature of their involvement in process improvement. Although a bit generic and incomplete, the list gives us a sense of how many different key authors and fields have understood the importance of processes.

- Management:
  — Porter (late 1980s, as cited in our Chapter 3)
  — Rummler, and Rummler and Brache (1980s through today)
- Business process reengineering (BPR) and redesign:
  — Hammer and Champy (1990s through today)
- Information technology (IT):
  — Work flow (late 1980s)
  — Packaged software (enterprise resource planning, ERP) (mid-1990s)
  — Software modeling (computer-aided software engineering, CASE) (late 1980s)
- Quality:
  — TQM (à la Deming and Juran, 1980s)
  — Six Sigma (1990s through today)

Performance Variables

Process goals, process design, and process management are the three performance variables that Rummler and Brache (1990) suggest be used to measure the effectiveness of processes.

Harmon (2003, p. 8) provides an interesting perspective by applying the IT capability maturity model to processes in general, showing five levels of the possible "is" state:

1. *Initial*: Chaotic and ad hoc, process not defined
2. *Repeatable*: Project management exists, process can be used again
3. *Defined*: Documented, used throughout organization on projects
4. *Managed*: Detailed process and results measures are understood and taken
5. *Optimizing*: Continuous process improvement

It is important to note Harmon's insistence that "each process exists to make a contribution to one or more Organization Goals" (p. 47). (We will elaborate on this shortly.) This agrees with our assertion that all six internal and the one external logics must be aligned to support the Economic and Strategy Logics of the organization.

It is also important to note that process design is responsible for only one-third of the effectiveness of a process. The three components are:

- Process goals
- Process design
- Process management

According to Rummler, one of the differences between process re-engineering and his approach is that re-engineering often fails to look at the process goals (most importantly) or at process management, leading to well designed processes that do not make contributions to organizational goals.

Process Goals are derived from Organization Goals, customer requirements and benchmarking information. (Rummler and Brache, 1900, p. 47)

Process Design is the component of processes we are most familiar with—mapping "is" and "should" states: the large diagrams built with flow charting or process mapping software.

Process Management consists of four components (Rummler and Brache, 1990, pp. 47–62):

- Goal management—measuring processes to see if they are meeting the desired goals
- Performance management—internal and external feedback on the performance of the processes
- Resource management—ensuring that resources are being allocated to processes in ways that allow processes to meet their goals
- Interface management—just as functional silos decrease performance, process silos can do the same. Interface management means ensuring that the interfaces and interactions among processes are being managed in ways that help complete the processes and achieve their goals, rather than hindering them.

The Elements of Process Logic

As already explained, all processes should add value to the output of the organization and assist in meeting its goals. To do so, authors speak of a *value chain*, the clustering and sequencing of processes in a way that allows them to add value.

For example, the Generic Value-Chain Model in the balanced scorecard (Kaplan and Norton, 1996, p. 96) is, in outline rather than flowchart form:

1. Customer need identified
2. Innovation process:
   a. Identifying the market
   b. Creating the product/service offering
3. Operations processes:
   a. Building the products/services
   b. Delivering the products/service
4. Postsale service process:
   a. Servicing the customer
5. Customer need satisfied.

Other authors use different classifications of the major processes in the value chain. However, if you look within each major process in the value chain, you always find the same subprocesses (for example, for those of you missing the sales process, it is found in almost all models under operations/deliver the goods).

There are some variations of the value chain across industries (one would not expect the value chain for Google to look like the one for McDonald's). Also, based on an organization's core competencies, some processes are quite detailed in their process flow maps (like supply chain management for McDonald's and R&D for pharmaceutical companies), whereas others have a much simpler map because they are outsourced and therefore are only managed.

We have chosen to use process categories that parallel the balanced scorecard categories:

- R&D processes
- Production/logistics processes
- Postsale processes

R&D Processes

You can ask two types of questions about R&D processes: What is the R&D strategy of the organization? What R&D processes does the organization follow?

In Table 8.2, we suggest the range of possibilities for answering the first question about the organization's R&D strategy. The develop-new-ones-based-on-market-research strategy is one that is used by the pharmaceutical industry. As Baby Boomers age, they are a large market that is prone to many of the illnesses associated with aging. Therefore, the industry focuses on developing new products

TABLE 8.2. R&D PROCESSES

	Options	Examples	Businesses
R&D process (product development)	**ASK: How do you provide new products and services?**		
	Develop new ones based on market research.	A single lightweight device that will provide phone, Internet, and paging services	Cisco Systems
	Invent new ones by pushing technology to new levels.	The copper chip	IBM
	Find existing or emerging ones and adapt them to your own strengths.	The Macintosh graphical user interface adapted as Windows	Microsoft
	Enhance your existing products/services by adding or extending features.	Software upgrades or new releases	All known software companies

(i.e., medicines) that will address the needs of that market. Apple, for example, used that strategy with the introduction of the iPod and iPhone products, but it generally follows the enhance-your-existing-products/services-by-adding-or-extending-features strategy.

The second question can be rephrased as, "What are all the possible R&D processes?" And that is a question no one can really answer, because the actual processes themselves differ by industry and company. Companies doing research with DNA certainly use different specific research processes from auto companies doing research on developing green automobiles.

However, most research processes fall into a handful of general categories. (Please note that this list, developed by the authors, has categories with different names in different industries, and some categories that are not used in all industries.)

- *Market research*: Are there customers who have a need for the product?
- *Basic research*: What is the structure of the DNA helix? How do cancer cells reproduce?
- *Applied research*: Given what we know about how cancer cells reproduce, what are possible ways of stopping that reproduction?
- *Design research and development*: Given that we know the customer need and what type of product might meet that need, how can we create it? This would include prototyping and rapid-prototyping processes.

- *Clinical trials*: Given that we think we have developed a product that we think works, we need to do a double-blind study to prove to a government agency that it does actually work.
- *Alpha testing*: Given that we think we have developed a product that almost works, let's put it out there and have users/customers help us make it work.
- *Beta testing*: Given that we think we have developed a product that works, let's make it available free to innovator and early adopter users for them to test it and tell us how well it works and what improvements we need to make before we release it.

Production/Logistics Processes

 Once your organization or your client's has designed a product/service, it must be built and delivered/executed.

As in research and development, the specific processes and even the categories of processes differ by industry and organization. Hammer and Champy (1993) suggest the subcategories we list in Table 8.3, which work well for a manufacturing

TABLE 8.3. PRODUCTION/LOGISTICS PROCESSES

Production and/or logistics processes	ASK: What happens inside the organization to turn sales and raw materials into products and services delivered to the customer? What are the 5 to 7 biggest cross-organizational flows of events and what groups participate in the process?	
	Possibilities:	What department or groups are involved?
	Product development (concept to prototype)	E.g.: Engineering only? Or also marketing, manufacturing, customer service, training, finance, customers, and even suppliers?
	Sales (prospect to order)	Sales and marketing only? Or also finance, engineering, manufacturing, customer service, customers?
	Supply chain (inbound and outbound materials)	Procurement and delivery only? Or also suppliers, engineering, manufacturing, sales, customer service?
	Manufacturing (parts to product)	Manufacturing only? Or also engineering, sales, customer service, training, suppliers, and even customers?
	Order fulfillment (order to payment)	Shipping and accounts receivable only? Or also suppliers, finance, sales, manufacturing, engineering, customer service, and customers?

organization that is rather self-contained. We have modified it here to include other possible process categories, especially detailing supply chain management processes following Porter (1985, p. 46–47) (inbound logistics, operations, outbound logistics, marketing and sales, service) and Poirier (1999, p. 9):

- Product development [concept to prototype (possibly in R&D) and then to actual deliverable product]
- Sales (prospect to order):
  — Sales force operations
  — Sales administration
  — Message creation:
    — For the public
    — Technical literature for the sales force
  — Media selection
  — Advertising development
  — Personal selling
  — Online selling
- Marketing Management
  — Product
  — Placement
  — Pricing
  — Promotion
  — Packaging
- Supply chain management [obtaining inputs (physical or data) needed to manufacture/create product; delivering product/service (output) to next partner organization in supply chain]
  — Forecasting and inventory planning
  — Vendor network rationalization
  — Production scheduling = addressed in other category, but considered here as well
  — Sales scheduling
  — Promotion process scheduling
  — Inbound logistics
  — Ordering
  — Transportation
  — Delivery
  — Handling
    — Unloading
    — Inspecting
    — Parts picking

- —Distribution scheduling
- —Outbound logistics (see Inbound)
- —Warehousing (only if used)
- —Delivery logistics (see Inbound)
- —Retailer processes
- —Repair processes
- Operations/manufacturing/creating/processing (This differs the most of all categories by type of industry.)
  - —Product creation (raw materials or parts to product)
    - —Component fabrication
    - —Assembly
    - —Fine-tuning and testing
    - —Maintenance,
    - —Facilities operation
  - —Information creation (raw data/program coded into mined data or programs)
  - —Services creation/delivery (processing people or things to meet the goal, from moving a package to giving a massage)
  - —Repair processes
- Order fulfillment (administrative—order receipt to shipment to delivery to payment)
  - —Receiving
    - —Confirming
    - —Filling
    - —Shipping
    - —Notifying

Production/logistics processes make up a great portion of what most, but not all, organizations do. We will see how some of these processes are actually done outside the organization in Chapter 9. It is unlikely that your organization has all of these processes, unless it is a large, multiproduct company like Kraft Foods, McDonald's, General Motors, Abbott Laboratories, or the like. Most companies specialize in the processes that are close to their core competencies, as FedEx specializes in delivery (though, since someone has to make the envelopes and labels, products are involved) or as Nike specializes in R&D and marketing.

Caveat: Based on Table 8.3, ask, "What happens inside the organization to make sales and turn raw materials into products and services delivered to the customer? What are the five to seven biggest cross-organizational flows of events? What groups participate in the process?" (We will repeat this near the end of the chapter.)

Postsale Processes

 Completing the sale and delivery of the product, as most organizations are aware in 2009, does not end the relationship with the customer if you ever want to see that customer again. The question is how does your company provide postsale support to customers: customer satisfaction, technical support, repair, updates, and returns.

In Table 8.4, we suggest that, as with R&D processes, both an attitude and a set of processes are involved.

The attitude can be measured on a scale of response. At one end is the reactive (and reactionary) position of some organizations: "OK, we know we are supposed to do this but we really don't want to so we are going to make it as hard as possible to get it." At the other end is the opposite response: "Thank you for buying from us, and here is how we can help you use the product and repair it should it break. With one phone call to a person in the United States who will answer on the second ring." All of us have experienced the frustration of the first attitude and turned to other providers. A few of us are even willing to pay a little extra (as explained in Product Logic) for the second type of response. Organizations with the latter orientation are called customer focused in the customer service

TABLE 8.4. POSTSALE PROCESSES

	Possibilities	Examples	Businesses
Postsale processes	ASK: Does your company provide postsale support to customers? In what ways (customer satisfaction, technical support, repair, updates, and returns)?		
	Minimal and reluctant	Many high-tech organizations, especially for Internet sales	Let's not mention them . . .
	Passive reactive: Complaint handling	Customer service and repair provided at customer's request	Most automobile manufacturers
	Active reactive: Complaint transformation	Move heaven and earth to satisfy the customer	Nordstrom's
	Proactive: Seek customers out and ask what could be better	Conduct regular focus groups of customers to solicit new product/service ideas and improvements	Sporting goods manufacturers: Skis Mountain bikes Motocross

literature, and they are known for both anticipating the problems and building the solutions into their products and processes. [For a more detailed discussion of customer-focused organizations, see Joby (2003).]

The specific processes vary by organization. In general, processes fall into the following categories and subcategories:

- Immediate follow-up (used heavily in online retail)
  — Customer satisfaction measurement
  — Follow-up of poor customer satisfaction
  — Offers of assistance
  — Recommendations for product/service use
  — Cross-selling of related products/services
- Return/exchange processes
  — Live: easiest to most difficult
    — Authorization
    — Customer sending
    — Company receiving
    — Financial crediting
    — Reshipping replacement product
  — Online: easiest to most difficult (same as live)
- Repair processes
  — Proactive versus reactive
  — Immediate, timely, slow
  — Service reps
  — Spare parts systems
- Update processes (especially for software)
  — Automatic
  — Notification
  — Request driven
- Medium-term follow-up processes (see Immediate follow-up)

Again, as we have said for the other two groups of processes, not all categories apply to all organizations, and the processes may be invisible to some customers. For example, some of these processes are available to recipients of FedEx packages (like package tracking); others must surely exist, like satisfaction, repairs, and the like, but may be available only to shippers, with still others available only to large shippers. Some organizations are clearly missing certain processes that should be there from the customer's point of view. When a customer fills out a satisfaction survey that is negative and does not hear back (or receives a you're-wrong response), the organization is unlikely to see the customer again.

Issues Related to Processes

Three additional issues are related to processes in general:

Not knowing processes. Despite all the literature and movements that Harmon (2003) pointed out starting in the 1980s and that the quality movement started even before then, some companies still cannot articulate the processes they use to accomplish the core competencies and the strategy and the Product Logic of the organization. In other words, most people in the organization cannot tell you how anything happens: how a product gets made, how research is done, how customer service is provided, how consulting services are delivered, or how products and services are sold.

Not valuing processes, or siloing. Part of the possible explanation for the first issue is that people in functional organizations value what happens in their function more than any cross-functional process. This is what Rummler and Brache call thinking in silos: using the farm metaphor of the large, independently standing and unconnected silos that hold grain and hay. Each function does what it does and then blindly hands it off to the next function; any errors or omissions in their work becomes the problem of the next work group. This thinking led Rummler and Brache and Hammer and Champy to push the focus on cross-functional processes and on process redesign and re-engineering.

Reconfiguring the supply chain processes. In addition to the redesign and re-engineering approaches to improving processes, Porter provides specific guidelines for reconfiguring supply and value chains:

- a different production process
- differences in automation
- direct sales instead of indirect sales
- a new distribution channel
- a new raw material
- major differences in forward or backward vertical integration
- shifting the location of facilities relative to suppliers and customers
- new advertising media (1985, p. 107)

Process redesign "fatigure". Fatigure is a combination of fatigue and failure. By now, the employees in many organizations have been through one (or probably several) process improvement exercises. They have spent a large amount of time creating "is" and "should" process maps, improving processes, presenting them to management, having them rejected or implemented, and having jobs change. They are tired. The bottom line is that after that work, according to Hammer and Champy (2003) in the revised and updated version of their book, different researchers have found a 50 to 70 percent failure rate with process re-engineering; that is, organizational performance did not improve with re-engineering, as predicted. So organizations are saddled with fatigue and failure when thinking about their business processes.

What You Should Do

You should take eight actions for Process Logic:

1. Identify the major R&D, production/logistics, and postsales processes of your organization.
2. For the major processes that are closest to your job assignment (for example, sales training or OD for manufacturing), identify the subprocesses involved.
3. Find any data that exists about the effectiveness of the existing processes.
4. Identify any disconnects in the Process Logic, processes that seem to be needed but are missing (keep these to yourself for now), as well as processes that are inefficient or redundant.
5. Determine what process redesign/improvement/re-engineering work has been done in the organization, what the results were, and what management and workers think of processes and redesign efforts.
6. Identify any disconnects you see between the Process Logic and the Product, Customer, and Strategy Logics.
7. Determine if any of Porter's eight ways to reconfigure value/supply chains have been tried or if they could solve any of the identified disconnects.
8. Identify process improvement initiatives that are needed in the organization, and develop (if there is not too much "fatigue") a strategy for your performance improvement department to become involved in or lead.

Measures for Process Logic

The news about the measures for Process Logic is good and bad (as it was for the Customer and Product Logics).

The good news is that you can use actual, solid, objective measures to assess how the organization is doing in this logic. And these are probably measures the organization already collects because they are important to the organization's success and therefore people track them regularly.

The bad news is twofold. First, the number of possible measures is very, very large—more than anyone can possibly track and make sense of. As you by now remember, both Stack (1994) and Kaplan and Norton (1996) caution that an organization can keep its eyes on only four to six measures at a time and that

TABLE 8.5. PROCESS MEASURES

Measures	**ASK: What are the key metrics your organization looks at to determine how well its Process Logic is working?**
	1. R&D processes:
	Products created (radically new, next generation, or enhancements: number each; percentage each; versus plan; versus competition)
	Cycle time (absolute; versus last product, versus competition; versus customer requirements, time from initiation to payback)
	Process time (absolute; versus last product, versus competition; versus customer requirements)
	Value-added activities (percentage)
	Rework or waste (unusable ideas [number; percentage])
	Coordination (unproduceable ideas [number; percentage])
	Innovative processes used (percentage rapid prototyping; etc.)
	Cost (absolute; versus last product, versus competition; versus customer requirements)
	2. Production and/or logistics processes:
	Quality (variance [amount; percentage]; defects [number; percentage]; rework [number; percentage; time]; unusable products [number; percentage])
	Cycle time (absolute; versus last product, versus competition; versus customer requirements)
	Process time (absolute; versus last product, versus competition; versus customer requirements)
	Value added activities (percentage)
	Coordination (order/supply/production/delivery match [number; percentage; timeliness; accuracy]; yield [percentage]; inventory [percentage; time 1 or 2])

TABLE 8.5. PROCESS MEASURES (*Continued*)

Innovative processes used [percentage rapid prototyping; etc.]

Cost [absolute; versus last product, versus competition; versus customer requirements]

Supplier/interim customer satisfaction

3. Postsale processes (repair/update and return):

Returns (variance [amount; percentage]; defects [number; percentage]; untimely [number; percentage; time]; wrong order [number; percentage])

Repairs/updates (amount needed [number; percentage]; done to customer satisfaction first time [number; percentage]; process cycle time

Value added activities [percentage])

Coordination (order/supply/production/ delivery match [number; percentage; timeliness; accuracy])

Innovative processes used (percentage rapid prototyping, etc.)

Cost (absolute; versus last product, versus competition; versus customer requirements)

4. Miscellaneous:

Effectiveness and efficiency

Sustainability

Consumption of resources

having a list of 20 measures to track at once is confusing, dispiriting, and useless for performance improvement. Unfortunately, we cannot help you narrow down which measures to focus on, because that answer depends on which measures your organization uses to track its performance.

Second, as with Product Logic, Process Logic has a large number of categories—processes—in which measures could be tracked. Again, we cannot help you narrow down the processes you should be seeking measures for, since that too depends on which processes your organization considers crucial.

As a result, providing you with a complete list of possible measures for Process Logic is impossible (and if it were possible, it would be impractical because it would double the length and price of this book). What we have opted to do, therefore, in Table 8.5, is to provide you with an illustrative list of measures under the three broad categories of processes.

Again, we suggest you first go through the table and see if there are measures that you know right away are things you should be tracking. Then, possibly using the table as a menu and conversation starter, consult the people in your organization who are responsible for tracking this information; find out what key measures are being tracked and what the goals and results are so far for the year. The people you are looking for are the ones who compile reports for leadership about the most critical processes for your organization: manufacturing, sales, production, and so on. Whatever it is will relate to your organization's core competencies.

Sample Worksheets for Process Logic

In Chapter 2, we introduced the Internal Scan Worksheet (Table 8.6). Here it is filled out through the Process Logic column for one of our clients. It is brief: just a few words summarizing each of the elements. This is the level of detail that we still encourage you to use to get the big picture without bogging yourself down in a major research project. Save your time and energy for more detailed analysis when you have a specific performance issue to investigate. Right after the Internal Scan Worksheet, you will see the Measures Worksheet (Table 8.7) filled out for the same client.

Process Logic Job Aid

This job aid (Table 8.8) summarizes strategy logic with graphics, definitions, questions to be answered, and examples. Use it when you are trying to identify the Process Logic for your own (or your client's) organization.

TABLE 8.6. SAMPLE INTERNAL SCAN FOR CREDIT CARD DIVISION OF A BANK

Assess and fill in the logic the business appears to be using.

ECONOMIC LOGIC	STRATEGY LOGIC	CUSTOMER LOGIC	PRODUCT LOGIC	PROCESS LOGIC	STRUCTURAL LOGIC
Cost structure • Variable: Cost of funds and delinquencies • To manage: Self-fund, control delinquencies **Financial focus** • Cost of goods sold **Profit Source** • Channel: Direct versus oil company cards versus Sears, etc.	**Mission and vision** • Provide profitable credit services to higher risk market **Initiatives/tactics** • Seek new customer-facing partners • Manage delinquencies tightly **Culture** • Do it now, ask forgiveness later **Core competency** • Collections **Growth strategy** • Alliances: Oil company, large retailer credit • Purchase: Other banks' delinquent portfolios **Pricing strategy** • High end of middle	**Market strategy** • Segment by economic groups • Target: $20K–$45K/ year • Low white-collar, high blue-collar • Some "high risk" credit **Customer need satisfaction** • Niche: Customer credit card **Relationship/ transaction strategy** • High volume of transactions key to income (fee-based)	**Differentiation** • Focus on needs of target group • Familiarity: Piggyback on oil company cards • Really good at controlling delinquencies (accept high-risk customers) **Image** • Familiar, reliable, "home folks"	**R&D/ product development** • Adapt others' innovations • Enhance existing products and services **Production/ logistics** • Sales • Credit granting • Processing transactions and billing • Collections • (Well-integrated) **Postsale** • Active–reactive exception handling: Disputes, credit problems	

- Do the logics in the six columns support each other or are they contradictory?
- If they are contradictory, does this have some bearing on the problem you were asked to solve?
- How can you test your assessment that these are the business logic(s) the company is using?
- Now review the logic in the light of your environmental scan. Do the six logics seem to be consistent with external realities?

Reprinted with permission of Lynn Kearny, 2009

TABLE 8.7. SAMPLE MEASURES WORKSHEET FOR CREDIT CARD DIVISION OF A BANK

Logic	Measures	Target	Current	Gap	Performance Problems	Interventions	Measured Results
Economic							
Strategy							
Customer							
Product							
Process	R&D innovation	1 new product not borrowed	0 new products	1 new product			
	Quality	10% error rate in credit granting	65% error rate in credit granting	55%			
	Cycle time from loan to collection	Average 30 days	Average 120 days	90 days			
	Dispute handling percentage	5% disagreements escalate to dispute	95% disagreements escalate to dispute	90% disagreements resolved			
Structural							

- What specific measures does the organization use for each type of logic? Write them in column 2.
- What is the target for each measure? Write it in column 3.
- What is the current number for each measure? Write it in column 4.
- What is the gap between target and current number for each measure? Write it in column 5.
- Those measures with the greatest, and most critical, gaps are the focus of the Performance Problem Analysis and Intervention Selection that take place next in the Performance Improvement process.

Reprinted with permission of Lynn Kearny, 2009

TABLE 8.8. SUMMARY JOB AID—PROCESS LOGIC

How the organization goes about creating the product/service

	Options	Examples	Businesses
R&D Process [Product Development] 	**ASK: How do you provide new products and services?**		
	Develop new ones based on market research.	A single lightweight device that will provide phone, Internet, and paging services	Cisco Systems
	Invent new ones by pushing technology to new levels.	The copper chip	IBM
	Find existing or emerging ones and adapt them to your own strengths.	The Macintosh graphical user interface adapted as Windows	Microsoft
	Enhance your existing products/services by adding or extending features.	Software	All known software companies
Production and/or Logistics Processes	**ASK: What happens inside the organization to turn sales and raw materials into products and services delivered to the customer? What are the 5 to 7 biggest cross-organizational flows of events and what groups participate in the process?**		
	Possibilities:	What Department or Groups Are Involved?	
	Product development [concept to prototype]	E.g.: Engineering only? Or also marketing, manufacturing, customer service, training, finance, customers, and even suppliers?	
	Sales [prospect to order]	Sales and marketing only? Or also finance, engineering, manufacturing, customer service, customers?	
	Supply chain [inbound and outbound materials]	Procurement and delivery only? Or also suppliers, engineering, manufacturing, sales, customer service?	
	Manufacturing [parts to product]	Manufacturing only? Or also engineering, sales, customer service, training, suppliers and even customers?	
	Order fulfillment [order to payment]	Shipping and accounts receivable only? Or also suppliers, finance, sales, manufacturing, engineering, customer service, and customers?	

(Continued)

TABLE 8.8. SUMMARY JOB AID—PROCESS LOGIC (*Continued*)

	Possibilities	Examples	Businesses
Postsale Processes	**ASK: Does your company provide postsale support to customers? In what ways? [customer satisfaction, technical support, repair, updates, and returns]**		
	Minimal and reluctant	Many high-tech organizations, especially for Internet sales	Let's not mention them . . .
	Passive reactive: Complaint handling	Customer service and repair provided at customer's request	Most automobile manufacturers
	Active–reactive: Complaint transformation	Move heaven and earth to satisfy the customer	Nordstrom's
	Proactive: Seek customers out and ask what could be better	Conduct regular focus groups of customers to solicit new product/service ideas and improvements	Sporting goods manufacturers
			Skis
			Mountain bikes
			Motocross
Measures	**ASK: What are the key metrics your organization looks at to determine how well its Process Logic is working?**		
	1. R&D processes:		
	Products created (radically new, next generation, or enhancements: number of each; percentage of each; versus plan; versus competition)		
	Cycle time (absolute; versus last product, versus competition; versus customer requirements, time from initiation to payback)		
	Process time (absolute; versus last product, versus competition; versus customer requirements)		
	Value added activities (percentage)		
	Rework or waste (unusable ideas [number; percentage])		
	Coordination (unproduceable ideas [number; percentage])		
	Innovative processes used (percentage rapid prototyping, etc.)		
	Cost (absolute; versus last product, versus competition; versus customer requirements)		

TABLE 8.8. SUMMARY JOB AID—PROCESS LOGIC (Continued)

2. Production and/or logistics processes:
   Quality [variance (amount; percentage); defects [number; percentage]; rework [number; percentage; time]; unusable products [number; percentage]]
   Cycle time (absolute; versus last product, versus competition; versus customer requirements)
   Process time (absolute; versus last product, versus competition; versus customer requirements)
   Value added activities (percentage)
   Coordination [order/supply/production/delivery match (number; percentage; timeliness; accuracy); yield (percentage); inventory (percentage time + or −)]
   Innovative processes used (percentage rapid prototyping, etc.)
   Cost (absolute; versus last product, versus competition; versus customer requirements
   Supplier/interim customer satisfaction

3. Postsale processes (Repair/Update and Return):
   Returns [variance (amount; percentage); defects (number; percentage); untimely (number; percentage; time); wrong order (number; percentage]
   Repairs/updates [amount needed (number; percentage); done to customer satisfaction first time (number; percentage); process cycle time]
   Value-added activities (percentage)
   Coordination [order/supply/production/delivery match (number; percentage; timeliness; accuracy)]
   Innovative processes used (percentage rapid prototyping, etc.)
   Cost (absolute; versus last product, versus competition; versus customer requirements)

4. Miscellaneous:
   Effectiveness and efficiency
   Sustainability
   Consumption of resources

Your Turn

Use the Process Logic Job Aid and the Internal Scan Worksheet to identify the Process Logic and measures operating in your organization or your client's. Ways to find out:

- Organization's Web site
- Annual report
- 10-K report
- Hoover's or Mergent (Most public libraries have a subscription.)
- Talk to members of the organization: particularly line managers, production people, quality control, accounting, and finance
- Any other sources suggested in this chapter

If you want a reproducible version of the worksheet (Table 8.9), there is one on the Web site at (www.Pfeiffer.com/go/kennethsilber). Copy it to your desktop, and either use it as is or modify it for the level of detail you need to work with. Consider creating an Excel spreadsheet.

Summary

In this chapter we have covered what is probably the highest leverage area for improving an organization's performance. Whether you are diagnosing organizational problems, directing a process improvement project, or helping others to deal with the HR issues and implications that invariably arise during such a project, you have an understanding of how critical good process management is. You know three parts must be dealt with for process work to be successful: process goals, process design, and process management. You are prepared to talk with business leaders about problems and opportunities that your expertise can help with.

Next we will get into the logic that supports all five of the others: Structural Logic.

TABLE 8.9. INTERNAL SCAN WORKSHEET

Assess and fill in the logic the business appears to be using.

ECONOMIC LOGIC	STRATEGY LOGIC	CUSTOMER LOGIC	PRODUCT LOGIC	PROCESS LOGIC	STRUCTURAL LOGIC

- Do the logics in the six columns support each other or are they contradictory?
- If they are contradictory, does this have some bearing on the problem you were asked to solve?
- How can you test your assessment that these are the business logic(s) the company is using?
- Now review the logic in the light of your environmental scan. Do the six logics seem to be consistent with external realities?

CHAPTER NINE

STRUCTURAL LOGIC

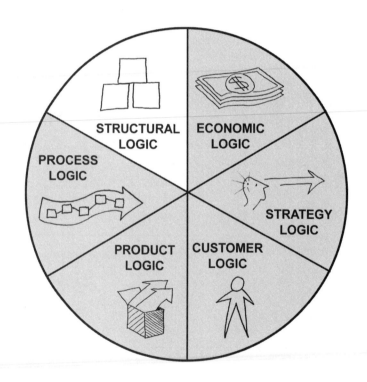

Structural Logic refers to how the organization combines and facilitates all the logics within the organization. Our view of learning and innovation is slightly different from the balanced scorecard view of learning and growth put forward by Kaplan and Norton (1996). They see the core measurements as being employee retention, satisfaction, and productivity, and the enablers as staff competencies, technology infrastructure, and climate for action (p. 129). See Table 9.1.

First, our view includes how the organization is structured, something you might have thought belonged in Strategy Logic, but we'll explain why it's here. Second, it includes how the organization uses information technology, which can be used to make all the logics run more smoothly, or they can be misused to make things more confusing and complex or, worse, actually to drive decisions in the other logics, including management of knowledge or intellectual capital. Third, our view includes human resources, the function of organization that provides—well—the human resources needed for all the other logics to work. Fourth, it includes learning and innovation, which is a category from the balanced scorecard, but is derived from the field of OD and organizational learning. It deals both with how individual learning and performance is improved and with how the organization as a whole learns. Finally, we will look into measures: how well the Structural Logic has been developed and how successful the organization is at implementing and achieving its strategy.

TABLE 9.1. ELEMENTS OF STRUCTURAL LOGIC

Organizational structure	
Information systems	
Human resources management	
Learning and innovation	
Measures	

Why Structural Logic Is Important to You and the Organization

As a whole, this logic may seem the most important of all to you personally because this is where you "live." For at least 90 percent of you readers, this logic is where your department in the organization is housed and where you spend a great deal of your time. And it is your job to be responsible for all or part of this logic. This is where people with problems of organizational and individual performance come for your help (even though the source of the problem may actually reside with one of the other logics).

Structural Logic is also important to you if there are many of your type of department in the organization and if all them are isolated or competing with you. For example, one of the authors worked for a training organization in an oil company that no longer exists. Since we were in information technology training and therefore totally powerless to change anything meaningful in the company, we identified all the other training and OD organizations within the company, something no one had ever done before. We were able to identify 29. We then met as a training council to see if we could leverage our knowledge and our different placement in the organization's structure to help each other and to change the way the organization functioned. What we learned, unfortunately, was that this was not possible because all 29 groups viewed themselves as "the best and only rightful" OD group in the company and that everyone wanted to go after everyone else's clients. Although we weren't happy, at least we knew where we stood and were able to take other steps to improve our position in the company.

This logic is also important to the organization. As you may recall from your reading in the Economic Logic Chapter, SG&A are the costs that are *not* directly attributable to the cost of goods sold. This Structural Logic is where most of those costs reside. And, unfortunately for us, it is also the first place that organizations look to reduce costs (usually by outsourcing) in tough economic times. So it is critical for all of us to take another look, from perhaps a different perspective, at a logic we think we already understand.

Caveat, Promise, and Focus

That preceding sentence might lead you to think that we are about to launch into an explanation of the HR, OD, HPT, and ID/training functions. We promise we are *not*. We assume that if you are reading this book, you have some level of expertise in some, if not all, of these areas and that you have colleagues with expertise in the areas in which you don't.

So we promise not to repeat everything you learned in HR 101 (or OD 101, or Training 101). We might provide a bullet list or two to remind you what is supposed to be there, as well as some measures for judging their quality, but that's as far as we'll go in stating what is obvious to you.

So the question is, "What are we going to talk about in this chapter?" The focus of this chapter will be on some elements of Structural Logic that might not have been in those courses or that are so important that *we believe they will impact the survival of your job, your department, and your company.*

The Elements of Structural Logic

Organizational Structure

 Organizational structure "describes how the overall work of the organization is divided into subunits and how these subunits are coordinated for task completion" (Cummings and Worley, 2009, p. 315). It consists of the boxes and arrows that make up the company organization chart. See Table 9.2.

Why Organizational Structure Is Important to You and the Organization

The structure of an organization is important to *you* because it defines where you are in the organizational pecking order. It illustrates how close you are organizationally to your clients, your bosses, the decision makers, and the other stakeholders in your projects. It tells you where you fit both horizontally and vertically in the organization. Vertically, it tells you how close your department is in the organization to having a seat at the table where decisions are made—how close you are to a vice presidential level. Horizontally, it tells you which vice president you report to. As we will see, all VPs are not equal. Are you in the HR organization under a VPHR, or are you in the line organization, under one of the VPs of the key organizational processes? Said another way, are you part of COGS or SG&A?

The organizational structure is important to the work you do and to the organization as a whole because it determines how the logics we have been discussing throughout this book interact (or do not interact) with one another. In Chapter 8 and again in this chapter, we stress the ideas of Rummler and Brache (1995) on the primacy of processes, not structure, in getting work done, and how "the white space" between vertical lines in an organization structure is where many process problems occur. Your organizational structure can silo

TABLE 9.2 ORGANIZATIONAL STRUCTURE

	Possibilities	Explanation
Organizational structure		**ASK: What does your organization chart look like? Why is it structured this way?**
	Traditional	
	Functional	VP and line organizations for marketing, R&D, manufacturing, HR, etc.
	Divisional	Resources needed to produce each product are organized under product's VP.
	Matrix	Across top of matrix are functions (R&D, HR, etc.), each headed by a VP. Down the side are products/services (products A, B, C, etc.), each headed by a coordinator.
	Modern	
	Process	Cross-skill teams are formed around each core process: e.g., R&D process or customer service process.
	Customer-centric	Customer is put at center of organization. Work groups are formed to focus on each customer group. Has adminstrative hub to coordinate work of various
	Network	Internal and external organizations that perform different competencies for the whole.

work, so that the many parts of a process are isolated from one another and thus hinder productivity, or it can facilitate communication and work flow across parts of a process to allow for effective process productivity, management, and improvement.

What Organizational Structure Is

According to Cummings and Worley (2009, p. 315), the division and coordination of the organization (as just defined), "should be designed to fit with at least four factors: the environment, organization size, technology, and organization strategy." Though Rummler and Brache might be more detailed about some of these factors and focus on the relation of the structure to business processes, philosophically these gurus agree. Organizational "form follows function"; you should design the structure of the organization last, after you have decided on all the other External and Internal Logics of the organization.

Businesses may choose from six types of organizational structures (Cummings and Worley, 2009). The first three are the traditional options; the second three are the more modern, OD- and HPT-based approaches.

Traditional

- Functional
- Divisional
- Matrix

Modern

- Process
- Customer-centric (versus product-centric)
- Network

We will describe each of these types in a little more detail, along with, as you would expect, the advantages and some disadvantages of each. As you will see, there is no perfect organizational structure for all organizations, but some structures fit certain situations better than do others (from Cummings and Worley, 2009, pp. 315–333).

Functional. Functional organizational structures divide the organization by its functions. So there is a VP and a department for research, manufacturing, engineering, marketing, finance, HR, etc., depending on the type of organization. Each function is staffed with specialists in the areas that the function addresses. Although this organizational structure promotes the maximum application of specialized skill to each function, it also has the potential to get in the way of thinking about cross-functional processes and can lead to the duplication of support services (e.g., a separate training organization in each function).

Divisional. Divisional organizational structures are also known as product or self-contained-unit structures. The organization may be divided based on:

- Products
- Services
- Customers
- Geography

Most of the resources necessary to produce a product, for example, are organized under a VP for that product. And all people concerned with producing that product report up through that organization.

Whereas in the functional structure all of the people in manufacturing report to the manufacturing division, in the divisional structure, manufacturing people for Product A report in the Product A hierarchy to the VP for Product A, and manufacturing people for Product B report through the Product B hierarchy to a VP for Product B.

Within the structure for each product are included all the functions needed to develop and produce and sell that product: research, sales, manufacturing, etc.

Some examples of companies organized in a divisional structure are General Electric and Dell.

Although this organizational structure allows each division to focus on its particular niche and promotes a Product A Team environment and culture, it also allows for the duplication of, and lack of communication among, similar functions across product lines (e.g., customer service, sales, and training practices).

Matrix. Matrix organizational structures are, in a sense, an attempt to combine the best aspects of the functional and divisional organizational structures, while minimizing the problems inherent in each. Across the top of the matrix are the different functions of the organization (research, manufacturing, marketing, customer service, etc.), each headed by a VP. Down the side of the matrix are the products/services produced by the organization (Product A, B, C, etc.), each headed by a coordinator. In each cell of the matrix resides the staff from a function who are specifically assigned to a product (e.g., the customer service staff assigned to Product A).

Originally designed by the aerospace industry for flexibility in a complex, changing product-mix environment, this matrix structure applies specialized knowledge to each product as required. It allows for movements of staff across products as needs change, and (from our perspective, most importantly) it allows for communication and consistency across different product teams as well across processes, thereby avoiding siloing and duplication. But we did say that no organizational structure is perfect, so here are the issues with matrix management. The most obvious is that each worker has two bosses: the functional boss and the product boss. Therefore at some point it is likely that the two bosses will have different priorities and different ideas of what should be done and how it should be done, leaving the worker with task interference and anxiety.

A matrix organization is very difficult to install in an organization that has never had it before, and there is long learning curve for people to operate effectively in this structure. Intel is an example of a well-established matrix organization. This structure works best when there is high pressure for information processing and sharing, when there is a broad range of products and services, when resources must be shared, and when there is real pressure from the outside (not from something the CEO read in an airline magazine about it) for both very different specialized products and highly specialized technical skills.

Process. The process organizational structure is a new approach that bases the organizational structure on the Process Logic of the organization (see Chapter 8). It forms teams of multiple skills around each of the organization's core processes (or core competencies, as discussed in Chapter 5), such as the research and development process, the customer service process, or the supply chain management process. At the head of each team of workers is a process owner, not a manager. This organizational structure has very little use for hierarchy and vertical structures, and therefore it doesn't have many management titles or boxes in a chart. Some of the key features of this structure are:

- Processes drive structure. . . .
- Work adds value. . . .
- Teams are fundamental. . . .
- Customers define performance. . . .
- Teams are rewarded for performance. . . .

- Teams are tightly linked to suppliers and customers. . . .
- Team members are well informed and trained. (Cummings and Worley, 2009, p. 323)

As an example, Healthways Corporation is organized around its five core processes: "understand the market and plan the business, acquire and retain customers, build value solutions, deliver solutions and add value, and manage the business" (Cummings and Worley, 2009, p. 325).

On the positive side of implementing this structure, the most obvious advantage is how the structure itself and the features that guide it are in line with the principles of business process improvement, organizational development, and human performance technology: customer evaluation, teamwork, rewards and consequences for performance, clear expectations, knowledge sharing, lack of siloing, employee involvement, fewer managers. But, again, no structure is perfect. In addition to threatening middle management, there are other barriers to establishing this organizational structure. The emphasis on skilled, empowered teams requires culture change, training on new skills, lengthier decision making, and a change in the mind-sets of all workers.

Customer-Centric. The customer-centric organizational structure is similar in philosophy to the process structure, but, instead of putting processes at the center of the organization structure, it puts the customers there (Galbraith, 2005). The focus is on satisfying the needs of key customer groups, and therefore there are work groups to focus on each customer group. They, in turn, are supported by product groups that help develop solutions for the customer groups. All are supported by an administrative structure that includes HR, finance, and R&D. Galbraith (2009) compares a customer-centric organization with a product centered one in the following way:

- Its goal is the best solution (versus product) for a customer . . .
- Its added-value is the way it uniquely packages all its products, services, support and other ancillary services for each customer (versus making product enhancements. . . .
- Its core processes are focused on the customer relationship and the integration of solutions (versus new product development) . . .
- Its structure is based on customer teams (versus product teams or process teams) . . .

This structure has the advantage of presenting a cohesive and targeted image and reality to the customer, and it allows the organization both to really understand its customers well and to customize novel solutions (real solutions, rather than just added products) for them. This structure has many of the same disadvantages of the process structure, plus the problem that customer teams can be so focused on their customer that they lose sight of the organization as a whole.

Network. The network organizational structure is related to the core competency and growth strategy elements of Strategy Logic (Chapter 5). For organizations that focus on core competencies and form alliances to grow and to carry out noncore competencies, some organization structure is still needed; however, none of the previous five forms will work. Network structure fills this need. The network organization has at its center an administrative hub that coordinates the work of the various other internal and external organizations that perform needed competencies for the organization. Four types of networks have been identified to date, synthesized from several scholarly articles by Cummings and Worley (2009, p. 329):

1. *Internal market network*: Within a single organization, each business unit is a separate profit center; it not only serves the other business units within the company, but it may also sell its services externally. ABB is a global business that is made up 50 businesses, divided into1,200 companies, in turn divided into 4,500 profit centers.
2. *Vertical market network*: Multiple organizations are linked to a central organization that coordinates their work and the flow of money, materials, etc. across the entire supply chain. We first discussed this in Strategy Logic, under core competencies. Nike, which focuses on core competencies internally, has different organizations to produce its shoes, to distribute them, to sell them, and to perform other functions. Nike uses alliances and partnerships as a growth strategy, giving the company access to skills and markets without having to develop core competencies in all these areas.
3. *Intermarket network*: These are alliances among different organizations in a variety of markets. The multiple industry groups provide synergies and allow entire industries to move well beyond their core competencies without having to individually contract for each portion of its production process (as contrasted with the vertical market).
4. *Opportunity network*: Like an ad hoc committee, an opportunity network is formed by bringing together a group of companies to accomplish a single goal. Once the goal is met, the organization disbands. In terms of Strategy Logic, this is the growth strategy we described as a joint venture. Many small high-tech firms in Silicon Valley work almost exclusively as members of joint ventures, combining skills in electronic engineering, programming, and

multiple patented electronic components to produce a system (or solution) that will do something valuable for a customer.

A network structure is a very flexible and adaptable approach to working in ever-changing global markets. Each organization can focus on its core competencies and find other ways to accomplish its other required processes. In network structures, it does not matter whether an internal or external organization performs many functions, especially the noncore functions. Thus what is considered outsourcing in a more traditional organizational structure is considered normal business practice in network structures. The organization that wants to focus on R&D and marketing can form a network with companies that produce the rest of the supply chain and support functions, some internal and some external, without the negative connotation associated with outsourcing. It can contract for training, for example, with any training organization, either one of its own business units or an external one, based on competence and cost. As you might expect, designing, implementing, and managing such an organization presents some unique challenges. The coordination of all the internal and external organizations and the creation of a corporate culture and loyalty are extremely difficult.

Issues Related to Organizational Structure

Which came first, the chicken or the egg? We started this section with the caveat that "form follows function" and later snidely referred to the CEO who adopts a new organizational structure because he read about it on an airplane. This represents the major issue in organizational structure. Everyone in the fields of management, strategy, OD, and HPT knows that, as in the organization of this very book, organizational structure or logic comes last, only after the company has done all the other hard work of deciding what it is about. And everyone also knows that, except for rare instances, every company decides its structure either before, or independently of, the design of the other six logics. And then everyone wonders why all the great ideas they have developed in those logics fall apart when they put them into practice in an organizational structure that is a complete mismatch.

What You Should Do

You should take six actions for this element of Structural Logic:

1. Classify the organizational structure of your company.
2. Find out how the organizational structure got to be what it is.

3. Identify the elements of the organizational structure that support (are aligned with) what the company says in the External and the other five Internal Logics, then identify those that get in the way (are not aligned).
4. In your own mind, determine if there is any chance of changing the structural elements that are not aligned; if there is none, identify possibilities for creating alternative structures or working around the structure.
5. Identify where you fit into the organizational structure and whether it helps you accomplish your department's mission.
6. In your own mind, determine if there is any chance of changing where your department sits in the organizational structure; if there is none, identify possibilities for creating alternative structures (e.g., alliances with other training/HR/OD organizations in the company) or for working around the structure.

Information Systems

 Information systems, in our context, consists of more than just computers. They are made up of all the processes and tools for gathering, storing, and disseminating knowledge within an organization. They include three areas we will discuss in detail (see Table 9.3):

- Match of technology to needs
- System usability
- Knowledge management and access

Why Information Systems Are Important to You and the Organization

The information systems (ISs) of an organization **_are_** important to you because you cannot do your job without information. We have spent the entire book telling you to gather information about each of the External and Internal Logics of your organization. If you cannot get it, you cannot do your job. Today, that information resides in computers, which use software. Somehow that software (a) has data or information input into it, (b) processes the information in some way(s), and (c) produces various outputs. So how the information technology systems are chosen, programmed, and controlled is important to you. Also important to you are what information is stored in the system, how it is decided what information to store, and how the information is gathered and input. Finally, it is important what information you and your department can access.

What Information Systems Are

Information systems are more than just the type of computer system your organization has. For example, we would bet that most of you work on large or

TABLE 9.3 INFORMATION SYSTEMS

	Possibilities	Examples
Information systems	**ASK: What are 5 to 7 key decisions most people in your organization have to make every day? How do they get the information they need to make those decisions?**	
	Match: Do the hardware, software, and processes involved in the company's information systems match and support the strategies and processes of the External Logic and the other five Internal Logics?	To enable Wal-Mart's just-in-time (JIT) inventory strategy, the IT system provides everyone in the company and all suppliers up-to-the-second inventory data for every stock keeping unit (SKU) in every store.
	System usability: Are the user interface design, online help design, and embedded training and documentation clear enough that everyone from the VP to the sales clerk can find anything they need without training or calling the IT help desk?	Why is the company intranet so hard to use, when the Amazon.com or eBay.com is so easy to use? What would you think if eBay required four hours of training before you put an item up for sale?
	Knowledge management: Does the organization capture and manage the knowledge of workers in knowledge management systems (KMS) in the context of its culture? Is information input, organized, and retrieved, and is the use of the KMS incentivized?	Accenture has a well publicized KMS through which any consultant can input a question about a client situation, find past similar situations, and receive current advice within 12 hours.

medium-sized computer systems, using Microsoft and/or SUN software, that you run some version of Windows, and that your organization has either PeopleSoft or SAP, as well as special applications that relate to your business. The focus of Structural Logic is on three questions:

- *Match*: The hardware, software, and processes involved in the company's information systems should match and support the strategies and processes of the External Logic and the other five Internal Logics. We will address this in more detail in the issues section.
- *System usability*: Is there anyone reading this book who has not either had to try to figure out how to use a new system application or been called on to write the training for a hard-to-use system? Is there anyone reading this book who has not wondered, "Why didn't they just ask me when they designed this system? I could have told them a lot about user interface design, and online help design, and embedded training." Speaking from our own personal experience (the authors and many of our friends have made considerable consulting income from designing training for hard-to-use and poorly documented information systems), the user interface and documentation for most information systems continue to be a problem for users. We will address this more in the issues section.
- *Knowledge management*: Many authors (Stewart, 1999; Svieby, 1997 especially) argue that the biggest asset of an organization is one that does not show up on the balance sheet: its intellectual capital. And therefore the organization needs to capture and manage the knowledge of workers in knowledge management systems (KMSs).

Based on the work of Nonaka and Takeuchi (1995), they argue the following points:

- The real value of an organization is in its intellectual capital.
- Intellectual capital is in two categories:
  — Patents, copyrights, and other formal legally protected inventions
  — The knowledge of its workers
- The knowledge of the workers is in two categories:
  — *Explicit*: The knowledge people know they know and probably have written down somewhere
  — *Tacit/implicit*: The knowledge people (especially experts) have in their brains, apply to their jobs, but don't consciously realize they know

- The major task of an organization is to capture and organize and make available to the whole organization the explicit and implicit knowledge of its workers.

1. The first step in the process (after organizing a group to do so) is to try to make the tacit/implicit knowledge explicit, using a process called cognitive task analysis (Note: If you are in HPT or training, cognitive task analysis is an important skill for you to possess.)
2. The second step is to capture the now explicit knowledge.
3. The third step is organize the knowledge in a useful way for easy retrieval by other workers.
4. The fourth step (sometimes combined with the third) is to put information into an information technology system.
5. The fifth step is make all the information in the KMS available to all workers.
6. The sixth step is to get users to use the knowledge management system

Issues with Information Systems

Cart Before the Horse. Just about everyone has a personal story about how the software available to them on their work computer does not allow them to do their job effectively. From wanting an Apple computer with superior graphics and film editing software (and having an old Windows machine without either), to wanting a Windows-based computer to run the latest version of SPSS for statistical analysis, all of us have experienced the mismatch between the software/hardware we have and the job we have to do.

The same issue can arise at the organization level. Just as we said with organizational structure and with information systems, form should follow function. The information systems the organization implements ought to be selected based on the other External and Internal Logics we have discussed, including organizational structure. It is impossible to implement the Strategy, Customer, Product, Process, and Structural logics, as well as certainly the measures, without a set of information systems that match those logics—or without systems that capture and provide the information required for those logics to function effectively. Yet time and again, we see organizations pick a software package (Peoplesoft is a common one, but there are many others, such as Aptify for Medical Applications), discover that the software does not support its current processes, and have to start redesigning processes, core competencies, structures, and other things to match the way the software functions. Clearly we are flogging a dead horse because most of your organizations have already bought and implemented an enterprise-wide information system, but we feel we should identify the issue of working backward.

Unusable System Interfaces/Documentation. *Caveat*: Poorly designed interfaces and documentation are *not* the fault of an evil cabal of IS professionals. IS people are, with a few exceptions, trained in the design of systems that perform the operations they are supposed to and in the coding languages used to write the programs. They are not trained in user interface design, online help design, or documentation writing. And since they wrote the systems, they understand how the systems work, so IS professionals are never confused by the interface, nor do they need to consult the help or documentation. So the question becomes, "What causes the plethora of poorly designed interfaces, help and documentation?" The most obvious answer is that IS and the end user client did not bring us into the project early enough to provide input on these matters, which are areas of expertise for many of us. The next question is, "Why not?" Here are some possible reasons we have run across:

- They do not know we exist.
- They do not like us.
- They do not recognize our level of expertise.
- They do not want another organizational unit muddying the waters.
- They are afraid we will add time and cost to the project.
- We do not have the clout to have a seat at the table (as discussed under Organizational Structure).
- We have not demonstrated our expertise in front-end help and interface design.
- We enable their behavior by always just saying "OK" when we get the fix-it-with-training request after the system is designed.

Some or all of these issues may be at play in your organization. Finding out which ones is crucial if you want to change the status quo and help provide usable information systems for users.

Knowledge Management Implementation. There are issues in several of the KMS development steps.

- *The second step*: Capturing the now explicit knowledge
  —The problem is that, for workers, there is little incentive and actually a nonincentive for giving up their knowledge to the system. It makes them dispensable to the organization.

—The solution is organizational incentives for giving up the knowledge, combined with job security.

- *The third step*: Organizing the knowledge
  —The problem is how best to organize the knowledge so that people can easily input new knowledge and easily retrieve knowledge when they need it.
  —Some people specialize in the design of knowledge management systems who know different ways to do this.
- *The fourth step*: Put information into a KMS that is available to all workers
  —This step is key because we are talking about information systems in this section of the book. It is crucial that the software system selected be one that is designed for knowledge management, be accessible to all to workers, and be easy to use for both inputting new knowledge in the appropriate place and for retrieving requested knowledge that matches the request and solves the problem of the requester.
- *The fifth step*: Making the KMS available to all workers
  —As highlighted in Table 9.3, in many organizations, the control of information is considered important: "Knowledge is power." This is opposite of the philosophy of intellectual capital and KMS, but it is still the norm in many organizations. Some company intranets, for example, do not even allow employees to see the company's Form 10K that we mentioned as a key data source in the first section of this book. Some organizations argue that they have good reasons for limiting access to some information (e.g., the loss of some key R&D data to industrial espionage in, say, the pharmaceutical industry could cost a company its competitive advantage and billions of dollars); indeed, a 2009 movie, *Duplicity*, starring Julia Roberts and Clive Owen, is about just such an occurrence.
  —The solution for each company is to find the delicate balancing point between appropriate access and security.
- *The sixth step*: Getting users to use the knowledge management system
  —Although we have discussed the issues for those inputting knowledge, other issues affect those who use the system to retrieve information. In addition to the obvious search strategy skills needed to get the information, there is a bigger issue: the cultural issue of being on record as asking for help. Many organizations punish people, either formally at performance review time, or informally by labeling the requester as the department dummy, the person who "doesn't know something and has to ask for help or information."
  —The solution to this problem is twofold. First, create a corporate culture (back in Strategy Logic, and coming soon in this chapter under Learning

and Innovation) that says it is OK to ask other people or systems for best practices or for problem-solving tips. Second, just as incentives were provided for putting information into the system, provide incentives for using the system to get information. Accenture is an example of a company that has a strong culture and incentive that support the use of the knowledge management system.

What You Should Do

You should take seven actions for this element of Structural Logic:

1. Find out who in your organization makes the decisions about which information technology systems (hardware and software) to purchase.
2. Find out the process the decision maker uses in making that decision.
3. Find out the organizational process for developing/purchasing new software systems. Who is involved at the kickoff meetings? What is the development process? How are timelines and budget developed?
4. Find out what the involvement of the training department in the development of software systems has been. When were they brought in? What role did they play? What was the attitude of the IS department and the clients to training?
5. Find out what your organization's knowledge strategy is: what knowledge has been collected, what KMS it is stored in, who has access to the knowledge in it, what the cultural and incentive supports are for participating.
6. Tabulate the answers to questions 1–5.
   a. Compare to the Strategy, Process, and other Internal Logic elements.
   b. Assess in terms of the continued well-being of your department.
7. Propose, but do not share with anyone yet, strategies for addressing the issues identified in item 6.

Human Resource Management

The *Handbook of Human Resource Management* defines HRM as:

the science and practice that deals with the nature of the employment relationship and all the decisions, actions, and issues that relate to that relationship. In practice, it involves an organization's acquisition, development, and utilization of employees, as well as the employees' relation to an organization and its performance." (Ferris, Rosen, and Barnum, 1995, pp. 2–3).

The U.S. Department of Labor's *Dictionary of Occupational Titles* says HRM:

[p]rovides the establishment with personnel assistance in identifying, evaluating, and resolving human relations and work performance problems within the establishment to facilitate communication and improve employee human relations skills and work performance. (1991, sec. 166.267.046. p. 111)

[p]lans and carries out policies relating to all phases of personnel activity; recruits, interviews, and selects employees; plans and conducts new hire orientation to foster positive attitude toward company goals; keeps records of insurance, pension plans, and personnel transactions; investigates accidents; conducts wage survey; prepares budget; meets to resolve grievances. . . . (pp. 108–109)

Why Human Resource Management Is Important to You and the Organization

This element of Structural Logic is probably the most important element in the whole book for you because it is where most people in the fields reading this book are housed in organizations. So understanding how your own organization works and is seen through organizational intelligence is critical to both your continued effectiveness and employment. As promised at the beginning of the chapter, there'll be no repeats of what you already know; we will leave this right here, assuming you already know its importance. See Table 9.4.

What Human Resource Management Is

Also in the spirit of that promise, all we will present here is a list of functions for the HRM element of Structural Logic. There is no consistent list of HR functions; each book slices and dices the tasks in different ways. We will present two as ways to review what you already know and to refer you to resources in case you do not already know.

The HR professional society, Society for Human Resource Management (SHRM, 2009), divides the various areas of HR as follows:

- Benefits
- Business leadership
- Compensation
- Consulting
- Diversity
- Employee relations
- Ethics and sustainability

TABLE 9.4. HUMAN RESOURCE MANAGEMENT

	Possibilities		Examples
Human resource management	**ASK: How do does the organization manage and support its people?**		
	The areas of HR according to SHRM:		**What is the firm actually doing?**
	Benefits	Ethics and sustainability	Recruiting, hiring, training, providing benefits to, firing, outplacing employees
	Business leadership	Global HR	
	Compensation	Labor relations	
	Consulting	Organizational and employee development	
	Diversity	Safety and security	
	Employee relations	Staffing management	

- Global HR
- Labor relations
- Organizational and employee development
- Safety and security
- Staffing management (www.shrm.org, retrieved March 19, 2009)

Many HR texts provide comprehensive listings of HR functions (DeCenzo and Robbins, 2006; DeNesi and Griffin, 2007; Dessler, 2007; Ivancevich, 2009; Mathis and Jackson, 2008). We have synthesized and chunked the HR functions described in the following list. Although the list represents the content of the texts cited, the actual wording and chunking in the following list are ours.

- Strategic HR management
  —HR policies
  —International HR
  —Risk management (safety and security)
  —Planning for disaster recovery
  —Legal compliance in all HR functions
  —Diversity and affirmative action
- Staffing, recruitment, and placement
  —Job analysis

  —Job description
  —Recruiting
  —Employee interviewing, testing, and measurement
  —Evaluating and selecting candidates
  —Hiring
  —Personnel placement
- Employee development
  —Orientation
  —Acculturating
  —Training
  —Performance appraisal and management
  —Career management
  —Job rotation and placement
- Compensation and incentives
  —Salaries/pay plans
  —Incentives and pay for performance
  —Benefits
- Managing employee relations
  —Employee rights
  —Union/management relations
  —Downsizing
  —Firing

Issues in Human Resource Management

Strategic Partnering Problems. It is frequently the case in organizational structures (see the discussion at the beginning of this chapter) that HRM is considered a necessary evil in an organization and that most people consider the role of HR to be simply hiring, firing, Equal Employment Opportunity Commission compliance, benefits, and related activities. It is considered to be just a staff function, an unnecessary cost added to SG&A, and a prime candidate for outsourcing to one of the large HR consulting firms. In such a view, HRM is not considered a true strategic partner that deserves a seat at the table as important decisions about the other External and Internal Logics are made. And that omission includes all components of HR, including OD and training.

This problem is the one that led us to write this book: to help HRM professionals see their function (and the rest of the organization) the way other specialized groups, such as marketing and IT see their own functions. The goal is to help HRM professionals explain the strategic importance we play in the organization, in terms that the decision makers at the top of the organization understand and respect.

Navel Gazing. We (the authors have worked in HR functions, so we can truly say *we*) contribute to this problem in three ways.

First, we speak a foreign language (actually at least four different foreign languages: HR-ese, Training-ese, OD-ese, and HPT-ese). So we can barely understand our colleagues, and the rest of the organization cannot understand us at all. We discussed this issue at the beginning of the book and explained why we have to learn to speak Business-ese like everyone else in the organization and keep our secret languages to ourselves.

Second, we suffer from what a colleague calls the Rodney Dangerfield Syndrome (we "get no respect, no respect at all"—for those under the age of 60). And sometimes we make the mistake of overcompensating and overstating the importance of what we do, as if we were the center of the organization. One of the authors worked at now defunct oil company at which, during an executive meeting, the VP of human resources reported a $500 million ROI [return on investment] for training; the CEO stopped him and asked, "Since our profit last year was $1 billion, does that mean if we did twice as much training, and left the oil business, we would end up with the same profit?" Needless to say, no one listened to HR for years following that episode.

Third and most important, we think only (or at least first and foremost) about our place in the Structural Logic portion of the organization. Sometimes we don't even understand our own Structural Logic piece of the organization (OD versus training versus HPT: how we calculate our ROI, how many training organizations there are, and so on). And if we do understand that, we do not make the attempt to understand how our Structural Logic relates to that of the rest of the organization. If you've made it this far in this book, you have taken the steps necessary to avoid this issue.

What You Should Do

You should take six actions for this element of Structural Logic:

1. Find out how your HRM function is organized.
   a. Who does each of the HR functions?
   b. Specifically who does:
      — Organizational improvement?
      — Process improvement?
      — Organizational development?
      — Training/instructional development?
      — Human performance technology?
2. Assess and choose a word to describe the tone of the relationship among the various organizational groups that perform this function: cooperative, competitive, don't know others exist, or some such term.

3. In your mind, think of a strategy that might improve the working relationship among all these groups.
4. Choose a word to describe the tone of the relationship between the HRM groups and the rest of the organization (and the rest of the logics): equal partner, stepchild, OD who?
5. In your mind, think of a strategy that can improve how the other logics and organizational units perceive HRM and its value-added contribution to the company.
6. Keep these strategies in your mind, but do not share them yet. If no one but you is ready, this will be a career-limiting move.

Learning and Innovation

 This is an element of Structural Logic in which our view differs from that of Kaplan and Norton (1996). Their focus is on individual learning. Ours is much wider, focusing on performance improvement at the individual and team levels, job design, and learning organizations, drawing on the fields of HPT, organizational psychology, and OD, in addition to Training. See Table 9.5.

As promised at the beginning of this chapter, we are not going to repeat all that those three fields, or even just some of the authors in them, have to say. Instead we will outline the salient ideas of key authors and expand on a limited set of authors whose ideas are frequently overlooked. For some readers this will be a review of what they already know, conveniently collected, packaged, and framed in a new way; for others, this can serve as advance organizer to future reading.

The learning and innovation element is divided into the following subelements:

- Individual and team performance improvement
  — Training
  — HPT performance improvement factors
- Organizational learning
  — HPT and OD job design
  — Learning organizations á la Senge
  — Single-loop, double-loop, and deutero organizational learning

Individual and Team Performance Improvement

This subelement focuses on how to improve the performance of groups of employees who do the work of the six Internal Logics.

TABLE 9.5 LEARNING AND INNOVATION

	Possibilities	Examples
Learning and innovation	**ASK: How does the organization improve its performance (what it knows and what it can do)?**	
	Individual and team performance improvement Training HPT performance improvement factors	Some organizations are moving from separate training, HPT, and OD departments to integrated departments that focus on providing internal clients with total solutions to improve performance: goals and incentives, organization and task design, workplace layout and equipment, references, and JIT tutorials, etc.
	Organizational learning HPT and OD job design Learning organizations (Senge) Single-loop, double-loop, and deutero organizational learning	An organization whose culture is to learn from mistakes and to change premises to ensure the same or similar mistakes will not happen again **A counterexample:** An organization that keeps repeating past mistakes and energetically defending them

Training. Traditionally, the approach to improve individual, and group, performance has been to send people to training. The rationale behind this strategy is that the way to improve performance is teach people the skills and knowledge they need to do their jobs.

To fulfill this mission, from about 1900 to March 2009, training has added to its teacher/instructor-led, classroom-based delivery mode, by incorporating (in approximately the following sequence) radio, film, filmstrip, and slides, learning labs, programmed instruction, computer-assisted instruction (round one, 1980s), simulation and games (round one, 1970s–1980s), e-learning and Web-based learning, online games and Second Life, podcasts, blogs and wikis, and Tweets (Silber, personal experience, 1965–2009). Training has become more systematic with the mid-1960s advent (yes, it's that old) of instructional design and development. Training has moved from a behaviorist to a cognitivist to, in some situations, a constructivist philosophy. It has moved from focusing on learning facts and operations to a focus on higher-order problem solving.

Performance Technology. The basic notion of HPT (human performance technology, a.k.a. HPI, or human performance improvement) is simple but profound. Poor worker performance is caused by a lack of skill and knowledge—which training is designed to fix—only a small percentage of the time (one hears the numbers 10 to 20 percent bandied about). In fact, as Gilbert pointed out in both his Performance and Behavior Engineering Models in *Human Competence* (1978), many other factors inside the worker, outside the worker, and within the organization as a whole impact human performance. The factors in the Behavior Engineering Model are in the following list form rather than in his matrix form (Gilbert, 1978, p. 88):

- Environment
  —Information
  —Clear expectations of desired performance
    —Accurate feedback about performance
    —Information about consequences of nonperformance
    —Guides and information needed to perform
  —Instrumentation
    —Appropriate and well designed workspace, furnishings, tools, and equipment
  —Motivation
    —Adequate and appropriate incentives for good performance
    —Removal of disincentives for good performance
    —Negative consequences for poor or nonperformance
- Internal Level
  —Motivation
    —Match between people's motives to work and the requirements of jobs
  —Capacity
    —Scheduling of work to match individuals' peak capacity
    —Addressing lack of physical capacity with prostheses, etc.
    —Selecting appropriate people for the job
  —Knowledge
  —Training

Gilbert later expanded on this original list in an article for the American Society for Training and Development, developing a list of what he called PROBE questions (Gilbert, 1982, cited in Dean and Ripley, 1997) that is more detailed and that more closely resembles the later list of Rummler.

Rummler (2007, p. 25; also in Rummler and Brache, 1990, p. 71) describes the factors that affect the "human performance system" in a slightly different way, from a systems perspective. They are presented in the following list, rather than in his flowchart format:

- A. Performance Specifications
  — Do performance standards exist?
  — Do performers know the desired output and the performance standards?
  — Do performers consider the standards attainable?
- B. Task Support
  — Can performers easily recognize the input requiring action?
  — Can the task be done without interference from other tasks?
  — Are job procedures and workflow logical?
  — Are adequate resources available for performance: time, tools, staff, information?
- C. Consequences
  — Are consequences aligned to support desired performance?
  — Are consequences meaningful from the performer's viewpoint?
  — Are consequences timely"
- D. Feedback
  — Do learners receive information about their performance?
  — Is the information they receive:
    — Timely?
    — Relevant?
    — Accurate?
    — Constructive?
    — Easy to understand?
    — Specific?
- E. Knowledge/Skill
  — Do performers have the necessary skills and knowledge to perform?
  — Do performers know why the desired performance is important?
- F. Individual Capacity
  — Are performers physically, mentally, and emotionally able to perform?"

The field of HPT therefore suggests that interventions to improve performance go beyond training and include elements to address each of the preceding elements that are missing during an analysis of the problem. This more holistic and systemic approach to solving individual and team performance problems is being adopted by a growing number of practitioners and training departments.

Organizational Learning

Organizational learning is the term used to refer to learning that occurs above the individual and team level. It suggests that organizations as entities can also learn and in fact must learn in order to survive.

HPT and OD Job Design

Both the fields of OD and HPT say that, independent of the preceding lists of performance factors that affect how people perform a *task*, how the organization designs the *whole* job in the first place is crucial.

Rummler's HPT focus in job design is on two factors (1990, pp. 160–161):

- The job design ("job model") must match organization design factors that come first:
  — Organization level relationship map
  — Process map
  — Process role/responsibility matrix
  — Function model
  — Function role/responsibility matrix
- The contents of the "job model"
  — Outputs
  — Critical dimensions
  — Measures
  — Goals

OD's focus in job design is on the people satisfaction side of the job. They say that well designed jobs should have the following characteristics:

- Congruence:
  — With the design of the overall organization and work groups within which the job falls
  — With the characteristics of the people who are likely to perform the job and get some satisfaction from doing it well
- Satisfaction:
  — Skill variety
  — Task identity (job completes the whole piece of work)
  — Task significance
  — Autonomy
  — Feedback

In addition, they suggest that, whenever possible, work should be organized so that it is performed by teams rather than by individuals to better meet these criteria (Cummings and Worley, 2009, pp. 114–115).

Learning Organizations á la Senge

According to Peter Senge, learning organizations are:

> organizations where people continually expand their capacity to create the results they truly desire, where new and expansive patterns of thinking are nurtured, where collective aspiration is set free, and where people are continually learning to see the whole together. (1990, p. 3)

His contention is that, in fact, organizations must become learning organizations or they will not survive. He and his colleagues have written extensively on characteristics of learning organizations. They have identified five key characteristics that allow for a company to be a learning organization:

- *Systems thinking*: A framework for seeing patterns and interrelationships rather than just part
- *Personal mastery*: Consisting of three parts:
  — Personal vision: As explained in Strategy logic, this is definite picture of what the future will look like
  — Creative tension: A gap between the vision and the current state that we are willing to work to close
  — Commitment to truth: A willingness to look beyond all the excuses we have for why we cannot do things and to face the truth about ourselves
- *Mental models*: An organized structure of how we see and act in the world, along with the willingness to test it and change it based on new data
- *Building shared vision*: The entire organization comes together to build a real vision that is based on the shared ideas of everyone in the organization
- *Team learning*: A view of teams as more than just having people work together, instead involving trust, mutual assistance, commitment, and shared vision

Single-Loop, Double-Loop, and Deutero Organizational Learning

Some of the most profound and basic ideas of organizational learning come from the work of Argyris and Schon (on whose academic and theoretical discussions much OD work is based), who identified three types of organizational learning.

They begin with the notion that every organization has what they call an "instrumental theory in use," which is what one gets when one looks at the organization's norms for "corporate performance . . . , strategies for achieving values . . . , and assumptions that bind strategies and values together" (1996, p. 14). This theory-in-use is like the combination of all the elements of the Economic and Strategy Logics.

They note that one problem with theories-in-use is that they frequently remain tacit/implicit (just as in our discussion of tacit/implicit knowledge in the Knowledge Management section). This means that they continue to operate unseen, unquestioned, and unchanged.

Single-Loop Learning. The first type of organizational learning is called single-loop (a term and distinction they acknowledge borrowing from Ross Ashby [Argyris and Schon, 1996, p. 21f]. This occurs when we face an organizational problem (for example, defects in a product), take corrective actions to fix that problem (for example, change the inputs and process and inspection), and stop. We do nothing to question the underlying organizational theory-in-use—we leave it implicit—to see if something more fundamental led to the problem in the first place (e.g., the corporate values are "get it done, at any quality, any way you need to, but get it done"). This type of learning can produce incremental improvements in organizations, but not underlying or systemic ones. The same problem can reoccur, or new problems in related areas can occur. Most organizations operate using single-loop learning. The U.S. auto industry is a prime example of organizations that think in this way.

Double-Loop Learning. Double-loop learning occurs when, faced with a problem, the organization not only immediately fixes the problem (the first loop) but then goes to the second loop and questions the underlying theory-in-use. It makes the theory-in-use explicit and asks what strategies, values, and/or assumptions allowed this problem to occur and what changes in the theory are necessary to become a transformed organization in which this kind of problem will never occur again. This type of learning transforms the organization, radically altering its assumptions, values, and strategies, leading to systemic changes throughout the organization. The Japanese auto industry and Apple Computer are examples of companies that use double-loop learning. The culture change that many organizations are trying to create with pronouncements and seminars actually require double-loop learning.

Deuterolearning. Finally, Argyris and Schon (1996, p. 29) borrow another term, *deuterolearning* (from Gregory Bateson), and apply it to organizations instead of individuals. It is what we know as learning to learn or metacognition in individual learning theory. Applied to the organization as a whole, this type of learning refers to the organization's ability to continually question and improve its single- and double-loop learning. Organizations that can do deuterolearning are truly learning organizations because they know how to find out and fix what is wrong now, how to change fundamental assumptions about the organization, and how to keep monitoring and improving those learning processes.

Issue in Learning and Innovation: Tower of Babel

Readers of this book who work in this logic come from many different disciplines. Each discipline has its own professional association, special language, unique theories, and certainty that it alone has the correct theory-in-use to the exclusion of every other discipline. This leads to people in HR, OD, HPT, and training not working in cooperation to execute Structural Logic to support the other logics. There is frequently competition for work instead of cooperation. There is very little sense of "let's work together on this" but rather turf wars about who gets to work with which client on which kind of problem. People rarely acknowledge that each discipline is (a) not really *that* different and (b) can bring a valuable perspective/theory/tool to bear on any organizational problem. Certainly, our use of different languages (terms, acronyms, models, principles, and beliefs) makes it difficult to discuss issues and sometimes even to know whether we are all in agreement or not. The overarching problem is what Senge calls our mental models: that we are right and therefore every other field must be wrong and that our field is really so different from every other.

The authors believe it is time for practitioners in Structural Logic to do some introspective double-loop learning—that is, question our own underlying assumptions, values, and strategies—and some deuterolearning—that is, asking ourselves how we learn about our field and the fields of others and how we can keep learning more about all the fields together.

What You Should Do

You should take six actions for this element of Structural Logic:

1. For individual learning, how does your organization (the company as a whole, not your departmental organization) address training and other performance improvement solutions?
   a. Who does those functions?
   b. How many departments are there?
   c. Where in the organization are they located?
   d. How do they work with each other?

e. How do they measure results?

f. How successful are they?

2. For organizational learning, how does your organization (the company as a whole, not your departmental organization) address job design and organizational learning?

a. Who does those functions?

b. How many departments are there?

c. Where in the organization are they located?

d. How do they work with each other?

e. How do they measure results?

f. How successful are they?

3. How do you personally and your department currently fit into this organizational mental model of how learning and innovation are done?

4. In your estimation, in what areas do learning and innovation currently support the rest of the organizational logics, and in what areas does it need improvement?

5. Identify your vision for how you believe you could and should fit into helping your organization do learning and innovation.

6. Do not share your findings from questions 4 and 5 with anyone yet; it could a career limiting move.

Measures for Structural Logic

As with Strategy Logic, measuring the results of Structural Logic are not as clear-cut as measuring the number and type of defects in the Product and Process Logics. But in Structural Logic there are more clear-cut measures than we encountered in the Strategy Logic.

There are two types of measures to use in measuring Structural Logic:

1. How many of the criteria does it meet? ("How good is our knowledge management system?")

   Meets *all* the criteria

   Meets *most* of the criteria

   Meets *none or few* of the criteria

2. How many did we do? ("How many projects did we do? How many problems did we solve?) This criterion can be expressed as a number or a percentage. ("In what percentage of our projects were we successful?")

The criteria for the measures for each element of Strategy Logic are presented in Table 9.6.

TABLE 9.6 MEASURES FOR STRUCTURAL LOGIC

Measures	ASK: How well does each element of Structural Logic meet these criteria?

	Rate each: all, most, few, or none
	
	1. Organization structure:
	  In alignment with other logics?
	  Meets the criteria for the organizational structure type chosen?
	
	2. Information systems:
	  Does technology match needs?
	  Does technology work?
	  Quality (variance [amount; percentage]; defects [number; percentage]; rework [number; percentage; time]; unusable products [number; percentage])
	  Cycle time (absolute; versus last product, versus competition; versus customer requirements)
	  Process time (absolute; versus last product, versus competition; versus customer requirements)
	  Value added activities (percentage)
	  Coordination (business process match [number; percentage; timeliness; accuracy])
	  Innovative processes used (percentage rapid prototyping, etc.)
	  Cost (absolute; versus last system; versus competition; versus customer requirements)
	
	2. Information systems (Continued):
	  Does system meet usability criteria?
	  Does KMS meet criteria for:
	    Making tacit/implicit knowledge explicit?
	    Capturing the knowledge?
	    Organizing the knowledge in a useful way?
	    Putting the information into an IT system?
	    Making all information in the KMS available to all?
	    Getting users to use the KMS?
	  Knowledge strategy (developed? consistent with other logics? satisfaction?)
	  Knowledge availability [to who needs it (percentage; number); when needed (process time; cycle time)]
	  Knowledge usability [relevance (percentage; amount; accuracy (percentage; amount)]
	  Accurate decisions made (number; percentage)
	
	3. HR management:
	  How many of the HRM functions are performed in the organization?
	  How well do the HRM functions support the other logics?

(Continued)

TABLE 9.6. MEASURES FOR STRUCTURAL LOGIC (*Continued*)

Measures	ASK: How well does each element of Structural Logic meet these criteria?
	4. Learning and innovation:
	Individual and team performance improvement (training and HPT factors)
	What percentage of individual/team performance improvement projects meet the client goals and actually solve the performance problem?
	On what percentage of the individual/team performance improvement projects do you measure business results?
	How many of the HPT performance improvement factors do you look at when solving individual/team performance improvement problems?
	Organizational learning:
	What percentage of job designs meet the Rummler criteria for job design?
	What percentage of job designs meet the OD criteria for job design?
	What percentage of the criteria for a learning organization does the organization meet?
	On what percentage of organizational problems does the organization do single-loop learning?
	On what percentage of organizational problems does the organization do double-loop learning?
	On what percentage of organizational problems do you do deuterolearning?

Sample Worksheets for Structural Logic

In Chapter 2, we introduced the Internal Scan Worksheet. Here it is in Table 9.7 with all the columns through Structural Logic filled out for one of our clients. It is brief: just a few words summarizing each of the elements. It is particularly important that you don't collect too much detail here. Because you know so much about (and spend so much time in) this logic, it is easy to get sucked in. Remember that this entire book is about building a robust understanding of the rest of the organization and about becoming conversant with the other six logics. Save your time and energy for that task, and do a light, high-level pass at this one. The same is true for the following measures worksheet, Table 9.8.

Structural Logic Job Aid

This job aid (Table 9.9) summarizes Structural Logic with graphics, definitions, questions to be answered, and examples. Use it when you are trying to identify the Structural Logic for your own (or your client's) organization.

Your Turn

Use the Structural Logic Job Aid and the Internal Scan Worksheet to identify the Structural Logic and measures operating in your organization or your client's. Here are some sources of information:

- Organization's Web site
- Annual report
- 10-K report
- Hoover's or Mergent (Most public libraries have a subscription.)
- Talk to members of the organization, particularly line managers, other HR people, IT, legal, and accounting.
- Any other sources suggested in this chapter

If you want a reproducible version of either worksheet, they are on the Web site at www.Pfeiffer.com/go/kennethsilber. Copy it to your desktop and use it. In the case of Structural Logic, we recommend you do not expand the level of detail, unless Structural Logic or some part of it is new to you.

TABLE 9.7. SAMPLE INTERNAL SCAN FOR CREDIT CARD DIVISION OF A BANK

Assess and fill in the logic the business appears to be using.

ECONOMIC LOGIC	STRATEGY LOGIC	CUSTOMER LOGIC	PRODUCT LOGIC	PROCESS LOGIC	STRUCTURAL LOGIC
Cost structure • Variable: Cost of funds and delinquencies • To manage: Self-fund, control delinquencies **Financial focus** • Cost of goods sold **Profit Source** • Channel: Direct versus oil company cards versus Sears, etc.	**Mission and vision** • Provide profitable credit services to higher risk market **Initiatives/tactics** • Seek new customer-facing partners • Manage delinquencies tightly **Culture** • Do it now, ask forgiveness later **Core competency** • Collections **Growth strategy** • Alliances: Oil company, large retailer credit • Purchase: Other banks' delinquent portfolios **Pricing strategy** • High end of middle	**Market strategy** • Segment by economic groups • Target: $20K–$45K/ year • Low white-collar, high blue-collar • Some "high risk" credit **Customer needs satisfaction** • Niche: Customer credit card **Relationship/ transaction strategy** • High volume of transactions key to income (fee-based)	**Differentiation** • Focus on needs of target group • Familiarity: Piggyback on oil company cards • Really good at controlling delinquencies (accept high-risk customers) **Image** • Familiar, reliable, "home folks"	**R&D/ product development** • Adapt others' innovations • Enhance existing products and services **Production/ logistics** • Sales • Credit granting • Processing transactions and billing • Collections • (Well-integrated) **Postsale** • Active–reactive exception handling: Disputes, credit problems	**Structure** • Functional **Information systems (ISs)** • Good IS match to operational needs, usability OK • No KMS **HR systems** • Basic, keeps up with competition's • Revolving door recruiting • Good comp package **Learning and innovation:** • Learning is reactive: Technical, regulatory, and competitive requirements only. • No HPT, no OD • Single-loop learning

• Do the logics in the six columns support each other or are they contradictory?
• If they are contradictory, does this have some bearing on the problem you were asked to solve?
• How can you test your assessment that these are the business logic(s) the company is using?
• Now review the logic in the light of your environmental scan. Do the six logics seem to be consistent with external realities?

Reprinted with permission of Lynn Kearny, 2009.

TABLE 9.8. SAMPLE MEASURES WORKSHEET FOR CREDIT CARD DIVISION OF A BANK

Logic	Measures	Target	Current	Gap	Performance Problems	Interventions	Measured Results
Economic							
Strategy							
Customer							
Product							
Process							
Structural	Structure	Meet all criteria for structure type	Meet only 50% of criteria for structure type	50% of criteria			
	System	Knowledge captured and stored	0% knowledge captured and stored	100% knowledge			
	HR management functions aligned	100% functions aligned	50 % functions aligned (hiring, promotion not)	50% functions			
	Performance improvement	HPT/OD solve 90% of problems	Training alone solves 30% of problems (only regulatory)	60% problems			
	Organizational learning	Meets 90% of criteria; all Type II learning	Meets 0% of criteria; all Type I learning	90% of criteria; 100% change in learning type			

- What specific measures does the organization use for each type of logic? Write them in column 2.
- What is the target for each measure? Write it in column 3.
- What is the current number for each measure? Write it in column 4.
- What is the gap between target and current number for each measure? Write it in column 5.
- Those measures with the greatest, and most critical, gaps are the focus of the Performance Problem Analysis and Intervention Selection that take place next in the Performance Improvement process.

TABLE 9.9. SUMMARY JOB AID—STRUCTURAL LOGIC

The organization's infrastructure: How it organizes itself to accomplish its work

	Possibilities	Examples
Organizational structure 	ASK: What does your organization chart look like? Why is it structured this way?	
	Traditional	
	Functional	VP and line organizations for marketing, R&D, manufacturing, HR, etc.
	Divisional	Resources needed to produce each product are organized under product's VP.
	Modern	
	Matrix	Across top of matrix are functions (R&D, HR, etc.), each headed by a VP. Down the side are products/services (product A, B, C, etc.), each headed by a coordinator.
	Process	Cross-skill teams are formed around each core process: e.g., R&D process or customer service process.
	Customer-centric	Customer is put at the center of organization. Work groups formed to focus on each customer group.
	Network	Has administrative hub to coordinate work of various internal and external organizations that perform different competencies for the whole.

TABLE 9.9. SUMMARY JOB AID—STRUCTURAL LOGIC (Continued)

Information systems	**ASK: What are 5 to 7 key decisions most people in your organization have to make every day? How do they get the information they need to make those decisions?**
	Match: Do the hardware, software, and processes involved in the company's information systems match and support the strategies and processes of the External Logic and the other five Internal Logics?
	To enable Wal-Mart's just-in-time (JIT) inventory strategy, the IT system provides everyone in the company and all suppliers up-to-the-second inventory data for every SKU in every store.
	System usability: Are the user interface design, online help design, and embedded training and documentation clear enough that everyone from the VP to the sales clerk can find anything they need without training or calling the IT help desk?	Why is the company intranet so hard to use, when the Amazon.com or eBay is so easy to use? What would you think if e-Bay required four hours of training before you put an item up for sale?
	Knowledge management: Does the organization capture and manage the knowledge of workers in knowledge management systems (KMSs) in the context of its culture? Is information input, organized, and retrieved, and is use of the KMS incentivized?	Accenture has a well publicized KMS through which any consultant can input a question about a client situation, find past similar situations, and receive current advice within 12 hours.
Human resource management	**ASK: How do does the organization manage and support its people?**
	The areas of HR according to SHRM:	**What is the firm actually doing?**
	Benefits	Recruiting, hiring, training, providing benefits to, firing, outplacing employees
	Business leadership	
	Compensation	Ethics and sustainability
	Consulting	Global HR
	Diversity	Labor relations
	Employee relations	Organizational and employee development
		Safety and security
		Staffing management

(Continued)

TABLE 9.9. SUMMARY JOB AID—STRUCTURAL LOGIC (*Continued*)

	ASK: How does the organization improve its performance (what it knows and what it can do)?
Learning and innovation	**Individual and team performance improvement** Training HPT performance improvement factors **Organizational learning** HPT and OD job design Learning organizations (Senge) Single-loop, double-loop, and deutero organizational learning	Some organizations are moving from separate Training, HPT, and OD departments to integrated departments that focus on providing internal clients with total solutions to improve performance: goals and incentives, organization and task design, workplace layout and equipment, references and JIT tutorials, etc. An organization whose culture is to learn from mistakes and to change premises to ensure the same or similar mistakes will not happen again. **A counterexample** An organization that keeps repeating past mistakes and energetically defending them.

TABLE 9.9. SUMMARY JOB AID—STRUCTURAL LOGIC (Continued)

Measures	ASK: How well does each element of Structural Logic meet these criteria?
	Rate each: all, most, few, or none
	1. Organization structure:
	In alignment with other logics?
	Meets the criteria for the organizational structure type chosen?
	2. Information systems:
	Does technology match needs?
	Does system meet usability criteria?
	Does KMS meet criteria for:
	Making tacit/implicit knowledge explicit?
	Capturing the knowledge?
	Organizing the knowledge in a useful way?
	Putting the information into an IT system?
	Making all information in the KMS available to all?
	Getting users to use the KMS?
	3. HR management:
	How many of the HRM functions are performed in the organization?
	How well do the HRM functions support the other logics?
	3. Learning and innovation:
	Individual and team performance improvement (training and HPT factors)
	What percentage of individual/team performance improvement projects meet the client goals and actually solve the performance problem?
	On what percentage of the individual/team performance improvement projects do you measure business results?
	How many of the HPT performance improvement factors do you look at when solving individual/team performance improvement problems?
	Organizational learning:
	What percentage of job designs meet the Rummler criteria for job design?
	What percentage of job designs meet the OD criteria for job design?
	What percentage of the criteria for a learning organization does the organization meet?
	On what percentage of organizational problems does the organization do single-loop learning?
	On what percentage of organizational problems does the organization do double-loop learning?
	On what percentage of organizational problems do you do deuterolearning?

© 2009. Reprinted with permission of Lynn Kearny.

TABLE 9.10. INTERNAL SCAN WORKSHEET

Assess and fill in the logic the business appears to be using.

ECONOMIC LOGIC	STRATEGY LOGIC	CUSTOMER LOGIC	PRODUCT LOGIC	PROCESS LOGIC	STRUCTURAL LOGIC

- Do the logics in the six columns support each other or are they contradictory?
- If they are contradictory, does this have some bearing on the problem you were asked to solve?
- How can you test your assessment that these are the business logic(s) the company is using?
- Now review the logic in the light of your environmental scan. Do the six logics seem to be consistent with external realities?

Summary

In this chapter we have given a quick helicopter view of territory that is probably already familiar to you but that is still a key part of any organization's success. Structural Logic is where most of us live and work on a daily basis. As members of the community, the authors have been a little rough in our remarks about the field's shortcomings, but it's tough love, delivered in the belief that we as HR professionals can contribute so much more if we solve some of our domestic problems. We hope it has been received in that spirit.

We have also spent some time examining parts of the HR field that are less well-known than they should be: human performance improvement and the work of Gilbert and Rummler. We strongly believe that HR, training, HPT, and OD hold many of the keys to the future for the organizations we serve. We believe that we can and should win the respect and influence to contribute on a higher level than we're usually asked to. We also believe that we all hold the keys in our own hands. Organizational intelligence was written to provide more of us with the passwords and the secret handshakes to gain access to the world of influence in our organizations.

We wish you the best, and welcome your questions, comments, and any experiences you are willing to share with us going forward.

PART THREE

CASE STUDY/RESEARCH

CHAPTER TEN

CASE STUDY

The Business Logic Model: Research at AptRentCo*

Kenneth H. Silber, PhD, CPT

Associate Professor, Educational Technology, Research and Assessment, Northern Illinois University, ksilber@niu.edu

and

Dr. X

Chief Learning Officer

AptRentCo

The Theoretical Model

The Business Logics Model has been developed over the last seven years, first by the investigator alone, and then with a coinvestigator (Silber, 1998; Silber and Kearny, 2005). It is a theoretical model that is a synthesis of the best existing

---

*This case study is based on a research study conducted by Dr. Silber. It has been disguised, with the cooperation of Dr. X, to remove any elements that might identify the company involved in any way, beyond saying it is one of the many leaders in real estate rental in the United States. All facts presented in the case study are real (if slightly altered to protect company identity); they are not fabricated; this is an actual use of the Business Logics Model. The name and format of the Business Logics Model used in the study were a prior version of that used in this book (circa 2005); thus it contains all the information that that version of the model called for. The astute reader will note that some of the categories and measures in prior versions were different from the current ones presented in this book. These changes do not lessen the value of the case study because it is an example of how the model presented in this book can be used to develop a rapid, accurate, and useful picture of an organization.

theories on organizational analysis, performance and success (Albrecht, 1994; Argyris and Schon, 1996; Charan, 2001; Kaplan and Norton, 1996; Porter, 1998; Rummler and Brache 1995; Senge, 1990; Silber, 1998; Stack, 1994). This model can be used to analyze organizations in the corporate as well as in education and government sectors (Silber and Kearny, 2005).

It contains seven constructs that define various components of organizational performance (called logics) that, according to the literature cited, are necessary for organizational function and success. Each construct contains a number of metrics on which an organization can measure its performance. The constructs, sample metrics, and data to be collected are summarized in the Table 10.1 folloeing table.

TABLE 10.1 PERFORMANCE METRICS DATA CHART

Construct	Sample Metrics	Sample Data to be Collected
External Logic	Substitutes; new entrants; technological trends	Number identified by organization; number addressed by plan
Economic Logic	Cost structure; financial focus; profit source	SG&A; COGS; EBITDA; profit per source
Strategy Logic	Mission; culture; core competencies; growth	Identified?; accuracy; aligned?; measurable?
Customer Logic	Market strategy; customer relationship strategy	Size of market share; new customers; complaints
Product Logic	Niche/broad; differentiation; image	Quality; price; knowledgeable?; novelty
Process Logic	R&D; production; logistics; postsale	Cycle time; waste; cost; coordination
Structural Logic	Structure; information technology; learning and innovation	Alignment; percentage of knowledge captured; rewards

The Research Method

The Research Questions

Based on the Business Logics Model, the study proposed to answer these questions:

- (a) what is the relationship between an organization's profile on these constructs and its performance on organizational success criteria?

- (b) what is the relationship between an organization's profile on these constructs and the success/failure of instructional design (ID) and human performance technology (HPT) solutions?

The case study research plan was based on Stake (1995) and Yin (2002). The study activities and results are as follows.

1. Revalidate the Model

For research as opposed to practical use, the model required one more round of validation by ID and HPT experts.

2. Select the Organizations

The investigator selected two corporate/educational organizations that were willing to participate in this theoretical model construct and success analysis. Finally, only AptRentCo was willing to participate

3. Collect Data

Data was collected from AptRentCo on how the organization defines itself on each construct: the metrics it uses to measure each construct and the current value of those metrics. Data about the ID and HPT solutions conducted in the organization in the last year, as well as about their success and/or failure, was also collected. The data was collected by review of documents and through interviews with Dr. X.

Data collection took place in the offices of AptRentCo, during the week of November 6–10, 2006. I sat with Dr. X and walked through each element of the model in sequence. For each element, he provided both a verbal response and documentation related to the element. He walked me through the document to ensure I understood it. I then entered the data on the form, and repeated it back for him to ensure that I had entered it correctly. Where I had not, he corrected my understanding, and I corrected the data entry. We then went on to the next element in the model.

When we finished walking through the model, we moved to talk about the training and HPT that had been successes and failures over the past year. He provided a complete verbal description of the projects, along with documentation of and his opinion about their success or failure. We addressed all the training/HPT initiatives his organization had conducted in the past year. We were occasionally interrupted by his need to conduct regular daily business, but we completed going through the entire model. I left the site with the data collection forms filled out and a six-inch stack of supporting documentation.

4. Analyze and Interpret the Data

Dr. Silber summarized the data collected using the constructs and metrics already in the model, generating a summary profile of the organization and of the ID/HPT solutions implemented in the organization.

The original intent of the analysis was to compare the organization's data profiles with those predicted by the model's constructs to identify similarities and differences on the following dimensions:

A. Presence or absence of a metric for a construct
B. Relative importance of each construct and metrics in it for the organization
C. Alignment among constructs and metrics
D. Levels of the metrics (desired and actual)
E. Congruence with HPT and management literature
F. Relationship of successful and failed HPT solutions to the Business Logics and metrics
G. What HPT solutions appeared to succeed and fail
H. What is the utility of the Business Logics Model
 I. What future research is appropriate
 J. How the model can be better applied to educational institutions

Due to participation of only one company, the data analysis had to be modified to eliminate any cross-organization comparisons. The data analysis is therefore focused on answering all the proposed questions by focusing on AptRentCo.

5. Results

The results are displayed in Tables 10.2 through 10.4 on the following pages.

6. Analysis

The data provided by AptRentCo was used to answering the analysis questions, as modified (explained in section 4) to eliminate cross-organizational comparisons and to focus on the internal workings of one organization.

A. Presence or Absence of a Metric for a Construct

It is clear, from the quantity, quality, and appropriateness of data provided for each Business Logic and metric, that AptRentCo consciously understands and addresses each of them and that it includes each of them in its planning, operational, evaluation, and publicly disseminated documents.

TABLE 10.2 CASE EXTERNAL SCAN WORKSHEET

External Factors Affecting the Business of AptRentCo

GENERAL TRENDS	KEY THREATS	THE INDUSTRY
Economic Supply- (versus demand-) driven business When interest rates go up, people can't buy, so they rent—but there is downward rent pressure. This affects the rents AptRentCo can ask. This affects the markets AptRentCo is in.		**New Entrants?** Low because AptRentCo stays in markets where supply is constrained
Demographic People with more money than time Echo boomers, 20–29		**Supplier Bargaining Power** High for operations (oil, gas, etc.) High for land and construction
Political Legal USHA REIT Laws Local rent control laws Landlord tenant laws	**KEY OPPORTUNTIES** High margin business Key protected markets 5 96% 20% of current renters are "up for grabs at renewal time," and $8 million to bottom line each 1% increase in renter retention	**Buyer Bargaining Power** High: Renters look at competitors in price band—walk away if too high High: Seasonal demand
Technological Not much construction tech change "How serve renters in a tech environ?" (e.g., providing all wired apts) Ability to use Internet to acquire renters (48% of leads) E-lease with minutes		**Threat of Substitutes** AptRentCo is a substitute itself, for people who cannot buy Condos and houses (as affected by economic logic) Movement to new town/market Other supplier's existing apartments New apartments constructed near existing AptRentCo sites
Sociocultural Non-English-speaking renters/workers A tight labor market High turnover rate New generation has limited understanding of customer-focused behaviors Cultural issues of U.S. teams serving non-U.S. culture residents (relating to women; bargaining)	**INDUSTRY GROWTH** Growing rapidly REITS control only 10% of apts. Small enough that all the players know each other	**Intensity of Rivalry** Competition is not only with big 10 REITs Market very fragmented—90% of apartments not owned by REITS Competition is market by market and submarket Competition is market by submarket (section of city invested in)

TABLE 10.3 CASE INTERNAL SCAN WORKSHEET

Logics of the Business of AptRentCo

ECONOMIC LOGIC	STRATEGY LOGIC	CUSTOMER LOGIC	PRODUCT LOGIC	PROCESS LOGIC	STRUCTURAL LOGIC
Cost Structure Most are fixed assets Compensation Most major maintenance Variable = casual maintenance	**Mission and Vision** To be the recognized industry leader in apartment investment and operations and to reinvent the industry through using the creativity of its people Only present in core protected markets Most profitable, not largest, markets: Expensive High entry barriers Long-term growth potential	**Market Strategy** Only market locations where can be profitable Affluence not sociodemographic marketing—can be illegal to do this Long-term relationships with customers—reduce turnover	**Product Strategy** Different types of apartments to meet variety of needs and incomes Year-round rentals "High-performing" apartments, with few defects and little need of repairs	**R and D Processes** Customer facing services: Variable lease pricing Resident portal (view accounts/pay) Leasing for the future	**Organizational Structure** CLO reports president, not HR—"have to be in operations for HPT to work" Separate from training delivery organizations Get training priorities by asking Operating VPs and executive committee
Financial Focus Mostly NOI (net operating income) SGA Information technology Training/HPT	**Objectives/Tactics** Field operations reflect NOI and values metrics Scorecards Targets	**Relationship** 80% of tenants will either stay or go no matter what AptRentCo does AptRentCo after the other 20% "up for grabs" Keeping a customer at lower rent amount may not be better than getting a new customer at higher rent amount	**Differentiation** Renter guarantees Service "Location" Flexible leasing terms No security deposit 100% move-in satisfaction Relocation guarantees	**Production and Postsale Processes** Leasing Move in Resident service requests Renewal Move out	**Information Systems** IT needed to meet customer needs and support work processes

TABLE 10.3 CASE INTERNAL SCAN WORKSHEET (*Continued*)

ECONOMIC LOGIC	STRATEGY LOGIC	CUSTOMER LOGIC	PRODUCT LOGIC	PROCESS LOGIC	STRUCTURAL LOGIC
Profit Source Same-store net operating income (NOI) Secondary is sales of Assets to move **money** to markets want to enter	**Culture** Reward/recognition tied to field targets Leadership rewards for high performance Leadership practices tied into evaluation system Employee engagement surveys		**Company Image** *Service* *Innovation (backed by research data)*		**Learning and Innovation–Skills** *Design some training (e.g., leadership programs)* *Focus on HPT solutions to improve skills:* *Explain dollar value of defects* *Job aids* *Feedback systems*
	Core Competencies *Apartment operations* *Source and buy apartments* *Nimble change management* *Technologically superior*				**Learning and Innovation—Human Capital** *Focus is process improvement* *Set metrics* *Gather data* *Report defect and dollar value* *Categorize defects as pre-ventables* *Set goals* *Redesign process, including IT* *Pilot* *Gather data* *Implement* *Feedback*

(*Continued*)

TABLE 10.3 CASE INTERNAL SCAN WORKSHEET (*Continued*)

ECONOMIC LOGIC	STRATEGY LOGIC	CUSTOMER LOGIC	PRODUCT LOGIC	PROCESS LOGIC	STRUCTURAL LOGIC
	Growth Strategy Key = internal organic growth with selected markets Acquisitions Joint ventures				**Learning and Innovation– Leadership** Aligned with values: Own the customer's experience Take responsibility Expect/inspect Educate/develop Support teams
	Pricing Strategy Price leader (in context of economy)				
	Alignment All elements aligned				

TABLE 10.4 CASE BUSINESS MEASURES WORKSHEET

Measures of the Business of AptRentCo

ECONOMIC LOGIC	STRATEGY LOGIC	CUSTOMER LOGIC	PRODUCT LOGIC	PROCESS LOGIC	STRUCTURAL LOGIC
Measures	**Measures**	**Measures**	**Measures**	**Measures**	**Measures**
Sales/revenue = percentage improvement = greatest lever	Are capital resources invested in the markets our strategy says we want?	Percentage of renewals at desired rent rates	Move-in survey	Leasing leads still open	Same measures as for other logics CLO because aligned with operational measures
Expenses = cost reduction = < 1/2 impact of revenue increase	Do field scorecards meet targets?	Move-in survey	Service request experience	Dollar value of open leads	
Net operating income (NOI)	Employee engagement survey scores	Service request experience	Resident survey	Move-in	Not ROI—too training focused—measures aligned with meeting business objectives
Total shareholder return	Leadership practices reflected in rewards	Resident survey	Property quality audit	Number of make ready defects	Training is < 3% of revenue
			Service request resolution score	Number of service requests first 14 days	
			Customer-focused phone calls	Dollar value of service requests	
				Move-in survey score	

B. Relative Importance of Each Construct and Metrics in It for the Organization

AptRentCo sees each of the logics and metrics as integrated in a systemic way. It therefore considers each of equal importance. Certainly, some of the logics and metrics are more important to different parts of the organization (e.g., net operating income and total shareholder return are most important to shareholders and senior management), but all parts of the organization recognize that these logics and metrics are interrelated, with a rise in one being the cause or result of the rise in another.

C. Alignment Among Constructs and Metrics

There appear to be no inconsistencies in the AptRentCo business logics and metrics. The Economic and Strategy Logics are aligned with each other and with the External Logics that affect the business. The Customer and Product Logics are aligned with the Strategy Logic. The Process and Structural Logics are aligned with the other four logics. In the HPT (Structural Logic) projects, for example, one sees project success measures that focus on the Process, Product, Customer, Strategy, and Economic Logics and metrics.

D. Levels of the Metrics (Desired and Actual)

Within the context of the constraints placed on the business of AptRentCo by External Logic, the levels of the metrics at which the organization is operating are good in some places and less than optimal in others. What is key at AptRentCo is that the organization knows where the levels of the metrics are below optimal and has HPT plans in place to raise those levels—as it has done, for example, with the leads and move-in experience metrics.

E. Congruence with HPT and Management Literature

The development of all the logics and metrics, including both the awareness of the factors involved and the aligned development of each of them, is solidly based on HPT and management literature. It is aligned with Albrecht, Argyris and Shon, Kaplan and Norton, Porter, Rummler and Brache, and Senge.

F. Which HPT Solutions Appeared to Succeed and Fail

The successful HPT solutions at AptRentCo are perfect case studies of the interventions suggested by HPT. They focus on the basic HPT interventions that provide the biggest performance improvement: identify the real problem and its magnitude, get agreement, set standards, communicate standards, provide feedback, provides tools and resources, provide incentives, evaluate results, and improve.

H. What Is the Utility of the Business Logics Model

This case study was successful in demonstrating that the Business Logics Model provides an extremely useful tool for developing a picture of an organization and identifying its performance issues. In one day of data collection (with a knowledgeable and cooperative organizational representative), an HPT consultant was able to develop a deep understanding of the workings of AptRentCo, its logics, its metrics, its performance against those metrics, its performance problems, and the types of interventions that succeeded in addressing those problems.

I. What Future Research Is Appropriate

It should not be surprising that an organization that understood the logics and metrics like AptRentCo was the organization that volunteered for this study. Other organizations backed out, either because the respondents did not know or have access to all this information or because the organization might have feared what its Business Logics and metrics portrait would look like.

Therefore the first piece of future research is to find an organization that does not present such a complete and blissful portrait but that is willing to undergo the Business Logics analysis anyway and to conduct a Business Logics Model of a less than optimal organization.

The second piece of research would be to try to find two matched organizations (in terms of business, size, etc.), but with one doing well and one doing not so well, and compare the logics, metrics, and HPT interventions.

The third piece of research would be conduct more widespread analyses, with the goals of developing a profile, based on the model constructs, of a successful and an unsuccessful organization.

AFTERWORD: WHAT TO DO WITH THE INFORMATION FROM THE BUSINESS LOGICS MODEL

We ended Chapter 9 by saying:

> We believe that we can and should win the respect and influence to contribute on a higher level than we're usually asked to. We also believe that we all hold the keys in our own hands. Organizational intelligence was written to provide more of us with the passwords and the secret handshakes to gain access to the world of influence in our organizations.
>
> We wish you the best, and welcome your questions, comments, and any experiences you are willing to share with us going forward.

This Afterword is a brief introduction to how to use the information you have gathered to get the seat at the table and to become a proactive business partner who helps improve bottom-line business results. Also, in every chapter, in the What You Should Do section, we have consistently been telling you to gather data, identify possible gaps, and/or list misalignments, but then *not* to share that information yet because it could be a career-limiting move.

This Afterword is a brief introduction to how to bring the information you have learned to the right people at the right time. We say *brief* because explaining more specifically how to use this information to get a seat at the table and telling people the problems of the organization in which you work (or for which you are consulting) is the subject of a whole other book. The subject has been touched on in various ways by Block (2000), Hale (2006), and others. Here we will just give you the headlines.

What You Know About Your Organization

If you have completed the Business Logics Model for your organization and given that information is power, then you are quite possibly the most powerful person in your organization. Because it is likely that you know more about your organization than any other single person in it (and that includes the CEO). Specifically:

- You know all about the Business Environment and Industry Structure in which the organization has to survive and prosper.
- You know about the organization's Economic Logic, including what some of its basic financial statements mean and what they tell you about possible issues in the company. And you know the right financial terms to use to tie what you do to financial measures the organization cares about.
- You know about the organization's Strategy Logic, especially its core competencies, culture, and growth strategy, which will help make some of the executive decisions that no one else understands seem rational to you.
- You know about the organization's Customer and Product Logics in great detail, especially how the organization measures success in these areas.
- You know about the Process Logic the organization uses to design, produce, sell, and service those products to customers and how the success of those processes is measured.
- You know all about the Structural Logic of the organization, including not only how it is organized (and where you fit and would like to fit in that structure), but also how knowledge is managed, how performance problems are solved, and how the organization itself learns and innovates.

So you can explain how your company works better than just about anyone else in it. But there's more. You also know most of the performance gaps and misalignments in the organization. You know where one element of a logic is not aligned with the other elements in that same logic, as well as where one logic is not aligned with the other six logics. Further, you know where the performance gaps in measures reside (e.g., not enough repeat customers, too many production defects, etc.).

In fact, you have a list, made during your analysis using the model, of just about everything in the organization that is "broken" and needs some sort of fixing, including the kind of HR, training, HPT, and OD solutions that we excel in providing.

What Not to Do

Having that knowledge makes you dangerous in the organization—a threat to people who perpetuate and try to hide performance problems. Therefore, lest we be responsible for your losing your job, we want to be very clear. Do *not* take all this information you have accumulated, walk into a meeting (either as an employee or consultant), and proceed to spend an hour telling everyone what's wrong with the organization. They will ignore the message and kill the messenger.

So What Do You Do?

You can now use this information in several ways that will not get you into trouble but that will instead make you a hero.

Picking Your Projects—Reactive

From now on, instead of just taking on any project that comes through the door, especially those that are asking for three days of training, pick projects that are aligned with the organization's logics, and the key measures. how do you know? First, you should be able to get an idea from the request and your knowledge of the logics and measures. But always ask the client "Which of the organization's key measures does this project relate to?" If they cannot answer you, or refer you to someone who can, then that is not a good sign. The client should know why fixing their problem will help the organization. Remember, for guidance on how to say "we are very busy, and have higher priority projects right now, but we will put you in the queue" nicely, consult the resources we mentioned above (Block and Hale).

- *Elevating the level of your projects (reactive):* Sometimes a client comes to you with a real need that you can see does impact a key logic and business measure, but the client doesn't see it that way. The client just wants the training or team-building session. Persuade the client that you agree there is a problem worth working on, but you would like to do a little analysis first. Based on your analysis, point out the real causes of the problem and the kinds of solutions that will really help the organization. Offer to work with the client on those meaningful problem solutions that will impact key organizational measures.

- *Seeking good projects (proactive):* The next level of evolution is actually to seek projects that will impact key logics and measures. Find friendly clients in the line organization with big problems and offer to work with them to solve them. The authors know one HPTer who used to walk around his organization saying, "Who has a million-dollar problem for us to solve?" He got plenty of takers, made many clients look good, and saved the organization a lot of money and problems.

- *Propose projects yourself:* You now know better than most people in the organization where the key performance deficiencies lay—in which logics and the real numbers. So you are actually in as good a position as your clients to raise questions (gently) about projects the organization could do to improve bottom-line results. Once you have identified some on your own, move immediately to the next couple of bulleted items before starting to do anything. This is to avoid jurisdictional disputes.

- *Partner—don't compete—with clients:* Partnering, one of the International Society for Performance Improvement's key values, should occur with all clients. Be an equal partner in solving the problem. Do *not* get sucked into the who-will-get-credit-for-this-ROI argument. If you and your client really work together and fix a major performance problem, and if you impact a key organizational measure, there'll be more than enough recognition for everyone involved.

- *Partner—don't compete—with other performance improvement departments;* Look at your Structural Logic analysis, and find all the other departments who have a mandate to do something similar to what you do (e.g., if you are in training, find all the other training departments, the OD departments, the quality departments, and the process redesign departments). If the authors' experiences over 60 years (that's total, not apiece) are any indication, you will find that you are competing with each other for clients, doing redundant work, and actually getting in each other's way. Although a giant peace hug will not happen overnight, begin to form alliances (see the Strategy and Structure Logics for how those work) with other departments, so that you can work together on difficult problems to really show major impact on measures, such as the successful process redesign involving getting process data (quality), redesigning jobs and processes (BPR/HPT/OD), and skill building (training). So why not start out working together?

- *Propose reorganizations:* After the peace hug has occurred as you discover the synergies of working together rather than fighting, consider making the hug formal. Also consider moving the location of these departments from the staff organization (like HR) to the line organization, as part of a revenue-generating department (like sales, manufacturing, and the rest), in which it is much easier to get access to, solve, and show contributions to solving serious and valuable business problems.

- *Get a seat at the beginning of every big project:* If you've ever been called in to develop training after a new IT system has been developed, you know the importance of this recommendation. Before any major initiative in any of the logics begins, from supply chain redesign to core competency identification to company branding, work your alliances and successes in the organization to be seated at the table, as an integral part of the project team, from day one. That's the way to have major impact on the key organizational measures and to truly demonstrate how you can add value.

- *Find out how the big decisions in your organizations get made:* How do R&D and new product decisions get made in your organization: in meetings, the golf course, the corporate jet? If you want to be part of those decisions, find out how you can get into that game. (Advice on how to do it is beyond the scope of this book.)

We could go on listing similar ways of using the information you have gathered from your Business Logics Model analysis. But you probably have the idea and have your own ideas about things you can do that make your organization work better. All we ask is that you do them. Remember, we didn't gather this information or write this book just to have a lot of information at our fingertips. Our goal, with the Model, with the book, and with all the fields involved in organizational performance improvement, has always been to help the organization improve its performance.

We have provided you with a tool for understanding your business, gathering key information about it, and speaking to others about it in language they will understand. The next step is yours.

THE AUTHORS

Kenneth H. Silber, Ph.D. CPT

Kenneth H. Silber, Ph.D. CPT, is President, www.silberperformance.com, and Associate Professor, Emeritus, Instructional Technology, Northern Illinois University. He is also an Adjunct Professor, Training and Performance Improvement at Capella University. For 45 years, he has been working in corporate, academic, and consulting settings to produce results for clients. Ken designed and implemented HPT interventions (ID-based and non-training) that have saved millions of dollars. He taught HPT/ ID skills to over two thousand students and employees. Ken has co-edited ISPI's ISPI Handbook *Training and Improving Workplace Performance,* edited ISPI's *From Training to Performance Series,* co-authored two chapters for ISPI's *HPT Handbook 3rd Edition,* co-authored *Writing Training Materials That Work,* published 60 articles and made over 100 presentations. He has earned his e-mail handle, wiseoldken@aol.com.

Lynn Kearny, CPT

Lynn Kearny, CPT, has headed her own performance consulting firm in Oakland California for over 25 years. She has wide experience assessing organizational needs and designing and developing performance improvement interventions. She also partners with clients to plan and graphically facilitate meetings and think tanks. She specializes in graphics to communicate complex and abstract ideas in a clear, memorable way. Lynn has worked in North America, Europe, Asia, and Africa. Clients include financial, manufacturing, retail, high- tech, governmental, and non-profit organizations. She has received numerous honors and awards from ISPI (International Society for Performance Improvement), including the coveted Outstanding Instructional Product award. Lynn served on ISPI's international board of directors and is currently faculty for both of ISPI's HPT Institutes. She has contributed chapters and articles and published five books relating to performance improvement.

She can be reached at lkearny@sprintmail.com, Web page at http://www .ifvp.org/directory/lkearny/index.htm.

REFERENCES

This list of references includes the actual sources cited in this text (including those cited in the case study). The authors are aware that readers checking editions and dates carefully will notice that in many cases the authors have cited years (and, in the text, the page numbers) of the editions they actually used to write the book. However, the authors both tend to have on their bookshelves original editions of books (e.g., Gilbert's original 1978 text), the original printings of books that have since been reprinted with later dates and new prefaces (e.g., Porter, 1985), and earlier editions of some textbooks than those that are currently available (e.g., Kotler, 1991).

Unless we felt the information in later editions changed substantively, we chose not to reference the later editions of certain books. So, if you should check a later edition of a book (e.g., Rummler and Brache, 1995 instead of 1990), you will find that our page references in the book do not match those in your edition. But they are accurate in the editions we used.

Addison, R., Haig, C, and Kearny, L. (2009) *Performance Architecture*. San Francisco, CA: Pfeiffer.

Albrecht, K. (1994) *The Northbound Train*. New York: AMACOM.

Argyris, C. and Schon, D. A. (1996). *Organizational Learning II*. Reading, MA: Addison Wesley.

Becker, M. J. (2007) "Relationship Power Line Enhanced Transaction to Relationship Marketing Continuum," *Mobile Marketing Association Journal*, August 21, 2007. Retrieved from http://www.mmaglobal.com/articles/relationship-power-line-enhanced-transaction-relationship-marketing-continuum-and-insights on March 23.

Block, P. (2000) *Flawless Consulting*, 2nd ed. San Francisco: Pfeiffer.

Bratton, B., et al. (1981) "Competencies for the Instructional/Training Professional," *Journal of Instructional Development, 5*, 14–15.

Burke, W. W., and Litwin, G. H. (1989) "A Model of Organizational Change and Performance," in Pfeiffer, J. W. (ed.), *1989 Annual: Developing Human Resources*, pp. 277–288. San Francisco, Pfeiffer.

Carleton, J. R., and Lineberry, C. S. (2004) *Achieving Post-Merger Success: A Stakeholder's Guide to Cultural Due Diligence, Assessment, and Integration*. San Francisco, Pfeiffer.

Chaoyun, C., and Schwen, T. (1997) "Critical Reflections on Instructional Design in the Corporate World," *Performance Improvement, 36*, 18–19.

Charan, R. (2001) *What the CEO Wants You to Know*. New York: Random House.

Clark, R. E., and Estes, F. (2002) *Turning Research into Results*. Atlanta, GA: CEP Press.

Clifton, R., Simmons, J., and Ahmad, S. (eds.). (2004) *Brands and Branding*. Princeton, NJ: Bloomberg Press.

Collins, J. C., and Porras, J. I. (1996) "Building Your Company's Vision," *Harvard Business Review, 74*, September–October, 2–13.

Cooke, R. A. (1993) *The McGraw-Hill 36-Hour Course in Finance for Nonfinancial Managers*. New York: Mcraw-Hill.

Cummings, T. G., and Worley. C. G. (2009) *Organization Development and Change*, 9th ed. Mason, OH: Cengage Learning.

Daljik, T. (ed.). (2005) *The Handbook of Niche Marketing: Principles and Practice*. New York: Routledge.

Dean P. J., and Ripley, D. E. (1997) *Performance Improvement Pathfinders*. Washington, DC: ISPI.

Deden-Parker, A. (1981) "Instructional Technology Skills Sought by Industry," *Performance and Instruction, 20*, 14–15.

Deden-Parker, A., Bratton, B., and Silber, K. H. (1980, April). Consulting Skills for Instructional Developers. Workshop conducted at the meeting of the Association for Educational Communications and Technology. Denver, CO.

DeCenzo, D. A., and Robbins, S. P. (2006) *Fundamentals of Human Resource Management*. 9th Edition. New York: John Wiley and Sons.

DeNisi, A. and Griffin, R. (2007). *Human Resource Management. 3rd Edtion*. Independence, KY: Cengage: South-Western College Publishers.

Dessler, G. (2007). *Human Resource Management*. 11th Edition. NY: Prentice-Hall.

ELearn Limited (Great Britain). (2005) *Business Environment*. London: Pergamon Flexible Learning.

Ferris, G. R., Rosen, S. D., and Barnum, D. T. (eds.). (1995) *Handbook of Human Resource Management*. Cambridge, MA: Blackwell Press.

Galbraith, J. (2005) *Designing the Customer-centric Organization*. San Francisco: Jossey-Bass.

Gilbert, T. (1978). *Human Competence*. New York: McGraw-Hill. (Reprinted 1995, Washington, DC: ISPI and 2008, San Francisco: Jossey-Bass.)

Hale, J. (2006) *The Performance Consultant's Fieldbook*, 2nd ed. San Francisco: Pfeiffer.

Hamel, G., and Prahalad, C. K. (1990) "The Core Competence of the Corporation," *Harvard Business Review*, May–June, 79–91.

Hamel, G., and Prahalad, C. K. (1996) *Competing for the Future*. Cambridge, MA: Harvard Business School Press.

Hammer, M. and Champy, J. (1993). *Reengineering the Corporation*. NY: Harper Business.

Hammer, M., and Champy, J. (2003) *Reengineering the Corporation*, revised, illustrated. New York: HarperCollins.

Harmon, P. (2003) *Business Process Change*. San Francisco: Morgan Kaufman.

Hartt, D. C., and Rossett, A. (2000) "When Instructional Design Students Consult with the Real World," *Performance Improvement, 39,* 36–43.

Hedberg, J. (1980) "Client Relationships in Instructional Design," *Programmed Learning and Educational Technology, 17,* 102–110.

Herbold, R. J. (2004) *The Fiefdom Syndrome*. New York: Currency Doubleday.

International Board of Standards for Training Performance and Instruction (IBSTPI). (1999) "1998 Instructional Design Competencies." Retrieved from http://www.ibstpi.org on December 1, 2004.

International Society for Performance Improvement (ISPI). (2002) "Standards for the Certified Performance Technologist". Retrieved from http://www.ispi.org on December 1, 2004.

International Society for Performance Improvement (ISPI). (2005) *HPT Principles and Practices Institute*. Washington, DC: International Society for Performance Improvement.

Ivancevich, J. (2009). *Human Resource Management*. 11th Edition. New York: McGaw-Hill/Irwin.

Jain, T., Trehan, M., and Trehan, R. (2006) *Business Environment*. New Delhi: VK Publications.

Joby, J. (2003) *Fundamentals of Customer-Focused Management: Competing Through Service*. Westport, CT: Praeger.

Johnson, J. T., Barksdale, H. C., and Boles, J. S. (2001) "The Strategic Role of the Salesperson in Reducing Customer Defection in Business Relationships," *Journal of Personal Selling and Sales Management, 21*(2), 123–134.

Kaplan, R. S., and Norton, D. P. (1996) *The Balanced Scorecard*. Cambridge, MA: Harvard Business School Press.

Katz, S. (1978) "The Politics of Instructional Technology," *NSPI Journal, 17,* 28–31.

Kaufman, R. (1999) *Mega Planning*. San Francisco: Sage Publications.

Kearny, L. (1994, April). "Wearing Business Glasses: How to Look at Your Organization Like a General Manager." Paper presented at the annual conference of the International Society for Performance Improvement, San Francisco, CA.

Kotler, P. (1991) *Marketing Management,* 7th ed. Englewood Cliffs, NJ: Prentice-Hall.

Mathis, R. L., and Jackson, J. H. (2008). *Human Resource Management*. 12th Edition. Independence, KY: Cengage: South-Western College Publishers.

McMath, R. M. and Forbes, T. (1998) *What Were They Thinking? Marketing Lessons You Can Learn from Products that Flopped*. New York: Times Business Books, a division of Random House.

Mintzberg, Henry. 1994. *The Rise and Fall of Strategic Planning*. NY: Free Press and Prentice Hall International.

Mintzberg, Henry. 1994. *The Rise and Fall of Strategic Planning*. NY: Free Press and Prentice Hall International.

Nadler L. (Ed). (1984) *The Handbook of Human Resources Development*. NY: John Wiley and Sons.

Nonaka, I. and Takeuchi, H. (1995) *The Knowledge Creating Company*. Oxford: Oxford University Press.

Palmer, A. and Hartley,B. (2008). *The Business Environment*. 6th Edition. New York: McGraw Hill Higher Education.

Pershing, J. (ed.) (2006). *Handbook of Human Performance Technology*. 3rd Edition. San Francisco, CA: Jossey-Bass/Pfeiffer.

Phillips, J. (1997) *Return on Investment*. Houston, TX: Gulf Publishing.

Poirier, C. (1999). *Advanced Supply Chain Management*. San Francisco: Berret-Koehler.

Porter, M. (1985, 1998). *Competitive Advantage*. New York: The Free Press.

Porter, M. (1980). *Competitive Strategy*. New York: Free Press.

Porter, M. E. (1985) *Competitive Advantage: Creating and Sustaining Superior Performance*" New York : The Free Press, Simon and Schuster Inc.

Powell, T. C. (1992, Feb.). "Organizational Alignment as Competitive Advantage," *Strategic Management Journal, (13)*2, 119–134.

Prahalad, C. K. (1993) "The Role of Core Competencies in the Corporation," *Technology Management*, Nov/Dec (36)6.

Price, R. D. (1978, April). "Preparing Instructional Developers for the Initial Client Conference." Paper presented at the meeting of the Association for Educational Communications and Technology, Kansas City, MO.

Reichheld, F. F., and (1996). *The Loyalty Effect.* Boston, MA: Harvard Business School Press.

Reichheld, F.F. Sasser, E. W. Jr. (1990), "Zero Defections: Quality Comes to Services," *Harvard Business Review, 68* (September-October), 105-111.

Rogers, E. (2003). *Diffusion of Innovations.* 5th Edition. New York: Free Press.

Rummler, G. (2007). *Serious Performance Consulting.* San Francisco: Pfeiffer.

Rummler, G. and Brache, A. (1990). *Improving Performance.* San Francsico: Jossey-Bass.

Rummler, G. and Brache, A. (1995) *Improving Performance.* 2nd Edition. San Francsico: Jossey-Bass.

Schein, E. (1999). *The Corporate Culture Survival Guide.* San Francisco: Jossey-Bass.

Senge, P. (1990) *The Fifth Discipline.* New York: Random House.

Silber, K. H. (1975, April). "People Skills Involved in Instructional Development." Paper presented at the meeting of the Association for Educational Communications and Technology, Dallas, TX.

Silber, K. H. (1978a). "Problems and Needed Directions in the Profession of Educational Technology," *Educational Communications and Technology Journal, 26*, 174–185.

Silber, K. H. (1978b, April). "Training Instructional Developers for the 80's." Paper presented at the meeting of the Association for Educational Communications and Technology, Kansas City, MO.

Silber, K. H. (1980a). "The Need for the Study of Approaches to Training Instructional Developers". *Journal of Instructional Development, 4*, 2–3.

Silber, K. H. (1980b). "The Need for the Study of Approaches to Training Instructional Developers." Paper presented at the meeting of the American Educational Research Association National Conference, Chicago, IL.

Silber, K. H. (1982a). "An Analysis of University Training Programs for Instructional Developers." *Journal of Instructional Development, 6*, 15–27.

Silber, K. H. (1982b). "Training Performance Technologists/Instructional Developers: An Analysis of University Training Programs." Paper presented at the meeting of the National Society for Performance and Improvement, San Diego, CA.

Silber, K. H. (1998). *Selecting Performance Improvement Interventions that Work to Improve the Organization's Key Metrics.* Chicago: Silber Performance Consulting.

Silber, K., and Bratton, B. (1984, April). Interpersonal Consulting Skills. Workshop conducted at the meeting of the National Society for Performance and Improvement, Atlanta, GA.

Silber, K.H. and Kearny, L. (2000, 2001, 2002, 2003, 2004, 2005, 2006, 2008) Seeing Organizations Through Business Glasses. Workshop and session conducted at the meeting of the International Society for Performance Improvement, Cincinnati, OH.

Silber, K. H. and Kearny, L. (2006). "Business Perspectives for Performance Technologists. in Pershing, J. (ed.), *Handbook of Human Performance Technology.* 3rd Edition. San Francisco, CA: Jossey-Bass/Pfeiffer.

Society for Human Resource Management (SHRM), (2009) (Retrieved from http://www .shrm.org/hrdisciplines/Pages/default.aspx on 3/5/2009.

Stack, J. (1994) *The Great Game of Business*. New York: Currency-Doubleday.

Stake, R. (1995) *The Art of Case Research*. Thousand Oaks, CA: Sage Publishing.

Sugrue, B. (2005) "Validated Practice: The Research Base for Performance Improvement," *Performance Improvement 43*(6) 8–13.

Stewart, T. (1999) *Intellectual Capital*. New Yark: Doubleday.

Stumpf, John (2009) CEO Wells Fargo Bank, SF Chronicle, 1/22/09, page C6.

Summers, L., Lohr, L., and O'Neil, C. (2002). "Building Instructional Design Credibility through Communication Competency." *TechTrends, 46*, 26–32.

Svieby, Erik (1997) *The New Organizational Wealth: Measuring and Managing Knowledge-Based Assets*. San Francisco: Berrett-Koehler.

Tosti, D. (2007, Jan). "Aligning the Culture and Strategy for Success. *Performance Improvement* 46, no. 1, 21–25.

Tosti, D. and Jackson, S. (1994, April) "Organizational Alignment: How It Works and Why It Matters." *Training*, 58–64.

U.S. Department of Labor Employment and Training Administration (1991*) Dictionary of Occupational Titles, Vol 1, 4th ed*. Washington DC: US Department of Labor.

Weitz, Barton A., and Kevin D. Bradford (1999), "Personal Selling and Sales Management: A Relationship Marketing Perspective," *Journal of the Academy of Marketing Science*, 27 (Spring), 241–254.

Yin, R. (2002). *Case Study Research: Design and Methods* 3rd ed. Newberry Park, CA: Sage Publishing.

INDEX

Page references followed by *t* indicate a table.